Securing the Enterprise

A Practical Guide for CISOs, CXOs, and IT Security Professionals

GS Jha

Apress®

Securing the Enterprise: A Practical Guide for CISOs, CXOs, and IT Security Professionals

GS Jha
Austin, TX, USA

ISBN-13 (pbk): 979-8-8688-1653-6　　　　ISBN-13 (electronic): 979-8-8688-1654-3
https://doi.org/10.1007/979-8-8688-1654-3

Copyright © 2025 by GS Jha

This work is subject to copyright. All rights are reserved by the Publisher, whether the whole or part of the material is concerned, specifically the rights of translation, reprinting, reuse of illustrations, recitation, broadcasting, reproduction on microfilms or in any other physical way, and transmission or information storage and retrieval, electronic adaptation, computer software, or by similar or dissimilar methodology now known or hereafter developed.

Trademarked names, logos, and images may appear in this book. Rather than use a trademark symbol with every occurrence of a trademarked name, logo, or image we use the names, logos, and images only in an editorial fashion and to the benefit of the trademark owner, with no intention of infringement of the trademark.

The use in this publication of trade names, trademarks, service marks, and similar terms, even if they are not identified as such, is not to be taken as an expression of opinion as to whether or not they are subject to proprietary rights.

While the advice and information in this book are believed to be true and accurate at the date of publication, neither the authors nor the editors nor the publisher can accept any legal responsibility for any errors or omissions that may be made. The publisher makes no warranty, express or implied, with respect to the material contained herein.

　　Managing Director, Apress Media LLC: Welmoed Spahr
　　Acquisitions Editor: Susan McDermott
　　Development Editor: Laura Berendson
　　Project Manager: Jessica Vakili

Distributed to the book trade worldwide by Springer Science+Business Media New York, 1 New York Plaza, New York, NY 10004. Phone 1-800-SPRINGER, fax (201) 348-4505, e-mail orders-ny@springer-sbm.com, or visit www.springeronline.com. Apress Media, LLC is a Delaware LLC and the sole member (owner) is Springer Science + Business Media Finance Inc (SSBM Finance Inc). SSBM Finance Inc is a **Delaware** corporation.

For information on translations, please e-mail booktranslations@springernature.com; for reprint, paperback, or audio rights, please e-mail bookpermissions@springernature.com.

Apress titles may be purchased in bulk for academic, corporate, or promotional use. eBook versions and licenses are also available for most titles. For more information, reference our Print and eBook Bulk Sales web page at http://www.apress.com/bulk-sales.

If disposing of this product, please recycle the paper

Table of Contents

About the Author xiii

Acknowledgments xv

Preface xvii

Introduction xix

Part I: Foundations of Cybersecurity: Understanding the Basics in an Evolving Landscape 1

Chapter 1: Introduction to Cybersecurity 3

How Did We Get Here? 3

Defining Digital Transformation 6

Transition from Digital Transformation to Secure Digital Transformation 7

Defining Cybersecurity 8

The Evolution of Cybersecurity Threats 10

    The Dawn of Malware 10

The Future of Cybersecurity Threats 12

    Cybersecurity Impacts by Numbers: A Snapshot 14

The Big Breaches 16

Cybersecurity Trends in 2025 (and Beyond) 20

Types of Data Compromised 23

The Importance of Cybersecurity in Today's World 23

Key Cybersecurity Principles 27

    1. Confidentiality 29

    2. Integrity 29

    3. Availability 29

    4. Accountability 30

TABLE OF CONTENTS

    5. Least Privilege 30

    6. Defense in Depth 31

    7. Proactive Risk Management 32

    8. Transparency and Communication 32

  Key Takeaways 33

Chapter 2: Core Cybersecurity Concepts 35

  Risk Assessment and Management 35

  Access Control 36

  Data Security 36

  Network Security 36

  Incident Response 37

  Cybersecurity Awareness and Training 37

  Threat Modeling and Risk Assessment 37

  Common Threat Modeling Methods and Key Steps 38

  Vulnerability Management 49

    Key Stages 50

    Benefits 51

    Key Considerations 51

  Incident Response Planning and Handling 51

    Key Stages 52

    Benefits 53

    Key Considerations 53

  Data Security and Privacy 54

    Key Aspects of Data Security 54

    Key Data Security Measures 54

    Importance of Data Security 54

  Data Privacy 55

    Core Principles 55

    Key Concepts 55

    Data Privacy Laws 55

    Key Considerations for Organizations 56

Access Control and Authentication	56
Authentication	57
Access Control	57
Network Security Fundamentals	58
Core Principles of Network Security	58
Key Network Security Fundamentals	58
Access and Authentication	58
Perimeter Security and Traffic Protection	59
Data Encryption	59
Vulnerability Management	59
Security Monitoring and Awareness	60
Importance of Network Security	60
Cryptography and Encryption	60
Key Takeaways	64

Chapter 3: The Threat Landscape: An Ever-Evolving Challenge 65

Key Cyber Threats	67
Why Understanding the Threat Landscape Is Crucial	67
The Complexity of the Digital World	67
1. Threats: The Actions or Events That Can Cause Harm	68
2. Vulnerabilities: Weaknesses That Can Be Exploited	73
3. Risks: The Consequences of Cyber Threats	73
Navigating the Evolving Threat Landscape	74
Key Takeaways	74

Part II: The Role of the Executive Leaders (CXO), CISO, and Board of Directors 77

Chapter 4: The Role of CXO/Executive Leaders 79

The Role of Executive Leaders in Secure Digital Transformation	79
The New Digital Landscape and Security Challenges	80
The Role of Executive Leadership in Driving Change	80

TABLE OF CONTENTS

Chapter 5: The Role of the Board of Directors 81
The Role of Board Members in Managing Cyber Risk 81
Why Is This Important? 82
Key Takeaways 82

Chapter 6: The CISO Role and Responsibilities 85
Defining the CISO Role 85
Key Responsibilities of a CISO 86
A Typical Workday for a CISO 87
Beyond the Daily Grind: Strategic Initiatives 88
Closing Thoughts: Why the CISO Role Is Crucial 88
Key Takeaways 89
Strategic Cybersecurity Planning and Governance 89
Key Elements of Strategic Planning 89
Strategic Planning in Action 90
Risk Management and Compliance: Safeguarding Organizational Integrity 91
Relationship Between Risk Management and Compliance 92
Security Operations and Incident Response 93
Integration of Security Operations and Incident Response 94
Technology and Architecture in Cybersecurity 94
People and Culture in Cybersecurity 95
Building a Strong Cybersecurity Culture 96
Communication and Advocacy in Cybersecurity 99
Cybersecurity Advocacy: Strengthening Digital Security 100
CIO's Role in Championing Cybersecurity with CISO and CXO 101
Key Takeaways 105

Chapter 7: Leadership and Communication 107
Building and Leading a High-Performing Security Team 107
Building a High-Performing Security Team 107
Leading a High-Performing Security Team 108
Communicating Security Risks and Strategies to Executives and the Board 109

Key Aspects of Effective Communication 110
Key Metrics and Reporting 110
Building Strong Relationships 111
Risk Assessment and Prioritization 111
Security Awareness for Executives and Boards 111
Why Effective Communication Matters 112
Stakeholder Management and Collaboration 112
Key Aspects of Stakeholder Management 112
Key Aspects of Collaboration in Cybersecurity 113
Importance of Stakeholder Management and Collaboration 114
Crisis Communication and Incident Response Communication 114
Key Aspects of Crisis Communication 115
Key Aspects of Incident Response Communication 115
Why Crisis and Incident Response Communication Matter in Cybersecurity 116
Key Takeaways 117

Chapter 8: CISO Skills and Competencies 119
Technical Expertise 119
Business Acumen 120
Communication and Interpersonal Skills 120
Leadership and Management Skills 121
Negotiation and Influencing Skills 121
Ethical Considerations and Decision-Making 121

Part III: Cybersecurity Frameworks and Standards 125

Chapter 9: The CISO in the Modern World 127
The Evolving Role of the CISO 127
Emerging Trends and Technologies Impacting the CISO Role 130
The Future of Cybersecurity Leadership 132
Key Metrics, KPIs, and Reporting 133
Key Takeaways 137

TABLE OF CONTENTS

Chapter 10: Key Cybersecurity Frameworks 139
    NIST Cybersecurity Framework 140
    ISO 27001 146
    COBIT 147
    CIS Controls 148
    MITRE ATT&CK 150
    Unified Kill Chain 154
    OWASP (The Open Worldwide Application Security Project) 163
    Key Takeaways 176

Chapter 11: Compliance and Regulations 179
    GDPR (General Data Protection Regulation) 182
    CCPA (California Consumer Privacy Act) 185
    CCPA vs. GDPR 187
    HIPAA (Health Insurance Portability and Accountability Act) 188
    SOX (Sarbanes-Oxley Act) 191
    PCI DSS (Payment Card Industry Data Security Standard) 192
    Key Takeaways 194

Chapter 12: Implementing and Maintaining a Security Program 195
    Develop a Cybersecurity Strategy 197
    Implement and Monitor Security Controls 197
    Conduct Security Audits and Assessments 197
    Implementing and Maintaining a Cybersecurity Program 198
    Cybersecurity Key Metrics, KPIs, and Reporting 200
    Key Takeaways 202

Part IV: Advanced Topics 203

Chapter 13: Cloud Security 205
    Cloud Computing Models (IaaS, PaaS, SaaS) 208
    Security Considerations in the Cloud 210

Key Cloud Security Considerations 210
Key Considerations for Cloud Security 211
Why Cloud Security Matters.. 211
Cloud Security Controls and Best Practices... 212
Key Takeaways.. 214

Chapter 14: Security Information and Event Management (SIEM) 217
SIEM Fundamentals 218
Implementing and Managing a SIEM Solution 220
Threat Detection and Response with SIEM 222
Threat Detection.. 222
Threat Response 223
Key Advantages of SIEM for Threat Detection and Response 225
Conclusion 226
Key Takeaways.. 226

Chapter 15: Artificial Intelligence (AI) and Machine Learning (ML) in Cybersecurity 229
AI/ML Applications in Threat Detection and Response.. 231
Ethical Considerations of AI/ML in Cybersecurity 233
Key Takeaways.. 235

Chapter 16: The Internet of Things (IoT) Security... 239
IoT Security Challenges and Vulnerabilities 240
Securing IoT Devices and Networks 241
Key Takeaways.. 243

Chapter 17: Blockchain and Cryptocurrency Security.. 247
Understanding Blockchain Technology 249
Security Challenges and Vulnerabilities in Blockchain 250
Securing Cryptocurrencies and Blockchain Applications................................... 253
Key Takeaways.. 255

TABLE OF CONTENTS

Chapter 18: Zero Trust Architecture 257
Understanding Zero Trust Architecture 258
Key Elements in a Zero Trust Architecture 258
Three Principles of Zero Trust? 259
The Five Pillars of Zero Trust 260
Why the Five Pillars of Zero Trust Matter 264
Seven Core Pillars of Zero Trust Architecture 264
Steps to Implementing Zero Trust Architecture 265
How to Implement Zero Trust Architecture 269
Step-by-Step Guide to Implementing ZTA 269
Examples of Zero Trust Architecture in Action 270
Key Benefits of Zero Trust Architecture 270
Conclusion 272
Key Takeaways 272

Chapter 19: Cybersecurity by Design 275
Prioritizing Security from Inception 276
Redefining Security As a Core Business Requirement 276
The Design Phase Is the Critical Juncture 277
Security Should Work Out of the Box 277
Secure by Design in Practice 278
Regulatory and Industry Support for Secure by Design 279
Moving from Aspiration to Action 279
Key Takeaways 280

Chapter 20: Data Privacy 281
Understanding Data Privacy vs. Data Security 282
Global Regulatory Landscape and the Role of Laws and Regulations 284
Core Principles of Data Privacy 284
Implementing a Data Privacy Program 285
Privacy-Enhancing Technologies (PETs) 286

Building a Culture of Privacy 287

Responding to Privacy Incidents 287

Key Takeaways 288

Part V: Cybersecurity Tabletop Exercises (TTXs) 291

Chapter 21: Tabletop Exercise: A Critical Tool for Incident Preparedness 293

Why Conduct a Cybersecurity TTX? 294

How a Typical TTX Works 295

Common Cybersecurity TTX Scenarios 296

Key Benefits of Conducting Regular TTXs 297

Key Takeaways 297

Chapter 22: David vs. Goliath: Cybersecurity's Constant Struggle 299

David's Strategic Advantages 300

Goliath's Vulnerabilities 300

Leveling the Playing Field 301

The Ongoing Battle 301

Key Takeaways 301

Glossary of Cybersecurity Terms 303

Resources and References 307

Index 309

About the Author

GS Jha is a seasoned IT and cybersecurity leader with over 25 years of experience driving transformational initiatives across global organizations. With a bachelor's degree in computer engineering from Pune University and a master's in computer science from Wayne State University, GS's academic journey laid the foundation for his expertise in technology and security. His commitment to leadership development continued at Northwestern University's Kellogg School of Management, where he earned an MBA in finance, strategy, and marketing, holding esteemed roles such as President of the India Business Club and Chairman of Kellogg Outdoor Adventure. Currently, he is furthering his knowledge by pursuing an MS in cybersecurity at Georgia Institute of Technology.

Throughout his illustrious career, GS has spearheaded IT transformations, regulatory compliance initiatives, and infrastructure modernization at industry-leading companies such as CareDx, Accuray, and Bio-Techne. Notably, at CareDx, his leadership delivered $13 million in IT cost reductions while aligning technology strategies to support $427 million in revenue while successfully leading and completing the company-wide, most critical, multi-year, pervasive three Sarbanes-Oxley Act (SOX) material weaknesses (MWs) remediation in collaboration with the Audit Committee, Internal Audit, KPMG, and Deloitte & Touche. His expertise spans ERP integration, cybersecurity frameworks, and operational excellence, making him a trusted advisor to executive teams and boards.

Beyond his professional achievements, GS exemplifies resilience and dedication in his personal pursuits. An avid endurance athlete, he has completed over 25 marathons, including the San Francisco and Austin Marathons. His adventurous spirit has also led him to summit Mount Kilimanjaro and Mount Shasta, embodying the determination and discipline that define his career.

ABOUT THE AUTHOR

GS Jha was awarded FedEx Information Technology Hall of Fame for leading the development of FedEx tracking software. The tracking software was launched at 1995 Miami Superbowl, and FedEx had three commercials.

Recognized as a finalist for the 2024 Bay Area CIO ORBIE Award and among the Top 10 Indian CIOs of the Year, GS is celebrated for his visionary leadership, mentorship, and ability to bridge the gap between technology and business. His passion for continuous learning and innovation makes him a transformative force in the rapidly evolving field of cybersecurity.

Acknowledgments

First and foremost, I am deeply indebted to my family for their unwavering encouragement, patience, and understanding throughout this project. Their belief in me and my vision has been a constant source of motivation.

I would also like to extend my thanks to the many colleagues, mentors, and professionals who have shared their insights and expertise with me over the years. Their real-world experiences and practical knowledge have been invaluable in shaping the content of this book.

A special thanks goes to the various organizations where I have had the privilege to work. These experiences have provided me with a unique perspective on the challenges and opportunities in the cybersecurity field.

I am also grateful to the numerous cybersecurity experts and thought leaders whose research, publications, and presentations have contributed to my understanding of this ever-evolving domain.

Finally, I want to thank you, the reader, for your interest in this book. I hope that it provides you with valuable insights and empowers you to navigate the complexities of the digital world with greater confidence and security.

—GS Jha

Preface

"If you are reachable, you are breachable." This adage is a stark reminder that in our hyper-connected digital age, every access point is a potential vulnerability. With the advancement and proliferation in computer technology, cybersecurity has evolved as a major threat and ongoing risk to individuals, businesses, and institutions of all sizes and forms on this planet. It is not a matter of if, it is a matter of when. According to data from various sources, a significant portion of Fortune 500 companies, estimated around 27%, have experienced data breaches within the last decade, indicating many companies have been breached in the past 10 years; however, the exact count of breaches is difficult to pinpoint due to the vast number of smaller breaches that may not be widely reported.

At the time writing was completed on this book (August 2025), an estimated several thousand companies are breached every day, with some reports stating that a company falls victim to a cyberattack roughly every 39 seconds, which translates to nearly 4,000 new cyberattacks occurring daily; however, the exact number can vary depending on how a "breach" is defined and the source of the data.

Our reliance on technology has transformed the way we live, work, and communicate. However, this transformation comes with significant challenges. The cyber threat landscape continues to grow in sophistication and scale, affecting individuals, businesses, and governments alike.

This book is my attempt to demystify the complexities of cybersecurity. It offers insights into the foundational principles, cutting-edge advancements, and the human elements that shape this field. Whether you are a business leader seeking to secure your organization, a technology professional, or simply someone concerned about digital safety, I hope this guide will empower you to navigate the evolving digital landscape with confidence.

Writing this book has been a deeply personal journey, reflecting over 25 years of experience in IT and cybersecurity. My goal is to shed light on not just the technical aspects but also the strategic and human considerations that are critical to success in this field. I believe that cybersecurity is more than just a technical challenge—it is a shared responsibility and an essential component of modern life.

Introduction

The digital revolution has transformed every aspect of our lives. From accessing information to conducting business and nurturing relationships, our world is now interconnected in ways unimaginable a few decades ago. However, this interconnectedness comes at a price: the persistent and growing threat of cyberattacks.

Cybersecurity threats are no longer a distant concern. Ransomware, data breaches, and cyber warfare have become everyday realities. These attacks can cripple businesses, expose sensitive information, and even disrupt national economies.

This book is a guide to navigating this evolving digital battleground. It explores

- The fundamental principles of cybersecurity
- Emerging threats and the technologies shaping the field
- The role of human behavior in creating vulnerabilities—and solutions

Whether you are an executive, IT professional, or someone who wants to understand how to protect themselves in the digital age, this book will provide actionable insights and strategies.

The digital world, a realm of ones and zeros, hums with unseen energy. On the surface, it is a place of endless possibilities—a global marketplace, a repository of knowledge, and a hub for creativity. But beneath this veneer lies a constant battle between builders and destroyers, between innovation and exploitation.

Every click, message, or transaction leaves a digital footprint—an opportunity for those with malicious intent to exploit vulnerabilities. From corporate boardrooms to personal devices, no one is immune to the rising tide of cyber threats.

This book invites you to step into this hidden war. We will explore the evolving tactics of cyber adversaries, the technologies that shape the future of security, and the strategies necessary to defend our digital lives. The battle for cyberspace is ongoing. Together, let us prepare for the challenges ahead.

PART I

Foundations of Cybersecurity: Understanding the Basics in an Evolving Landscape

Cybersecurity begins with a solid foundation. In this part, we will explore how the digital landscape has evolved, why cybersecurity is critical, and the principles that form the backbone of effective security strategies.

CHAPTER 1

Introduction to Cybersecurity

Cybersecurity has evolved from a niche technical concern to a strategic priority for organizations worldwide. As digital transformation accelerates, businesses, governments, and individuals face unprecedented challenges in safeguarding sensitive data and systems.

The shift to cloud computing, remote work, and distributed IT environments has expanded the attack surface for cybercriminals. Traditional security measures are no longer sufficient in this dynamic landscape. Organizations must adopt multilayered approaches to stay resilient.

This chapter explores how cybersecurity has transformed over the years, the impact of major breaches, and why it is now a boardroom discussion rather than just an IT concern.

How Did We Get Here?

In today's rapidly evolving digital landscape, organizations face increasing pressure to leverage information technology (IT) to stay competitive. However, this reliance on technology has also brought about significant challenges in safeguarding sensitive data and systems. Cybersecurity, once primarily a technical concern within data centers, has become a complex and critical strategic issue as the modern enterprise has become increasingly distributed. With employees working remotely, applications deployed across various platforms, and data residing in the cloud and on-premises, the attack surface has expanded significantly.

The legacy approach is unbale to adapt to the world we live in today. Many organizations, however, still have this type of technology in place and are therefore frequent targets of cyberattacks. Workers are considerably more mobile now, and many work from home. The third-party systems are integrated as part of digital transformation to digitize the workflows resulting in larger attack surface resulting in many weaker links in the system for hackers to break into. Organizations have tried to adapt by using virtual private networks (VPNs) to extend the company's network to employees and third-party service providers' locations. While VPNs do offer certain levels of protection, they also have been the cause of numerous breaches given their public exposure and network-level access. Ultimately, VPN increase the exposure to bad actors by creating new opportunities for them to gain access to the company's network. Couple this predicament with the adoption of the public cloud and SaaS. Because the traditional architecture puts users and applications on the same network, this means that the company network is now extended to all of those disparate cloud locations as well. As the old network model grows, it creates a huge surface that enables lateral movement for users as well as for attackers.

This older architecture, commonly known as hub-and-spoke and castle-and-mote security, as shown below, is still in place at many organizations today.

Legacy architectures represent a castle and moat, which fail to provide security in a mobile and cloud world.

"If you're reachable, you're breachable." There are still many ways for attackers to break into a castle or even trick its owners into letting them in. The problem is, once they are in, they can see, explore, and steal anything inside by default.

This has necessitated a multilayered approach to cybersecurity, encompassing traditional security measures like firewalls and proxy servers, as well as newer technologies designed to protect end-user devices, cloud environments, and data centers. Data loss prevention (DLP) engines have also become crucial in safeguarding sensitive information from unauthorized access and exfiltration.

Due to these developments, a leadership role of ever-growing importance has emerged: the Chief Information Security Officers (CISOs). The CISO's ultimate responsibility is protecting and setting policies for an organization's people, computer hardware, software, and information assets. This security-specific focus caused the CISO role to begin separating from IT and the rest of the executive team and the board.

Starting in 2010, the pace of technological innovation accelerated significantly with the emergence and rapid growth of cloud computing. Market share and investment gradually shifted away from traditional in-house data centers toward infrastructure-as-a-service (IaaS) providers like Amazon Web Services (AWS), Google Cloud Platform (GCP), and Microsoft Azure. Concurrently, organizations began embracing Software as a Service (SaaS) platforms, adopting solutions from companies such as Microsoft, Google, Salesforce, Workday, and Zoom.

Cost efficiency, faster time-to-market, increased developer productivity, and the ability to harness immense computing power were the primary drivers behind the widespread adoption of cloud computing. These benefits provided organizations with a significant competitive edge in the market. However, this migration to the cloud also resulted in a more distributed IT landscape, with organizational resources spanning their own data centers, various IaaS/SaaS solution providers, and multiple geographical locations.

From a cybersecurity perspective, the distributed nature of data across various locations, including on-premises, cloud providers, and across different geographical regions, posed a significant organizational risk. Ensuring comprehensive data protection across this extended landscape became a paramount challenge. Furthermore, many cloud services and platforms inherently support data sharing capabilities, which, while enabling collaboration and innovation, also necessitate robust security controls and enforcement mechanisms to prevent unauthorized access and data breaches. Traditional network and security architectures, designed for more static and centralized IT environments, proved inadequate in addressing the dynamic and distributed nature of modern IT infrastructures. These legacy systems struggled to keep pace with the evolving threat landscape and the rapid expansion of cloud adoption.

CHAPTER 1   INTRODUCTION TO CYBERSECURITY

As a consequence of these evolving technologies and increased connectivity, there have been several high-profile, well-publicized cyber breaches and data breaches. These incidents have resulted in significant financial losses, reputational damage, and legal repercussions for the organizations involved. Some of these breaches have led to severe consequences for security professionals. For example, the former Uber CISO was successfully prosecuted for his role in the company's data breach. Similarly, the CISO of SolarWinds faced legal action following the company's major breach in 2020. These cases have created a heightened sense of legal and personal liability for cybersecurity professionals across the industry, particularly for CISOs. Boards of directors are also increasingly concerned about their own potential legal exposure in the event of a cyber breach. Recognizing this growing concern, the Securities and Exchange Commission (SEC) issued a landmark ruling in July 2023 that formalizes the disclosure requirements for publicly traded companies in the event of a cyber breach. This ruling provides greater clarity on the legal expectations for organizations and their security leaders in managing and disclosing cybersecurity risks.

As cybersecurity risks have become increasingly critical, boards of directors are now demanding a deeper understanding of their organization's cyber risk exposure, the investments required to mitigate those risks, and the timelines for implementing necessary security controls. Cybersecurity has become a prominent agenda item in board meetings, with discussions often centering on risk assessments, mitigation strategies, and the organization's overall cybersecurity posture.

In recognition of the growing importance of cybersecurity, some forward-thinking boards have taken steps to formalize their oversight of cyber risk. This includes the creation of dedicated audit committees or task forces specifically focused on cybersecurity or broader risk management, which allows for more in-depth analysis and proactive risk mitigation.

Defining Digital Transformation

Digital transformation is the process of using digital technologies to change how a business operates, its culture, and how it interacts with customers. It's a way for businesses to adapt to changing market and business needs.

Digital transformation is a widely used term that encompasses a broad range of organizational changes, impacting the CXO role more than any other executive function. Wikipedia defines it as "the adoption of digital technology by an organization to improve non-digital products, services, or operations, with the goal of enhancing innovation, customer experience, or efficiency."

The COVID-19 pandemic accelerated the urgency for businesses to evolve to remain competitive. While "transformation" is often used as a buzzword, organizations must embrace technological advancements to maintain relevance in a landscape where success is increasingly tied to digital capabilities. Digital has become synonymous with modernization.

At its core, digital transformation seamlessly integrates all aspects of an organization—its suppliers, employees, and physical assets. Although it drives innovation and efficiency, it also introduces significant risks.

Ensuring a secure digital transformation is challenging as cyber threats continue to grow, employees work remotely, and applications become more decentralized. To succeed, transformation must extend beyond digital adoption to include robust security strategies. This requires modernizing application, network, and security architectures to align with cloud adoption and workforce mobility trends. Ultimately, this enhances productivity, reduces risks, and lowers costs and complexity. A core objective of security transformation is safeguarding data and controlling access. This is the foundation of the shift from "digital transformation" to "secure digital transformation."

Transition from Digital Transformation to Secure Digital Transformation

Transitioning from a standard "digital transformation" to a "secure digital transformation" involves prioritizing cybersecurity measures throughout the entire process of adopting new technologies and changing business practices, ensuring data protection and user privacy are central to every digital initiative, rather than an afterthought.

Successful organizations are embracing secure digital transformation to stay competitive in a rapidly evolving landscape. Achieving this requires modernizing applications, networks, workforce strategies, and security architectures. Secure transformation enhances agility and competitiveness by enabling faster decision-making, improving user productivity, and reducing security risks. When implemented correctly—leveraging established frameworks like NIST CSF, ISO 27001, MITRE ATT&CK, Unified Kill Chain, and Zero Trust Architecture (ZTA)—it can also significantly lower overall costs and complexity.

CHAPTER 1   INTRODUCTION TO CYBERSECURITY

Secure digital transformation is not a single project or product—it is an ongoing journey. It demands a cultural shift and a change in mindset. Organizational inertia can be a major obstacle, as employees often prefer familiar practices. To overcome this, the executive leadership team must drive secure digital transformation from the top down, ensuring alignment across all levels of the organization.

Defining Cybersecurity

This chapter lays the groundwork for understanding cybersecurity, providing a foundation for deeper exploration of critical topics and technologies.

At its core, cybersecurity is the practice of safeguarding computer systems, networks, and data from unauthorized access, misuse, disruption, modification, or destruction. It involves a comprehensive set of technologies, processes, and practices aimed at protecting sensitive information, ensuring system integrity, and maintaining the availability of critical services.

Key Concepts

In cybersecurity, CIA stands for Confidentiality, Integrity, and Availability—a foundational model guiding information security practices. The CIA triad provides organizations with a structured framework to identify security risks and implement safeguards to protect critical assets.

- **Confidentiality**: Ensures that information remains private and accessible only to authorized individuals. This involves security measures such as encryption, access controls, and data masking to prevent unauthorized disclosure.

- **Integrity**: Maintains the accuracy and completeness of information. This includes measures like data validation, intrusion detection systems, and regular backups to prevent unauthorized modifications.

- **Availability**: Guarantees that systems and data remain accessible to authorized users when needed. Organizations achieve this through disaster recovery planning, load balancing, and fault tolerance mechanisms.

The Evolving Landscape

The cybersecurity landscape is in a constant state of evolution, influenced by several key factors:

- **Technological Advancements**: The rise of cloud computing, the Internet of Things (IoT), and artificial intelligence (AI) has introduced new vulnerabilities and expanded potential attack surfaces.

- **Increased Reliance on Technology**: As businesses and individuals become more dependent on digital infrastructure, the potential impact of cyberattacks grows significantly.

- **Sophistication of Cyber Threats**: Cybercriminals continuously refine their techniques, leveraging ransomware, phishing, and social engineering to exploit vulnerabilities.

- **Global Interconnectedness**: The highly connected digital world allows cyber threats to spread rapidly, causing widespread disruptions across industries and borders.

The Importance of Cybersecurity

Cybersecurity is essential for individuals, businesses, and governments alike:

- **Individuals**: Protecting personal data, financial information, and online privacy is crucial in an era of frequent data breaches.

- **Businesses**: Ensuring business continuity, protecting intellectual property, and maintaining customer trust are top priorities.

- **Governments**: Safeguarding national security, critical infrastructure, and sensitive citizen data is imperative to maintaining public safety and stability.

The Human Factor

Despite technological advancements, human error remains one of the biggest cybersecurity vulnerabilities. Simple mistakes—such as clicking on malicious links, using weak passwords, or neglecting software updates—can lead to significant security breaches.

To mitigate these risks, cybersecurity education and awareness programs are essential. By fostering a culture of security awareness, individuals and organizations can make informed decisions and adopt safer online practices, strengthening overall resilience against cyber threats.

CHAPTER 1   INTRODUCTION TO CYBERSECURITY

The Evolution of Cybersecurity Threats

Cybersecurity threats have evolved significantly since the early days of computing. What once began as harmless pranks and curiosity-driven explorations has transformed into highly sophisticated cyberattacks, driven by organized crime syndicates and nation-state actors, posing severe global risks.

Early Days: Viruses and Worms

The Dawn of Malware

The early era of computing saw the emergence of basic malware, including viruses and worms, which laid the foundation for modern cyber threats.

- **Viruses**: Malicious programs that attached themselves to legitimate software, spreading through infected files and requiring user interaction to propagate
- **Worms**: Self-replicating programs that exploited system vulnerabilities to spread autonomously across networks, often causing widespread disruptions

Early Cybersecurity Measures

Initial cybersecurity efforts primarily focused on containment, relying on antivirus software and firewalls to detect and isolate known threats. While these defenses were effective against early malware, evolving threats soon demanded more advanced security strategies.

The Rise of Organized Crime

- **Financial Gain**: As the internet expanded and ecommerce grew, cybercriminals increasingly targeted financial gain.
  - **Phishing**: Fraudulent emails or messages designed to deceive users into disclosing sensitive information like passwords and credit card details
  - **Ransomware**: Malicious software that locks a victim's files through encryption and demands a ransom payment for restoration
  - **Data Breaches**: Large-scale theft of sensitive organizational data, often monetized through financial fraud or sales on the dark web

The Era of Advanced Persistent Threats (APTs)

- **State-Sponsored Attacks: Nation-states increasingly use cyberattacks for espionage, sabotage, and political influence.**

- **Advanced Persistent Threats (APTs)**: Highly sophisticated, targeted attacks by well-funded adversaries, often involving prolonged infiltration and data theft

- **Cyber Espionage**: Theft of intellectual property, military intelligence, and other sensitive corporate and government data

- **Cyber Warfare**: Disrupting critical infrastructure, including power grids, transportation systems, and financial networks

The Rise of the Internet of Things (IoT)

The proliferation of IoT devices—from smartphones to smart homes—has expanded attack surfaces, enabled botnets for DDoS attacks, and raised significant data privacy concerns, including

- **New Attack Surfaces**: The explosion of IoT devices (smartphones, smart homes, connected cars) has vastly expanded attack vectors.

- **IoT Botnets**: Networks of compromised IoT devices used for DDoS attacks and other malicious activities.

- **Data Privacy Concerns**: The widespread collection and use of IoT data raise significant security and privacy risks.

The Age of Artificial Intelligence (AI)

We've entered the age of AI-enabled cybersecurity, where speed, intelligence, and adaptability are nonnegotiable. AI won't eliminate the need for skilled cybersecurity professionals—it will amplify their capabilities. Success lies in combining human judgment with machine precision, using AI to strengthen defenses while remaining vigilant to its limitations and risks.

Cybercriminals increasingly leverage AI to automate sophisticated attacks—crafting personalized phishing emails, developing self-mutating malware that evades defenses, and creating deepfakes to deceive and manipulate.

- **AI-Powered Attacks: Cybercriminals are increasingly leveraging AI to automate and enhance attack sophistication.**

- **AI-Driven Phishing**: Crafting highly personalized and convincing phishing emails using AI

- **AI-Powered Malware**: Developing self-mutating malware capable of evading traditional security defenses

- **Deepfakes**: Creating realistic but fraudulent audio and video content to deceive and manipulate

The Future of Cybersecurity Threats

The future of cybersecurity threats is poised to become increasingly complex and sophisticated, driven by rapid technological advancements and the expanding digital footprint of organizations. As artificial intelligence and machine learning become more integrated into business operations, threat actors are also leveraging these tools to launch more targeted and adaptive attacks. The rise of quantum computing poses a looming challenge to current encryption standards, while the proliferation of IoT devices expands the attack surface exponentially. Additionally, geopolitical tensions and cyber warfare are expected to intensify, making critical infrastructure and supply chains prime targets. To stay ahead, cybersecurity strategies must evolve to be more proactive, intelligence-driven, and resilient, emphasizing continuous monitoring, Zero Trust Architectures, and cross-sector collaboration.

Emerging cyber threats driven by rapid advances demand resilient systems and robust cybersecurity awareness to counter human vulnerabilities in an ongoing arms race. Examples include

CHAPTER 1 INTRODUCTION TO CYBERSECURITY

- **Continued Evolution**: The rapid pace of technological advancement will drive increasingly complex cybersecurity threats.

- **Focus on Resilience**: The shift is moving from pure prevention to building systems that can endure and recover from cyber incidents.

- **The Human Factor**: Cybersecurity awareness and training remain critical in mitigating risks tied to human error and social engineering.

- The evolution of cybersecurity threats is a continuous arms race—as technology advances, so do cybercriminals. Staying ahead requires innovation, adaptation, and a proactive approach to security and education.

CHAPTER 1   INTRODUCTION TO CYBERSECURITY

Cybersecurity Impacts by Numbers: A Snapshot

Cybercrime is projected to cost the global economy a staggering $10.5 trillion annually, making it one of the most lucrative and damaging criminal enterprises in history. This surge is fueled by increasingly sophisticated threats such as ransomware, phishing, AI-powered attacks, and business email compromise, which now affect organizations of all sizes and sectors. The World Economic Forum's 2025 Outlook highlights how geopolitical tensions, emerging technologies, and supply chain interdependencies are compounding the complexity of the threat landscape.

Key statistics highlight the scale and impact of cybersecurity threats and defenses include

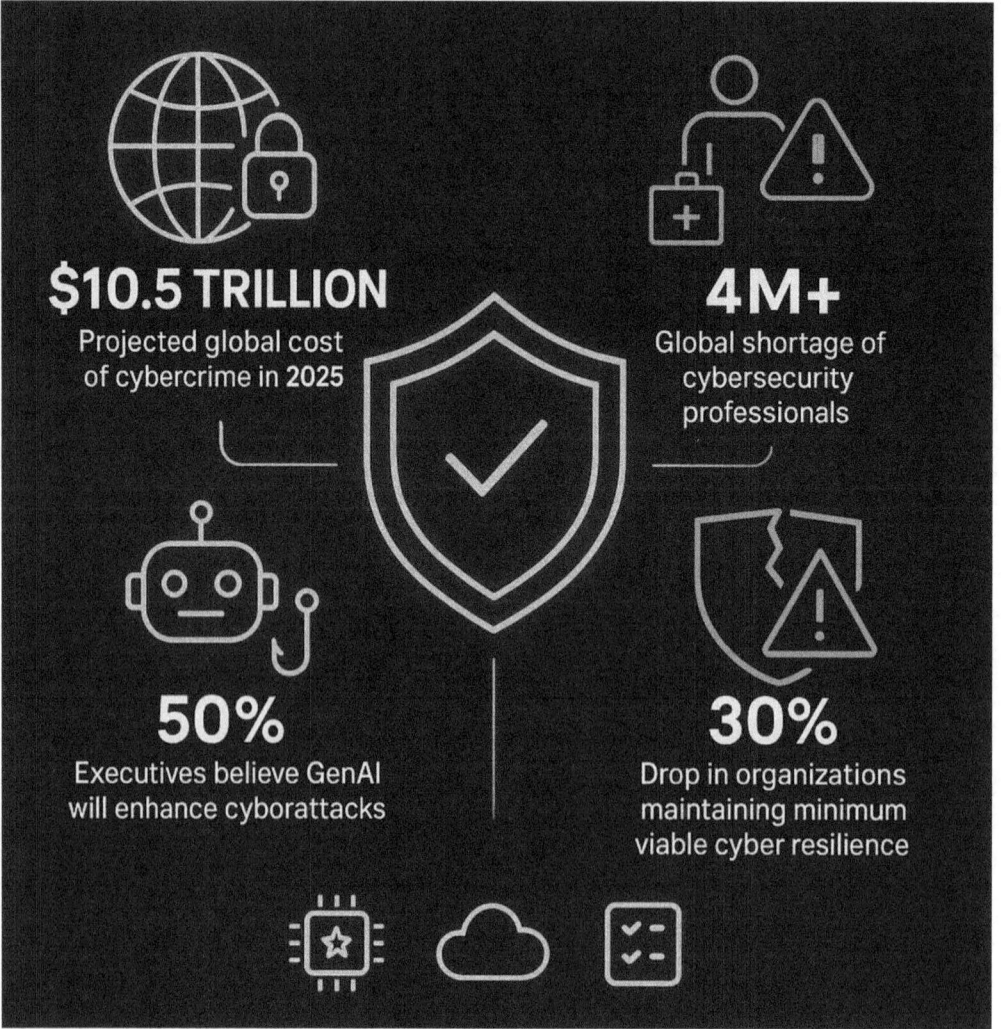

- **Cost of Cybercrime**
  - The annual global cost of cybercrime is projected to exceed $10.5 trillion by 2025 up from $8.4 trillion in 2022 and $23 trillion by 2027.
  - The average cost of a data breach in 2024 was $4.88 million.
- **Data Breaches**
  - The frequency of data breaches continues to rise.
  - Millions of personal records are compromised each year.
- **Cybersecurity Workforce**
  - A global cybersecurity skills shortage remains a critical challenge.
  - Millions of professionals are needed to fill security roles worldwide.
- **Cybersecurity Spending**
  - Organizations are making significant investments in cybersecurity, yet threats continue to evolve.

Key Cybersecurity Statistics

- **Data Breaches**: The number of data breaches rose by 200% between 2013 and 2022. In 2024, the average cost per breach was $4.88 million.
- **Vulnerabilities**: A new security vulnerability is identified and published every 17 minutes.
- **Malware**: More than 450,000 new malware variants are detected daily worldwide.
- **Human Error**: 68% of data breaches can be traced back to human error.
- **Password Security**
  - 37% of employees use their employer's name in their password.
  - 44% of users recycle passwords across personal and business accounts.

CHAPTER 1   INTRODUCTION TO CYBERSECURITY

- **Cybercrime Costs**: Cryptocrime is projected to cost $30 billion by 2025.
- **Cybersecurity Market**: The cybersecurity industry is expected to grow to $300 billion by 2024.
- **Cyber Insurance**: One in three US companies has purchased data-breach or cyber liability insurance.

The Big Breaches

The most devastating cyber breaches in history include the following (see Tables 1-1, 1-2, and 1-3):

- **Yahoo (2013–2016)**: Over three billion accounts were compromised, exposing personal data such as email addresses and passwords.
- **Equifax (2017)**: Affected 148 million people, exposing Social Security numbers, birthdates, and addresses.
- **Facebook (2019)**: A data breach exposed the personal information of 533 million users, including names, locations, birthdates, and phone numbers.
- **Marriott International (2014–2018)**: Guest reservation data for approximately 383 million guests was compromised, including passport numbers and credit card information.
- **Capital One (2019)**: Exposed the personal and financial information of 100 million customers, including Social Security numbers, bank account details, and credit card information.
- **SolarWinds (2020)**: A sophisticated supply chain attack implanted malware into widely used software, affecting government agencies and private companies globally.
- **Accellion (2020)**: A zero-day exploit targeted a file server, affecting multiple companies. The total cost remains undisclosed.
- **Microsoft Exchange Server (2021)**: A series of vulnerabilities allowed hackers to access and steal emails, calendars, and sensitive data.

- **Colonial Pipeline (May 2021)**: A ransomware attack disrupted fuel supply across the US East Coast, causing widespread shortages.

- **Kaseya (July 2021)**: A supply chain ransomware attack affected over 1,500 businesses worldwide.

- **T-Mobile (August 2021)**: A breach exposed the personal data of 50 million customers, including Social Security numbers and driver's license details.

- **Facebook (October 2021)**: Over 500 million user records were leaked due to a security misconfiguration.

- **Electronic Arts (December 2021)**: Credential abuse led to the theft of 780GB of gaming source code and development tools.

- **Microsoft (2022)**: A zero-day exploit compromised user accounts and cloud infrastructure.

- **Twitter (2022)**: A zero-day vulnerability led to the exposure of over 5.4 million user profiles.

- **Apache Log4J (2022)**: A critical zero-day exploit impacted millions of devices and enterprise applications worldwide.

- **DC Health Link (2023)**: A misconfiguration exploit exposed the healthcare data of US government employees.

- **UnitedHealth Group's ChangeHealth (2024)**: In February 2024, a ransomware attack on Change Healthcare, a subsidiary of UnitedHealth Group, compromised the protected health information of millions of people. UnitedHealth estimated that 190 million people were impacted by the breach and UnitedHealth paid a $22 million ransom to BlackCat/ALPHV ransomware group.

- **Fidelity Investments (2024)**: A third-party data breach impacted over 28,000 customers.

- **Integris Health (2024)**: A cyberattack exposed the personal information of nearly 2.4 million patients.

CHAPTER 1   INTRODUCTION TO CYBERSECURITY

Table 1-1. Top Ten Data Breaches in 2023

	Organization name	Sector	Location	Known records breached	Month of public disclosure
1	DarkBeam	Cybersecurity	UK	>3,800,000,000	September
2	Real Estate Wealth Network	Construction/real estate	USA	1,523,776,691	December
3	Indian Council of Medical Research (ICMR)	Healthcare	India	815,000,000	October
4	Kid Security	IT services/software	Kazakhstan	>300,000,000	November
5	Twitter (X)	IT services/software	USA	>220,000,000	January
6	TuneFab	IT services/software	Hong Kong	>151,000,000	December
7	Dori Media Group	Media	Israel	>100 TB	December
8	Tigo	Telecoms	Hong Kong	>100,000,000	July
9	SAP SE Bulgaria	IT services/software	Bulgaria	95,592,696	November
10	Luxottica Group	Manufacturing	Italy	70,000,000	May

CHAPTER 1 INTRODUCTION TO CYBERSECURITY

Table 1-2. *Top Ten US Data Breaches in 2024*

	Organization name	Sector	Location	Known records breached	Month of public disclosure
1	National Public Data	Data management	USA	>1,300,000,000	
2	AT&T	Telecom	USA	>183,000,000	
3	T-Mobile	Telecom	USA	>31,500,000	
4	Community Clinic of Maui	IT services/software	USA	>123,000	
5	Infosys McCammish Systems	IT services/software	USA	>805,000,000	
6	United Health	Healthcare	USA	>100,000,000	
7	Young Consulting	Software	USA	1,000,000	
8	Ticketmaster	Sales and distribution	USA	>40,000,000	
9	Evolve Bank	Banking and finance	USA	7,600,000	
10	Dell	Hi-tech	USA	49,000,000 customers and 10,000 employees	

Table 1-3. Top Ten Data Breaches in 2024

	Organization name	Sector	Location	Known records breached	Month of public disclosure
1	Change Healthcare	Healthcare	USA	Over 190 million	Feb-24
2	Snowflake	Technology	USA	Data from over 100 customers	May-24
3	UK Ministry of Defence	Government	United Kingdom	Approximately 270,000 personnel records	May-24
4	Ascension	Healthcare	USA	Approximately 5.6 million individuals	May-24
5	MediSecure	Healthcare	Australia	Not specified	Not specified
6	Synnovis-NHS UK	Healthcare	United Kingdom	Disrupted services	Jun-24
7	CrowdStrike-Microsoft Outage	Technology	USA	Service disruption	Not specified
8	Transport for London (TfL)	Transportation	United Kingdom	Systems targeted; customer data reportedly unaffected	Aug-24
9	Ivanti	Technology	USA	Mass zero-day exploits	Not specified
10	Salt Typhoon	Cybersecurity	China	State-sponsored cyber activities	Not specified

Cybersecurity Trends in 2025 (and Beyond)

Cybersecurity in 2025 is marked by rapid technological advancements, evolving threats, and shifting geopolitical landscapes. The cybersecurity landscape in 2025 underscores the need for proactive strategies, continuous adaptation, and collaborative efforts to safeguard against evolving threats.

CHAPTER 1 INTRODUCTION TO CYBERSECURITY

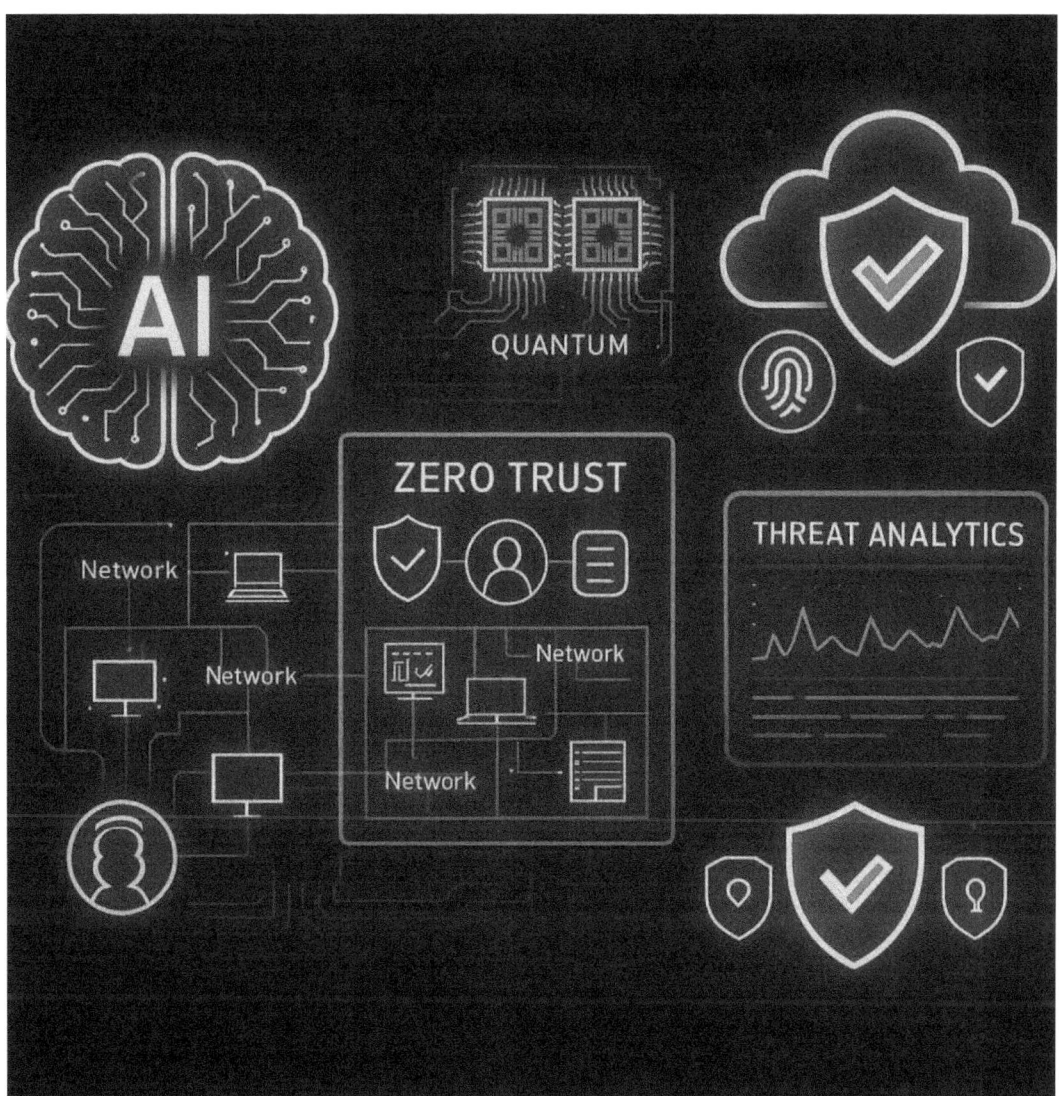

Industry analysts estimate that the global cost of cybersecurity will reach a staggering $10.5 trillion in FY 2025. To put that into perspective, this is larger than the GDP of many major countries, a significant percentage of global IT spending, etc. If cybersecurity were a country, it would be third economy in the world after the United States and China. This figure underscores the immense financial implications of cyber threats for organizations worldwide.

The $10.5 trillion encompasses a wide range of expenses, including

1. **Direct Costs**: Recovery from cyberattacks, business disruption, legal and regulatory fines

2. **Indirect Costs**: Reputational damage, loss of customer trust, decreased productivity

3. **Preventative Costs**: Investments in security technologies, personnel, training, and compliance

It is important to note that while the $10.5 trillion figure is a prominent projection, other estimates exist. For instance, some reports suggest that the global cost could be in the range of $1.2 to $1.5 trillion by the end of 2025. These varying figures highlight the difficulty in fully quantifying the total impact of cybercrime. However, all indicators point toward a continued and substantial increase in the financial burden caused by malicious cyber activities.

CHAPTER 1   INTRODUCTION TO CYBERSECURITY

Types of Data Compromised

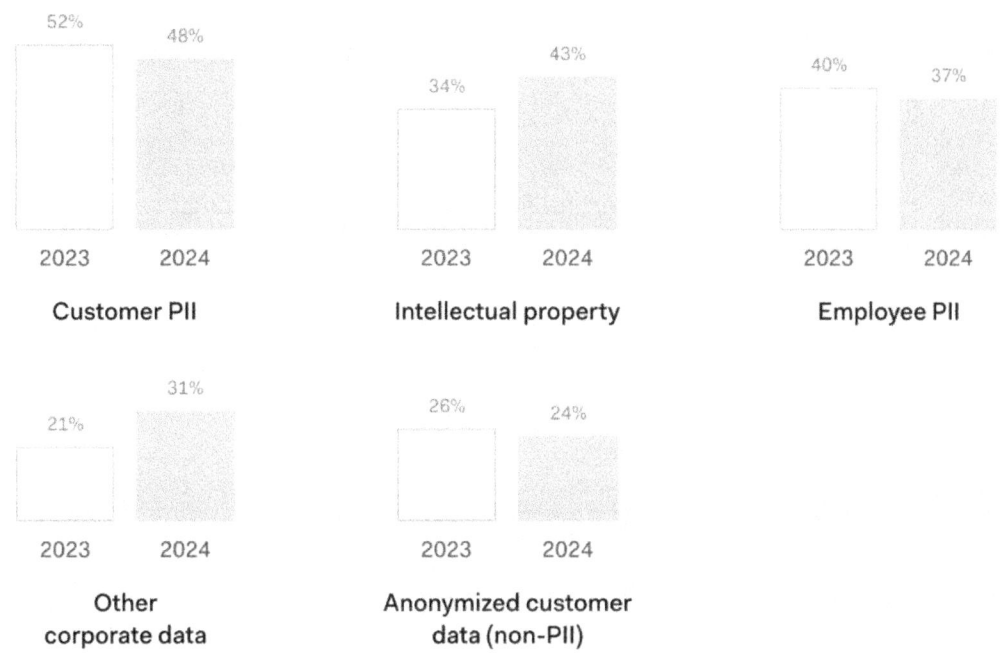

Source: IBM Report 2024

The figure above shows the types of data compromised by percentage.

These are just a few examples of the many significant cyber breaches that have occurred in recent years. These events highlight the importance of strong cybersecurity measures to protect sensitive information and mitigate the risks associated with cyberattacks.

The Importance of Cybersecurity in Today's World

In today's hyper-connected world, cybersecurity is not a luxury—it is an absolute necessity. Technology is deeply embedded in every aspect of life, from personal communication and financial transactions to critical infrastructure and national security. A strong cybersecurity posture is no longer just a technical requirement; it is a fundamental pillar of social, economic, and political stability.

CHAPTER 1   INTRODUCTION TO CYBERSECURITY

The Ubiquity of Technology

Technology affects every aspect of our lives, including

- **Personal Life**: Smartphones, laptops, and connected devices facilitate everything from social interactions and entertainment to online shopping and remote work.

- **Businesses**: Organizations of all sizes depend on technology for operations, communication, data storage, and customer engagement.

- **Critical Infrastructure**: Essential services, including power grids, transportation, healthcare, and financial markets, increasingly rely on interconnected systems.

- **Government**: Governments use technology for national security, law enforcement, and public service delivery, making them prime cyberattack targets.

The Escalating Threat Landscape

The cyber threat landscape is constantly evolving, with attackers becoming increasingly sophisticated and malicious:

- **Ransomware Attacks**: Cybercriminals encrypt critical data, demanding ransom payments for its release, crippling businesses and infrastructure.

- **Data Breaches**: The theft of sensitive personal and financial information can have devastating consequences for individuals and organizations.

- **Supply Chain Attacks**: Attackers exploit software supply chain vulnerabilities to infiltrate and compromise multiple organizations.

- **Nation-State Actors**: Advanced Persistent Threats (APTs) from state-sponsored actors target critical infrastructure and government systems for espionage and sabotage.

- **Emerging Threats**: The rise of artificial intelligence (AI) and the Internet of Things (IoT) introduces new vulnerabilities and attack vectors.

The Consequences of Cyberattacks

The consequences of cyberattacks can be devastating, affecting individuals, businesses, and even critical infrastructure. Here's a breakdown of the potential impacts:

For Individuals

- **Identity Theft**: Cybercriminals can steal personal information like social security numbers, bank account details, and passwords to open fraudulent accounts, make purchases, or apply for loans in your name.

- **Financial Loss**: You could lose money through unauthorized transactions, scams, or ransomware attacks that encrypt your files and demand payment for their release.

- **Loss of Privacy**: Cyberattacks can expose your personal data, browsing history, and online activity, leading to privacy violations and potential embarrassment.

- **Emotional Distress**: The stress and anxiety caused by a cyberattack can be significant, especially when dealing with identity theft or financial loss.

For Businesses

- **Financial Losses**: Businesses can suffer significant financial damage due to data breaches, ransomware attacks, and disruption of operations. Costs can include
  - **Direct costs**: Ransom payments, legal fees, regulatory fines, IT recovery expenses
  - **Indirect costs**: Loss of revenue, damage to reputation, customer churn

- **Reputational Damage**: A cyberattack can severely damage a company's reputation, leading to loss of customer trust and negative publicity.

- **Operational Disruption**: Cyberattacks can disrupt business operations, causing downtime, delays, and loss of productivity.

- **Legal and Regulatory Issues**: Companies that fail to protect customer data may face legal action and hefty fines for noncompliance with data protection regulations.

For Critical Infrastructure

- **Disruption of Essential Services**: Cyberattacks can target critical infrastructure like power grids, hospitals, and transportation systems, potentially causing widespread disruption and endangering lives.

- **National Security Threats**: Cyberattacks can be used to steal sensitive government information, disrupt critical services, or even sabotage infrastructure, posing a threat to national security.

Examples of Real-World Consequences

- **Colonial Pipeline Attack**: A ransomware attack in 2021 shut down the largest fuel pipeline in the United States, causing widespread fuel shortages and price increases.

- **Equifax Data Breach**: In 2017, a massive data breach at Equifax exposed the personal information of nearly 150 million people, leading to identity theft and financial losses.

- **WannaCry Ransomware Attack**: In 2017, the WannaCry ransomware attack infected hundreds of thousands of computers worldwide, disrupting businesses and healthcare organizations.

Protecting Yourself and Your Business

- Use strong passwords and enable multifactor authentication.
- Keep your software updated.
- Be cautious of phishing emails and suspicious links.
- Install antivirus and anti-malware software.
- Back up your data regularly.
- Educate yourself and your employees about cybersecurity best practices.
- Develop an incident response plan to prepare for potential cyberattacks.

The Importance of Proactive Measures

Given the increasing threat landscape, proactive cybersecurity measures are essential:

- **Robust Cybersecurity Frameworks**: Implementing and maintaining frameworks like NIST and ISO is crucial for organizations of all sizes.

- **Continuous Monitoring and Threat Intelligence**: Real-time system monitoring and intelligence gathering help detect and mitigate threats proactively.

- **Cybersecurity Education and Training**: Employees must be trained on cybersecurity best practices, including recognizing phishing emails and using secure passwords.

- **International Cooperation**: Collaboration across nations is essential to combat global cyber threats and share intelligence and best practices.

- **Research and Development**: Advancements in AI-powered threat detection, encryption, and risk mitigation help organizations stay ahead of emerging cyber threats.

Cybersecurity is no longer a niche concern—it is central to national and global security, economic stability, and individual safety. By understanding the evolving threat landscape, implementing robust security measures, and fostering a culture of cybersecurity awareness, we can mitigate risks, protect critical systems, and create a more secure and resilient digital future.

Key Cybersecurity Principles

This chapter provided a general overview of key cybersecurity principles. Specific implementation details may vary depending on the organization's size, industry, and risk tolerance.

Cybersecurity is an ever-evolving field, but certain fundamental principles remain crucial for safeguarding digital assets and mitigating risks. It explored some of the key cybersecurity principles that organizations of all sizes should embrace: confidentiality, integrity, availability, accountability, least privilege, defense in depth, protective risk management, and transparency and communication.

CHAPTER 1   INTRODUCTION TO CYBERSECURITY

The first three confidentiality, integrity, and availability constitute the CIA framework as shown in the diagram below; a cornerstone of information security, it outlines three fundamental principles essential for protecting information and systems. **Confidentiality** ensures that sensitive information is accessible only to authorized individuals, preventing unauthorized disclosure. This is achieved through measures like encryption, access controls, and data anonymization. **Integrity** focuses on maintaining the accuracy, completeness, and trustworthiness of information throughout its life cycle. It aims to prevent unauthorized modification or destruction of data, often implemented through hashing, digital signatures, and version control. Lastly, **availability** guarantees that authorized users can access information and systems when needed. This involves implementing robust infrastructure, redundancy, backup and recovery plans, and protection against denial-of-service attacks. Together, these three principles form a comprehensive approach to safeguarding information assets.

1. Confidentiality

Protecting sensitive information from unauthorized access, use, disclosure, disruption, modification, or destruction. This includes customer records, financial data, intellectual property, and employee information.

Implementation

- **Encryption**: Use strong encryption algorithms to secure data in transit and at rest.

- **Access Control**: Enforce multifactor authentication (MFA), role-based access control (RBAC), and least privilege to restrict access.

- **Data Loss Prevention (DLP)**: Deploy DLP tools to monitor and prevent unauthorized data transfers.

2. Integrity

Ensuring the accuracy and completeness of information while preventing unauthorized modifications or deletions.

Implementation

- **Hashing**: Use hashing algorithms to verify data integrity and detect unauthorized changes.

- **Change Management**: Establish a formal change management process to track and control system and data modifications.

- **Input Validation**: Implement user input validation to prevent malicious data from entering systems.

3. Availability

Ensuring authorized users can access systems and data when needed.

Implementation

- **Redundancy**: Maintain redundant systems and backups to ensure business continuity during disruptions.

- **Disaster Recovery Planning**: Develop and regularly test disaster recovery plans to minimize downtime during emergencies.
- **Regular Maintenance**: Conduct routine system updates and maintenance to address vulnerabilities and optimize performance.

4. Accountability

Establishing clear cybersecurity responsibilities within an organization.
Implementation

- **Security Policies**: Create and enforce comprehensive security policies covering acceptable use, data handling, and incident response.
- **User Training**: Provide ongoing cybersecurity awareness training to help employees recognize threats and follow best practices.
- **Incident Response Plan**: Develop and regularly test an incident response plan to efficiently handle security breaches.

5. Least Privilege

The Principle of Least Privilege (PoLP) is a fundamental concept in information security that dictates that a user, entity, application, or system should be granted only the minimum necessary access rights or permissions required to perform its legitimate functions and nothing more, as illustrated in the following Venn diagram.

In simpler terms, it's about giving out only the "keys" that are absolutely essential for someone or something to do their job and no extra keys that could lead to unauthorized access or potential harm.

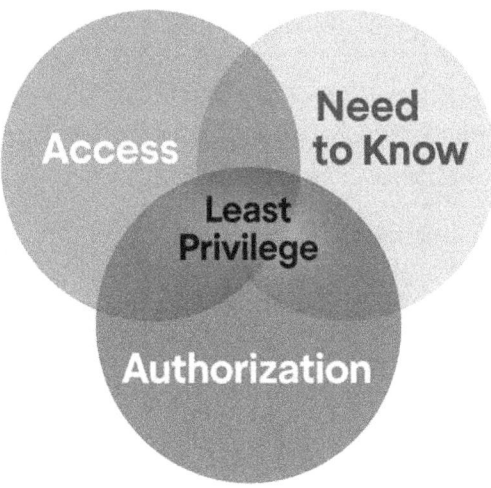

Implementation

- **Role-Based Access Control (RBAC)**: Implement RBAC to assign permissions based on job roles and responsibilities.
- **Regular Access Reviews**: Conduct regular access reviews to ensure that user permissions remain appropriate and up-to-date.

6. Defense in Depth

Utilizing multiple layers of security controls to safeguard systems and data against various threats.

Implementation

- **Firewalls**: Use firewalls to regulate network traffic and block unauthorized access.
- **Intrusion Detection Systems (IDS)**: Deploy IDS to continuously monitor network activity for malicious behavior.
- **Antivirus and Anti-Malware Software**: Ensure all devices are equipped with up-to-date antivirus and anti-malware solutions.

7. Proactive Risk Management

Continuously identifying, assessing, and mitigating cybersecurity risks to minimize potential threats and vulnerabilities.

Implementation

- **Threat Modeling**: Regularly conduct threat modeling exercises to identify vulnerabilities and attack vectors.
- **Vulnerability Scanning**: Perform scheduled scans to detect and remediate security weaknesses.
- **Security Information and Event Management (SIEM)**: Use SIEM tools to aggregate, analyze, and correlate security logs for real-time threat detection and response.

8. Transparency and Communication

Ensuring open and transparent communication with stakeholders regarding cybersecurity risks and incidents.

Implementation

- **Incident Reporting**: Establish clear procedures for reporting and managing security incidents.
- **Communication Plans**: Develop structured plans to inform stakeholders about security incidents and mitigation strategies.

By following these key cybersecurity principles, organizations can strengthen their security posture, safeguard critical assets, and reduce the impact of cyber threats.

Key Takeaways

Cybersecurity has drastically changed from a technical, IT-focused issue to a **critical, strategic priority** for organizations of all types and sizes.

- **Digital Transformation's Impact**: The increasing reliance on technology, especially cloud computing, remote work, and distributed systems, has significantly **expanded the attack surface** for cybercriminals. Traditional security measures are no longer adequate.

- **Multilayered Approach Is Essential**: Organizations must adopt **comprehensive, multilayered cybersecurity strategies** to protect their data and systems in this dynamic threat landscape.

- **Boardroom Concern**: Cybersecurity is no longer just an IT department issue. It's now a **major business risk** that requires attention and discussion at the highest levels of leadership (the boardroom).

- **Shifting Landscape**: The modern enterprise is distributed, with employees working remotely, applications in various locations, and data spread across clouds and on-premises servers. This **complexity demands a new approach to security**.

CHAPTER 2

Core Cybersecurity Concepts

Core concepts in cybersecurity include confidentiality, integrity, and availability (CIA), as well as network security and vulnerabilities.

This chapter provides an in-depth exploration of essential cybersecurity principles crucial for professionals and organizations seeking to enhance their security posture. Building upon foundational cybersecurity definitions, the following sections delve into core concepts that underpin effective security practices.

Risk Assessment and Management

- **Identifying Vulnerabilities**: Conducting comprehensive security assessments to identify weaknesses in systems, networks, and applications. Common methods include vulnerability scanning, penetration testing, and risk assessments.

- **Threat Modeling**: Analyzing potential threats and their impact on organizational assets. This helps prioritize mitigation efforts and allocate resources effectively.

- **Risk Mitigation**: Implementing technical, administrative, and physical controls to minimize the likelihood and impact of cyber threats.

Access Control

- **Authentication**: Verifying user and device identities before granting access. Methods include passwords, biometrics, and multifactor authentication (MFA).

- **Authorization**: Enforcing access privileges to ensure individuals only have access necessary for their job functions.

- **Least Privilege**: Granting users the minimum required access to reduce potential damage from compromised accounts.

Data Security

- **Data Encryption**: Transforming data into an unreadable format to prevent unauthorized access—essential for protecting data in transit and at rest

- **Data Loss Prevention (DLP)**: Preventing unauthorized data transfers through monitoring, blocking, and classification policies

- **Data Backup and Recovery**: Regularly backing up critical data and maintaining disaster recovery plans to ensure business continuity

Network Security

- **Firewalls**: Devices that filter network traffic based on predefined rules, creating a barrier between internal and external networks.

- **Intrusion Detection and Prevention Systems (IDPS)**: Monitor and respond to malicious network activity, blocking or alerting on threats.

- **Virtual Private Networks (VPNs)**: Establish secure, encrypted connections over public networks, ensuring safe remote access.

Incident Response

- **Incident Detection**: Identifying and responding to security incidents through log monitoring, intrusion detection, and threat intelligence feeds

- **Incident Handling**: Containing, investigating, and remediating incidents by isolating affected systems, collecting evidence, and restoring functionality

- **Post-incident Activities**: Conducting root cause analysis to implement corrective actions and improve future response capabilities

Cybersecurity Awareness and Training

- **Educating Employees**: Raising awareness of cybersecurity risks such as phishing, social engineering, and secure password practices

- **Promoting a Security Culture**: Encouraging all employees to understand their role in safeguarding organizational assets

These foundational cybersecurity concepts provide a framework for building and maintaining a strong security posture. By adopting these principles, organizations can mitigate risks, protect valuable assets, and ensure resilience against evolving cyber threats.

Threat Modeling and Risk Assessment

Threat modeling is a structured approach to identifying, analyzing, and mitigating security threats in a system or application. This process involves thinking like an attacker to anticipate vulnerabilities.

Risk management is the overall process of identifying, assessing, and controlling risks in an organization. It involves making informed decisions on allocating resources to minimize threats effectively.

Common Threat Modeling Methods and Key Steps

1. **Define Objectives and Scope**

    Begin by clearly articulating the purpose of the threat modeling initiative. Identify what you aim to achieve—whether it's uncovering architectural weaknesses, ensuring compliance, improving secure development practices, or reducing business risk.

    Define the scope of the assessment, specifying

    - The systems, applications, and infrastructure components involved
    - The business units, user roles, and third parties interacting with the system
    - Key business processes and data flows under review

    A well-defined scope ensures focused analysis and efficient use of resources.

2. **Identify and Prioritize Assets**

    Catalog all critical assets within the defined scope, such as

    - Sensitive data (PII, IP, financial data)
    - Core applications
    - Infrastructure components (servers, APIs, networks)
    - User identities and credentials

    Evaluate the value of each asset in terms of confidentiality, integrity, and availability (CIA), and prioritize them based on their business importance and exposure to risk.

3. **Create an Architecture Overview (Aligned with the VAST Model)**

    Develop a visual representation of the system using architectural diagrams that highlight

    - Key components (e.g., front end, back end, databases, services)
    - Data flows between components
    - Trust boundaries (e.g., user to app, app to database, internal to external)

Ensure the diagrams are

- **Visual**: Easily understandable for technical and nontechnical stakeholders.
- **Agile**: Flexible and capable of evolving as the system changes.
- **Simple**: Avoid unnecessary complexity; focus on actionable details.

This step enables a shared understanding of the system's attack surface.

4. **Identify Threat Actors**

   Analyze potential adversaries who might target your system. Include

   - **External**: Cybercriminals, nation-states, hacktivists, competitors
   - **Internal**: Disgruntled employees, contractors, accidental insiders

   Assess each actor's

   - **Motivations** (e.g., financial gain, disruption, espionage)
   - **Capabilities** (technical skill, resources)
   - **Access vectors** (insider privileges, phishing, malware)

   Understanding threat actors informs prioritization of security controls.

5. **Decompose Application and Identify Threats (STRIDE Methodology)**

   Break down the application into granular components to analyze

   - Interactions between components
   - Data transmission points
   - Entry and exit points

   Use the **STRIDE** framework to identify potential threats:

   As shown below, the STRIDE model is a threat modeling methodology used in cybersecurity to identify and categorize potential threats to a system or application. It's an acronym where each letter represents a different category of threat:

CHAPTER 2   CORE CYBERSECURITY CONCEPTS

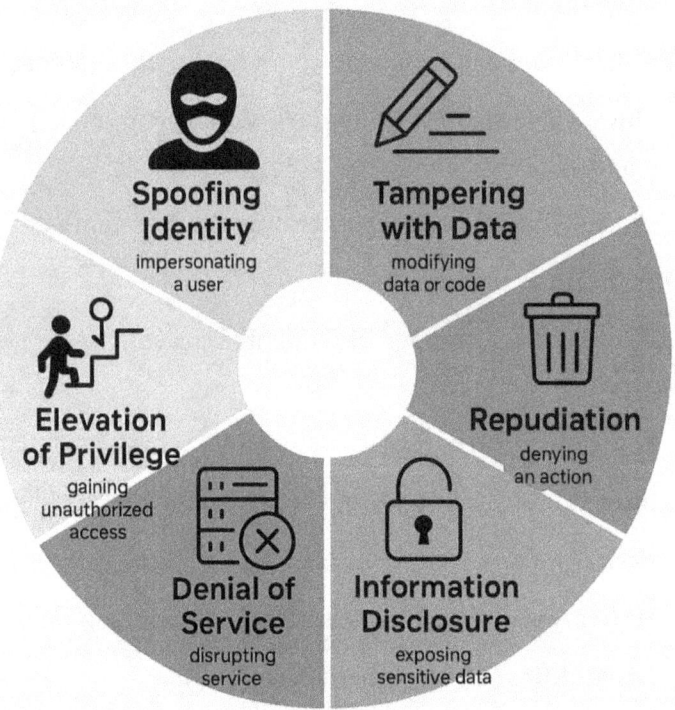

- **S: Spoofing**—This threat involves an attacker impersonating a legitimate user, system, or process. The goal is to gain unauthorized access or deceive the system into believing they are someone or something they are not.
    - **Example**: An attacker sends an email that appears to be from a trusted colleague, tricking the recipient into revealing sensitive information.
- **T: Tampering**—This refers to the unauthorized modification or alteration of data. It can apply to data at rest (stored), data in transit (being sent), or data being processed.
    - **Example**: An attacker modifies a financial transaction amount as it's being transferred between accounts.

- **R: Repudiation**—This threat occurs when an attacker can deny having performed an action, and the system lacks sufficient proof to contradict their denial. This impacts accountability and non-repudiation.
    - **Example**: A user denies making a purchase on an ecommerce site, and there's no logging or digital signature to prove they did.
- **I: Information Disclosure**—This involves the unauthorized exposure or leakage of sensitive information. This can range from confidential business data to personal user information.
    - **Example**: A misconfigured database allows anyone to view customer credit card details.
- **D: Denial of Service (DoS)**—This threat aims to make a system, application, or resource unavailable to its legitimate users. This is often achieved by overwhelming the system with traffic or exploiting vulnerabilities that cause it to crash.
    - **Example**: An attacker floods a web server with so many requests that legitimate users cannot access the website.
- **E: Elevation of Privilege**—This threat allows an attacker to gain higher levels of access or permissions than they legitimately should have. This often leads to an attacker being able to perform actions they wouldn't normally be authorized to do.
    - **Example**: A standard user exploits a software bug to gain administrative rights on a system.

Complement STRIDE analysis with

- Attack trees and misuse cases
- Threat intelligence feeds
- Historical vulnerability data

6. **Analyze Threats and Vulnerabilities**

   The **DREAD framework** is a risk assessment model used in threat modeling to evaluate and prioritize security threats based on five key factors: **Damage potential, Reproducibility, Exploitability, Affected users**, and **Discoverability**. Each factor is scored on a consistent scale (typically 1 to 10), and the total score helps determine the relative risk of a threat. For example, a vulnerability that is easy to exploit (high Exploitability), causes significant harm (high Damage potential), and affects many users will score higher and warrant more urgent mitigation. While DREAD provides a structured and quantitative approach to prioritizing threats, it has been largely deprecated in favor of simpler models like STRIDE or qualitative risk matrices, due to concerns around subjectivity and inconsistent scoring. However, it remains a useful educational tool and starting point for understanding risk prioritization in security assessments.

   Assess each identified threat using the **DREAD** model to quantify risk:

   - **Damage**: Potential business or technical impact
   - **Reproducibility**: Ease of recreating the exploit
   - **Exploitability**: Effort required to launch the attack
   - **Affected Users**: Number of impacted individuals/systems
   - **Discoverability**: Likelihood of the vulnerability being found

Additionally, apply the **LINDDUN** framework for privacy threat analysis:

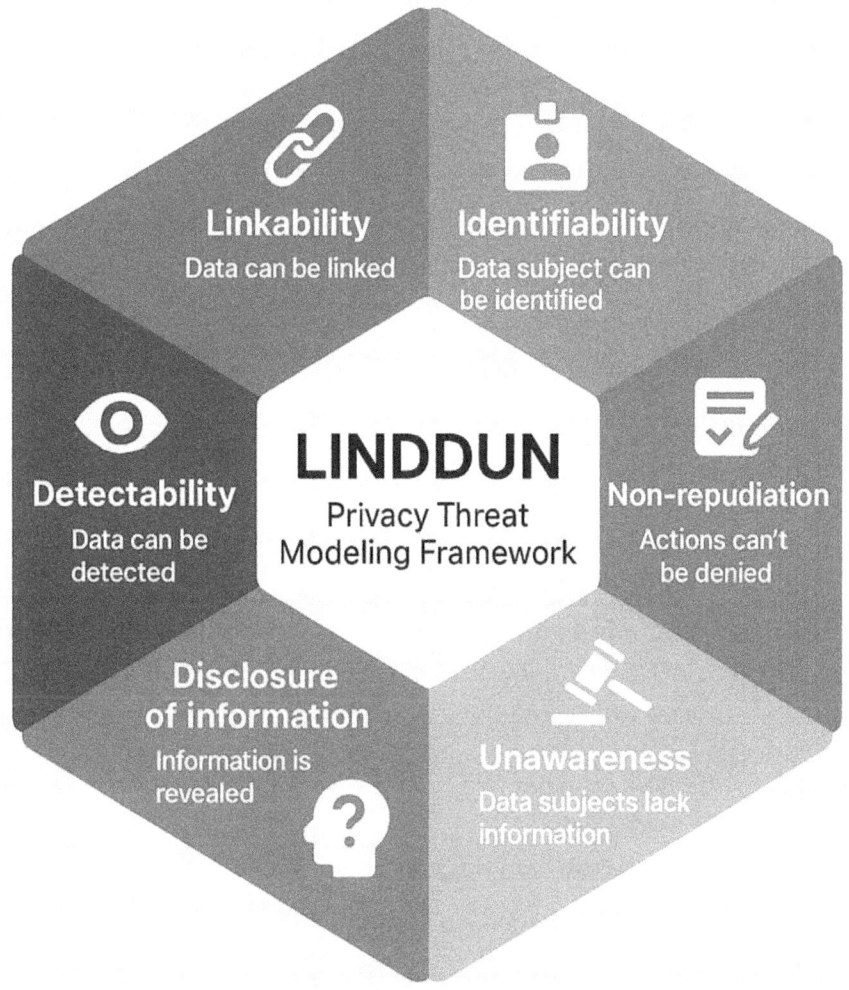

LINDDUN is a privacy threat modeling framework designed to systematically identify and mitigate privacy risks in software systems. The acronym stands for **Linkability, Identifiability, Non-repudiation, Detectability, Disclosure of information, Unawareness, and Noncompliance**—each representing a category of privacy threat. Unlike security-focused frameworks that center on protecting systems from unauthorized access, LINDDUN focuses specifically on how personal data might be exposed, misused, or mishandled. It guides architects and developers through a structured process: starting with a system's Data Flow Diagram (DFD), mapping each component to applicable privacy threats, and then developing appropriate countermeasures. LINDDUN is particularly useful in privacy-by-design efforts and is complementary to threat modeling tools like STRIDE, offering a dedicated lens for protecting user data and aligning with privacy regulations such as GDPR.

- **L: Linkability**—The ability to link two or more actions, data items, or identities that were intended to be unconnected.
    - **Example**: Anonymized health records can be linked to individuals if they contain similar patterns or rare conditions.
- **I: Identifiability**—The possibility to uniquely identify an individual from a dataset.
    - **Example**: A dataset with ZIP code, birthdate, and gender can uniquely identify many individuals.
- **N: Non-repudiation**—The inability of a subject to deny having performed an action. While useful in security (e.g., digital signatures), this may violate privacy when individuals cannot plausibly deny involvement.
    - **Example**: Logging user activities in a system without allowing for anonymity.
- **D: Detectability**—The ability to detect the presence of an individual or their data in a system, even without identifying them.
    - **Example**: An attacker notices that a certain user's data traffic pattern spikes at a specific time.
- **D: Disclosure of Information**—Unauthorized or unintended exposure of personal or sensitive data.
    - **Example**: A data breach that leaks customer financial details.
- **U: Unawareness**—The data subject is unaware of how their data is collected, used, or shared.
    - **Example**: Users agreeing to vague or hidden data collection in app permissions.

- **N: Noncompliance**—Failure to comply with privacy policies, user consent terms, or data protection regulations (like GDPR or HIPAA).
  - **Example**: Sharing data with third parties without user consent.

Perform

- Static and dynamic code analysis
- Vulnerability scans
- Manual code reviews
- Penetration testing

This multilayered analysis gives a comprehensive view of security and privacy risks.

7. **Perform Attack Modeling (Using PASTA Methodology)**

   The **PASTA (Process for Attack Simulation and Threat Analysis)** framework is a risk-centric threat modeling methodology designed to help organizations identify, analyze, and mitigate cyber threats early in the development life cycle. It consists of **seven sequential stages**, starting with defining business objectives and technical scope and progressing through decomposition of the application, threat enumeration, vulnerability analysis, attack modeling, risk analysis, and finally, countermeasure implementation. Unlike traditional threat models that focus solely on technical vulnerabilities, PASTA integrates **business impact analysis and attacker profiling**, making it especially useful for aligning security efforts with organizational risk tolerance and compliance goals. Its structured, repeatable process helps security teams simulate real-world attack scenarios and prioritize mitigation strategies based on potential impact.

   Adopt the **PASTA (Process for Attack Simulation and Threat Analysis)** framework to simulate real-world attack scenarios:

   1. **Define Business Objectives**: Align threat modeling with business priorities.
   2. **Define Technical Scope**: Identify system architecture, assets, and boundaries.

3. **Decompose Application**: Detail components and workflows.
4. **Analyze Threats**: Map identified threats to attack scenarios.
5. **Analyze Vulnerabilities**: Review vulnerabilities and weaknesses.
6. **Simulate Attacks**: Model potential exploits to assess impact.
7. **Conduct Risk and Impact Analysis**: Score risk likelihood and business impact.
8. **Evaluate Countermeasures**: Recommend actionable mitigations.

This approach provides context-rich insights, balancing technical depth with business relevance.

8. **Evaluate Risk and Impact**

    Consolidate findings into an overall risk posture by evaluating

    - The severity of threats and vulnerabilities
    - The likelihood of exploitation
    - The business impact (e.g., financial loss, reputational damage, legal exposure)

    Use risk matrices or heatmaps to visually communicate risk levels to stakeholders.

9. **Develop and Prioritize Countermeasure**

    Identify and recommend security controls and mitigations such as

    - Authentication hardening
    - Access controls and least privilege enforcement
    - Data encryption and tokenization
    - Input validation and output encoding
    - Network segmentation
    - Security monitoring and alerting

Assess each control's
- Effectiveness
- Implementation effort
- Cost vs. benefit

Prioritize actions based on risk severity, business priority, and resource availability.

10. **Validate, Review, and Iterate**

    Review the threat model with key stakeholders:
    - Validate threat assumptions and countermeasures.
    - Identify missing scenarios or new threats.
    - Incorporate feedback from developers, security teams, and business leaders.

    Threat modeling should be a **living process**, revisited during
    - Major system changes
    - Software release cycles
    - New threat intelligence emergence

11. **Communicate Results and Build Awareness**

    Prepare clear, actionable reports for different audiences:
    - **Executives**: High-level risks and business implications
    - **Developers**: Technical vulnerabilities and required fixes
    - **Security Teams**: Monitoring and incident response needs

    Deliver training sessions to ensure teams understand
    - Their roles in addressing threats
    - How to implement and test mitigations
    - How to respond to emerging threats

12. **Implement and Continuously Monitor**

    Operationalize the threat model by integrating it into

    - Software development life cycle (SDLC)
    - DevSecOps pipelines
    - Change management and incident response processes

    Establish monitoring mechanisms to

    - Detect deviations from expected behavior
    - Alert on indicators of compromise
    - Feed real-time insights back into the threat model

    Continuously update the threat model as systems evolve, ensuring it remains relevant and effective against the dynamic threat landscape.

Risk Management Key Steps
The key steps of risk management include

- **Risk Identification**: Identify potential risks across various areas, including financial, operational, reputational, and security risks.
- **Risk Assessment**: Analyze and prioritize risks by evaluating their likelihood and potential impact.
- **Risk Response**: Develop and implement appropriate strategies to address identified risks:
  - **Risk Avoidance**: Eliminate the risk by choosing not to engage in certain activities (e.g., avoiding entry into a high-risk market).
  - **Risk Mitigation**: Minimize the likelihood or impact of the risk through preventive measures (e.g., implementing cybersecurity controls).
  - **Risk Acceptance**: Acknowledge the risk and its potential consequences when mitigation is impractical or cost prohibitive.
  - **Risk Transfer:** Shift the risk to a third party, such as through insurance or outsourcing.
- **Risk Monitoring and Control**: Continuously track, reassess, and adapt risk management strategies to ensure ongoing effectiveness.

Threat modeling is an important part of the overall risk management process. By identifying and analyzing potential threats, organizations can better understand their risk exposure and develop effective risk mitigation strategies.

Vulnerability Management

Vulnerability management is a process that identifies, assesses, and fixes security weaknesses in an organization's systems. It is a key part of an organization's security program, and helps to prevent cyberattacks and data breaches.

As shown below, vulnerability management is a continuous, cyclical process of identifying, classifying, prioritizing, remediating, and mitigating software vulnerabilities. It is a proactive security approach that minimizes the risk of exploitation.

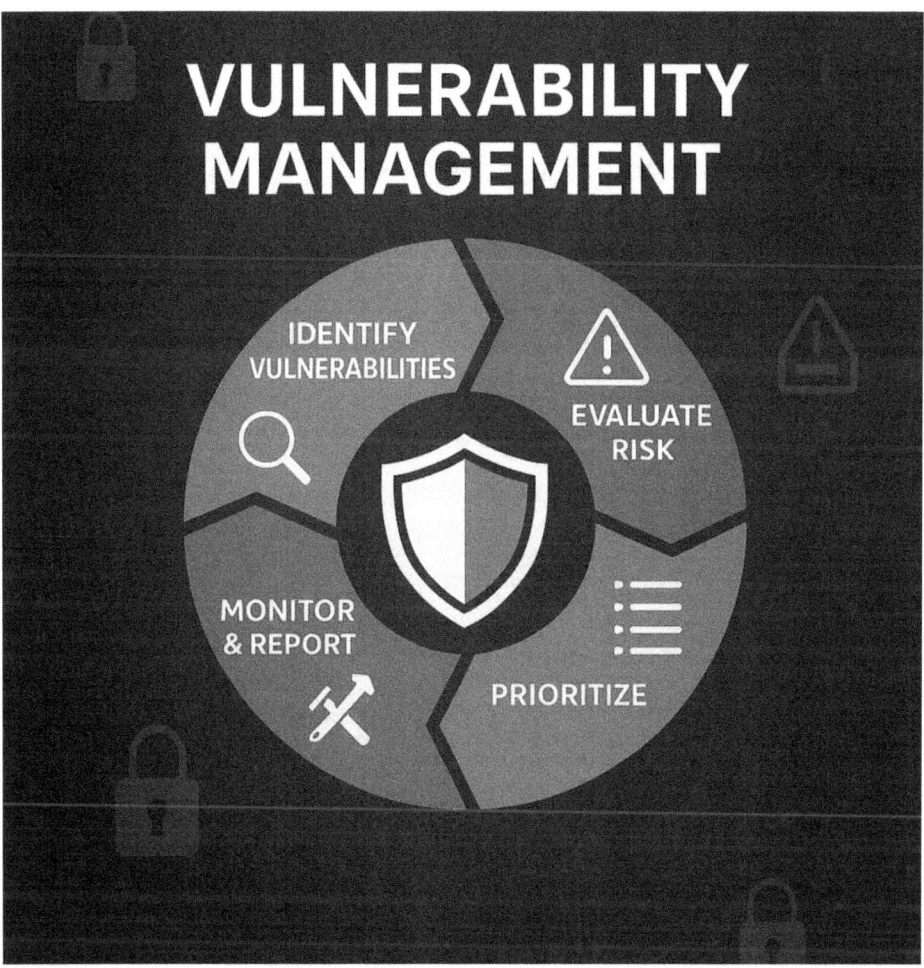

CHAPTER 2   CORE CYBERSECURITY CONCEPTS

Key Stages

- Identify
  - **Asset Discovery**: Identify all systems, applications, and devices within the organization.
  - **Vulnerability Scanning**: Use automated tools to detect vulnerabilities such as missing patches, weak configurations, and outdated software.
  - **Threat Intelligence**: Gather intelligence from sources like security advisories and threat feeds to stay updated on emerging threats.
- Classify and Prioritize
  - **Risk Assessment**: Evaluate the severity and impact of vulnerabilities.
  - **Prioritization**: Rank vulnerabilities based on exploitability, business impact, and criticality.
- Remediate
  - **Patching**: Apply security updates to fix known vulnerabilities.
  - **Configuration Management**: Implement secure configurations to harden systems.
  - **Access Control**: Strengthen user access restrictions to limit exposure.
- Mitigate
  - **Intrusion Detection and Prevention Systems (IDPS)**: Detect and prevent cyberattacks.
  - **Security Information and Event Management (SIEM)**: Monitor security events and detect anomalies.
  - **Incident Response**: Develop a plan to respond effectively to security incidents.

- Reporting and Monitoring
  - **Regular Reporting**: Track vulnerability status and remediation progress.
  - **Continuous Monitoring**: Adjust vulnerability management based on new threats and assessments.

Benefits

- **Reduced Risk of Breaches**: Addresses vulnerabilities before attackers exploit them
- **Improved Security Posture**: Strengthens overall security defenses
- **Regulatory Compliance**: Ensures compliance with security regulations and standards
- **Cost Savings**: Prevents financial losses from data breaches and downtime
- **Enhanced Reputation**: Demonstrates a commitment to security and customer trust

Key Considerations

- **Automation**: Automate vulnerability management for efficiency.
- **Integration**: Integrate with other security tools for real-time risk visibility.
- **Continuous Improvement**: Regularly refine strategies based on evolving threats.

Incident Response Planning and Handling

Incident Response Planning and Handling (IRPH) refers to the process of creating a structured plan to detect, analyze, respond to, and recover from security incidents like cyberattacks or data breaches, with the goal of minimizing damage and restoring normal operations as quickly as possible; this includes proactive preparation, identifying potential threats, implementing detection mechanisms, and defining clear steps to contain, eradicate, and recover from incidents when they occur.

Incident Response Planning is a structured approach to detecting, responding to, and recovering from security incidents like cyberattacks, data breaches, and system outages. The goal is to minimize damage, downtime, and financial loss while strengthening security posture.

Key Stages

- Preparation
  - **Identify Threats and Vulnerabilities**: Conduct threat modeling, risk assessments, and vulnerability scans.
  - **Develop an Incident Response Plan**: Define roles, responsibilities, and response procedures.
  - **Assemble an Incident Response Team**: Assign roles like incident commander, technical lead, and legal counsel.
  - **Establish Communication Protocols**: Ensure clear communication among stakeholders.
  - **Conduct Training and Drills**: Simulate incidents with tabletop exercises.
- Identification
  - **Detection**: Use SIEM, IDPS, and log monitoring to identify security events.
  - **Initial Assessment**: Determine incident scope and impact.
- Containment
  - **Isolate the Threat**: Restrict infected systems or networks to prevent spread.
  - **Control Damage**: Apply emergency containment measures, such as disabling compromised accounts.

- Eradication
  - **Remove the Root Cause**: Patch vulnerabilities and eliminate malware.
  - **Data Recovery**: Restore data from verified backups.
- Recovery
  - **System Restoration**: Resume normal operations securely.
  - **Business Continuity**: Ensure minimal disruption to critical operations.
- Lessons Learned
  - **Post-incident Review**: Analyze response effectiveness and identify improvements.
  - **Plan Updates**: Update response plans based on lessons learned.

Benefits

- **Reduced Downtime**: Faster recovery minimizes business disruptions.
- **Financial Protection**: Limits monetary losses from breaches.
- **Improved Security Posture**: Identifies and mitigates security gaps.
- **Regulatory Compliance**: Helps meet legal reporting requirements.

Key Considerations

- **Regular Testing and Updates**: Keep incident response plans up-to-date.
- **Clear Communication**: Ensure transparent messaging with stakeholders and the public.
- **Cross-Team Collaboration**: IT, security, legal, and PR teams must work seamlessly.

CHAPTER 2   CORE CYBERSECURITY CONCEPTS

Data Security and Privacy

Data security protects information from unauthorized access, use, modification, or destruction. It ensures confidentiality, integrity, and availability (CIA) through technology, policies, and training.

Key Aspects of Data Security

- **Confidentiality**: Ensures only authorized users can access sensitive data using encryption and access controls
- **Integrity**: Prevents data tampering with validation and checksums
- **Availability**: Ensures data is accessible via backups and disaster recovery plans

Key Data Security Measures

- **Access Control**: Enforce MFA, role-based access control (RBAC), and least privilege.
- **Data Encryption**: Encrypt data at rest and in transit.
- **Data Loss Prevention (DLP)**: Block unauthorized data transfers and leaks.
- **Security Awareness Training**: Educate employees on phishing and social engineering threats.
- **Incident Response Planning**: Ensure readiness to handle data breaches.

Importance of Data Security

- **Protects Sensitive Information**: Safeguards personal, financial, and intellectual property data
- **Ensures Business Continuity**: Prevents disruptions caused by security incidents

- **Compliance**: Meets regulatory requirements like GDPR, CCPA, and HIPAA
- **Builds Trust**: Strengthens customer and stakeholder confidence

Data Privacy

Data privacy protects individuals' rights by ensuring proper handling of personal information.

Core Principles

- **Notice**: Inform users about data collection practices.
- **Choice**: Provide options for data use and sharing.
- **Access**: Allow users to view and correct personal data.
- **Security**: Protect data from unauthorized breaches.
- **Enforcement**: Ensure compliance with privacy laws.

Key Concepts

- **Personal Data (PII)**: Identifiable information (e.g., name, SSN, email)
- **Data Processing**: Collecting, storing, sharing, and deleting data
- **Data Controller**: Organization that determines how data is used
- **Data Processor**: Third-party handling data on behalf of a controller

Data Privacy Laws

- **GDPR (EU)**: Strictest data protection law worldwide
- **CCPA (California, USA)**: Grants consumer privacy rights

CHAPTER 2   CORE CYBERSECURITY CONCEPTS

Key Considerations for Organizations

- **Data Protection Officers (DPOs)**: Oversee privacy compliance.
- **Employee Training**: Educate staff on privacy policies.
- **Incident Response Plans**: Prepare for data breaches.

Access Control and Authentication

Authentication verifies identity, while access control defines permissions. Together, they protect data, systems, and networks.

Working of Authentication and Authorization

Authentication

Confirms users are who they say they are

Authorization

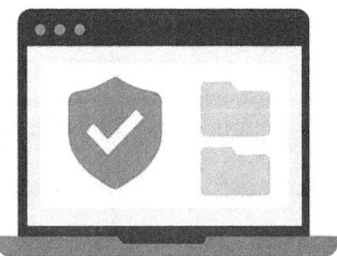

Gives users permission to access a resource

Authentication

What It Is: The process of verifying a user's identity to confirm that they are who they claim to be.

Methods

- **Something You Know**: Passwords, PINs, security questions
- **Something You Have**: Security tokens, smart cards, mobile phones
- **Something You Are**: Biometrics (fingerprints, facial recognition, voice recognition)
- **Multifactor Authentication (MFA)**: Combining two or more methods for enhanced security

Access Control

What It Is: Determining what resources a user can access after their identity has been authenticated. It ensures appropriate permissions based on roles and responsibilities.

Methods

- **Role-Based Access Control (RBAC)**: Assigns permissions based on a user's role (e.g., administrator, employee, customer)
- **Attribute-Based Access Control (ABAC)**: Grants access based on user attributes, resource type, and context (e.g., time of day, location)
- **Least Privilege**: Ensures users only have the minimum necessary access to perform their job functions

How They Work Together

1. **Authentication**: The user presents credentials (e.g., username and password).
2. **Verification**: The system validates the credentials using authentication methods.
3. **Authorization**: If authentication is successful, access control mechanisms determine what the user can access based on assigned permissions.

Importance

- **Data Protection**: Prevents unauthorized access to sensitive information
- **System Security**: Safeguards critical systems from cyber threats
- **Compliance**: Helps organizations meet regulatory standards (e.g., GDPR, HIPAA)

Network Security Fundamentals

Network security fundamentals include firewalls, access control, encryption, and intrusion prevention systems.

Network security is the practice of protecting networks from unauthorized access, threats, and disruptions to safeguard sensitive data and maintain system integrity.

Core Principles of Network Security

- **Confidentiality**: Ensures sensitive data is only accessible to authorized users
- **Integrity**: Maintains data accuracy by preventing unauthorized modifications
- **Availability**: Ensures network services remain accessible to legitimate users

Key Network Security Fundamentals

Access and Authentication

- **Access Control**: Restricts network resource access based on identity and authorization levels
- **Authentication**: Verifies user identities through passwords, biometrics, and MFA

- **Authorization**: Assigns specific permissions based on user roles
- **Least Privilege**: Grants only the minimum access necessary to reduce risk

Perimeter Security and Traffic Protection

- **Firewalls**: Filter incoming and outgoing network traffic based on predefined rules.
- **Intrusion Detection/Prevention Systems (IDS/IPS)**: Monitor and block suspicious activities.
- **Virtual Private Networks (VPNs)**: Establish secure, encrypted connections over public networks.

Data Encryption

- **Encryption in Transit**: Protects data traveling over a network (e.g., HTTPS, VPNs)
- **Encryption at Rest**: Secures stored data on servers and databases

Vulnerability Management

- **Regular Vulnerability Scans**: Identify security weaknesses and prioritize remediation.
- **Patch Management**: Ensure software and operating systems are updated with security patches.
- **Network Segmentation**: Divide networks into isolated segments to limit potential breaches.

Security Monitoring and Awareness

- **Security Information and Event Management (SIEM)**: Collect and analyze security logs for threat detection.
- **Security Awareness Training**: Educate employees on phishing threats, password security, and suspicious activity reporting.

Importance of Network Security

- **Protecting Sensitive Data**: Safeguards customer data, financial records, and intellectual property
- **Maintaining Business Continuity**: Ensures operations aren't disrupted by cyberattacks
- **Protecting Reputation**: Builds trust with customers, partners, and stakeholders
- **Meeting Compliance Requirements**: Helps organizations adhere to regulatory standards

By implementing strong network security measures, organizations can reduce cyber risks, safeguard critical assets, and maintain a secure, reliable infrastructure.

Cryptography and Encryption

Cryptography is the practice and study of secure communication techniques that allow information to be protected from unauthorized access. Derived from Greek words meaning "hidden writing," its core purpose is to ensure confidentiality, integrity, authenticity, and non-repudiation of data. This is achieved through the use of complex mathematical algorithms, often involving encryption (converting readable plaintext into unreadable ciphertext) and decryption (reversing the process). Modern cryptography broadly encompasses symmetric-key algorithms, where the same key is used for encryption and decryption, and asymmetric (public-key) algorithms, which utilize a pair of mathematically related public and private keys. Cryptography is fundamental to securing nearly every aspect of our digital lives, from online banking and secure web browsing (HTTPS) to digital signatures, cryptocurrencies, and end-to-end encrypted messaging. Its goal is to achieve various security objectives, including

- **Confidentiality**: Ensuring that only authorized individuals can access information

- **Integrity**: Guaranteeing that information has not been altered or tampered with

- **Authentication**: Verifying the identity of a sender or the authenticity of data

- **Non-repudiation**: Preventing someone from denying that they sent a message or performed an action

Cryptography encompasses a wide range of techniques and algorithms, not just for hiding data but also for generating digital signatures, creating secure hash functions, and enabling secure multiparty computation.

Encryption is a core process within cryptography, transforming readable data, known as plaintext, into an unreadable or unintelligible form, called ciphertext. This transformation is accomplished using a specific algorithm (a set of mathematical rules) and an encryption key. The key acts as a secret parameter, critical for both the encryption and subsequent decryption processes. Without the correct key, the ciphertext remains indecipherable, thus ensuring confidentiality and preventing unauthorized access to sensitive information. There are two primary types of encryption: symmetric-key encryption, where the same key is used for both encryption and decryption, and asymmetric-key (or public-key) encryption, which employs a pair of distinct but mathematically linked keys—a public key for encryption and a private key for decryption. Encryption is indispensable for securing digital communications, protecting data at rest (e.g., on hard drives), and enabling secure transactions across networks like the internet. In essence, encryption is a method or tool used to achieve one of the primary goals of cryptography (confidentiality).

CHAPTER 2   CORE CYBERSECURITY CONCEPTS

Here's a breakdown:

Cryptography

- **Broader Concept**: Encompasses all aspects of secure communication, including
    - **Encryption**: Transforming data into an unreadable format
    - **Decryption**: Recovering the original data from the encrypted form

- **Digital Signatures**: Verifying the authenticity and integrity of data
- **Hashing**: Creating a unique digital fingerprint of data
- **Key Management**: Securely generating, distributing, and storing cryptographic keys

Encryption

- **Specific Technique**: The core method for achieving confidentiality in cryptography.
- **Involves**
  - **Algorithms**: Mathematical rules used to transform plaintext into ciphertext
  - **Keys**: Secret values used in the encryption and decryption process

Types of Encryptions

- **Symmetric-Key Encryption**: Uses the same key for both encryption and decryption. Examples: AES and DES.
- **Asymmetric-Key (Public-Key) Encryption**: Uses two different keys—a public key for encryption and a private key for decryption. Examples: RSA and Elliptic Curve Cryptography (ECC).

Applications of Cryptography and Encryption

- **Securing Data in Transit**: Protecting data transmitted over networks (e.g., HTTPS, VPNs)
- **Securing Data at Rest**: Protecting data stored on devices (e.g., file encryption, database encryption)
- **Authentication**: Verifying the identity of users and devices
- **Digital Signatures**: Ensuring the authenticity and integrity of digital documents

In essence:

- Cryptography is the overarching field of secure communication.
- Encryption is a fundamental technique within cryptography used to protect data confidentiality.

Key Takeaways

- **Core Concepts**: Cybersecurity is built on the principles of confidentiality, integrity, and availability (CIA), as well as addressing network security and vulnerabilities.
- **Risk Assessment and Management**: This is a critical component, encompassing
    - **Identifying Vulnerabilities**: Discovering weaknesses in systems, networks, and applications through methods like vulnerability scanning, penetration testing, and risk assessments
    - **Threat Modeling**: Analyzing potential threats and their impact on organizational assets to prioritize mitigation efforts
    - **Risk Mitigation**: Implementing controls (technical, administrative, and physical) to reduce the likelihood and/or impact of cyber threats
- **Holistic Approach**: The image suggests a holistic approach to cybersecurity, considering various elements like access control, data security, network security, incident response, and cybersecurity awareness.

CHAPTER 3

The Threat Landscape: An Ever-Evolving Challenge

The threat landscape refers to the constantly changing and expanding collection of potential cybersecurity risks, including malicious actors, attack methods, and vulnerabilities, that organizations face, requiring continuous adaptation and vigilance to stay ahead of emerging threats and protect sensitive data.

CHAPTER 3   THE THREAT LANDSCAPE: AN EVER-EVOLVING CHALLENGE

As shown above, the threat landscape is a constantly changing environment that demands continuous vigilance and adaptation. Both organizations and individuals must stay informed about emerging threats and vulnerabilities to maintain a strong security posture. By understanding its components and implementing the right security measures, we can navigate the digital world with greater confidence and resilience.

Key Cyber Threats

- **Malware and Its Types**: Viruses, worms, Trojans, ransomware
- **Social Engineering Attacks**: Phishing, spear phishing, whaling
- Denial-of-Service (DoS) and Distributed Denial-of-Service (DDoS) Attacks
- Advanced Persistent Threats (APTs)
- Insider Threats
- **Emerging Threats**: IoT security, cloud security, AI/ML in cybersecurity

Why Understanding the Threat Landscape Is Crucial

1. **Proactive Defense**: Identifying potential threats and vulnerabilities allows organizations to implement preventive security measures.
2. **Risk Assessment**: A comprehensive understanding of threats enhances risk assessment, helping prioritize security investments.
3. **Incident Response Planning**: Knowing the threat landscape enables organizations to prepare and respond effectively to security incidents.
4. **Resource Allocation**: Helps organizations allocate resources efficiently to address critical vulnerabilities first.

The Complexity of the Digital World

The digital world is embedded in our daily lives, from communication and commerce to national security and infrastructure. However, this interconnectedness also introduces a complex, evolving set of cyber threats.

CHAPTER 3   THE THREAT LANDSCAPE: AN EVER-EVOLVING CHALLENGE

The threat landscape represents the intricate web of dangers that individuals and organizations face in cyberspace. It consists of three core components:

1. Threats: The Actions or Events That Can Cause Harm

Threats come from multiple sources, including malicious actors, cyber tools, and attack methods:

- **Malicious Actors**: Individuals or groups intending to cause damage, ranging from lone hackers to nation-state cyber operations and organized cybercriminals.
- Some of the known malicious actors
  - **Malware**: Includes viruses, ransomware, spyware, and Trojans, all designed to infiltrate and disrupt systems (see Table 3-1).

Table 3-1. Types of Malware

Malware Type	What It Does	Real-World Example
Ransomware	Disables the victim's access to data until ransom is paid	RUYK
Fileless Malware	Makes changes to files that are native to the OS	Astaroth
Spyware	Collects user activity data without their knowledge	DarkHotel
Adware	Serves unwanted advertisements	Fireball
Trojans	Disguises itself as desirable code	Emotet
Worms	Spreads through a network by replicating itself	Stuxnet
	Gives hackers remote control of a victim's device	Zacinlo
Keyloggers	Monitors users' keystrokes	Olympic Vision
Bots	Launches a broad flood of attacks	Echobot
Mobile Malware	Infects mobile devices	Triada
Wiper Malware	Erases user data beyond recoverability	WhisperGate

- **Phishing Attacks**: Deceptive attempts to trick users into revealing sensitive information through emails, messages, or fake websites. Phishing is a cyberattack that leverages email, phone, SMS, social media, or other forms of personal communication to entice users to click a malicious link, download infected files, or reveal personal information, such as passwords or account numbers.

  While the most well-known phishing attacks usually involve outlandish claims, such as a member of a royal family requesting an individual's banking information, the modern phishing scam is far more sophisticated. In many cases, a cybercriminal may masquerade as retailers, service providers, or government agencies to extract personal information that may seem benign such as email addresses, phone numbers, the user's date of birth, or the names of family members.

  Phishing is one of the most common types of cyberattacks, and its prevalence continues to grow year over year (Table 3-2). COVID-19 dramatically increased cyberattacks of all kinds, including phishing attacks. During the lockdown period, people generally spent more time online and also experienced heightened emotions — the virtual recipe for an effective phishing campaign. According to the FBI, phishing was the top form of cybercrime in 2020, with incidents nearly doubling compared to 2019.

Table 3-2. *Types of Phishing*

Phishing Types	What It Does
Spear Phishing	Considered one of the most dangerous phishing attacks as it uses personalized information about the target to increase the likelihood of success
Business Email Compromise (BEC)	Often targets high-level employees within a company by posing as a trusted business partner or executive to request wire transfers
Smishing	Phishing attacks carried out via text messages, often appearing as urgent notifications from a bank or other trusted entity
Vishing	Phishing attacks conducted through phone calls, where the attacker might impersonate a company representative to solicit sensitive information
Clone Phishing	A copy of a legitimate email is sent with malicious links or attachments to trick the recipient into clicking on them

- **Social Engineering**: Manipulating individuals into performing unauthorized actions or divulging confidential information. A social engineering attack is a cybersecurity attack that relies on the psychological manipulation of human behavior to disclose sensitive data, share credentials, grant access to a personal device, or otherwise compromise their digital security.

  Social engineering attacks pose a great threat to cybersecurity since many attacks begin on a personal level and rely on human error to advance the attack path. By invoking empathy, fear, and urgency in the victim, adversaries are often able to gain access to personal information or the endpoint itself. If the device is connected to a corporate network or contains credentials for corporate accounts, this can also provide adversaries with a pathway to enterprise-level attacks.

  With cyber criminals devising ever-more manipulative methods for tricking people and employees, organizations must stay ahead of the game. In this post, we will explore ten of the most common types of social engineering attacks:

1. Phishing
2. Whaling
3. Baiting
4. Diversion Theft
5. Business Email Compromise (BEC)
6. Smishing
7. Quid Pro Quo
8. Pretexting
9. Honeytrap
10. Tailgating/Piggybacking

- **Denial-of-Service (DoS) Attacks**: Overwhelming networks or systems with traffic, making them inaccessible to legitimate users. A DoS attack is a malicious cyberattack where an attacker floods a target system, like a website or server, with excessive traffic, rendering it unavailable to legitimate users by overwhelming its processing capabilities and essentially preventing access to the service, effectively "denying" service to intended users.

- Types of DoS attacks:

    a. **SYN Flood**: Sending numerous connection initiation requests without completing the handshake, consuming server resources.

    b. **ICMP Flood**: Sending large amounts of ICMP (Internet Control Message Protocol) packets to overwhelm the target.

    c. **Buffer Overflow**: Exploiting a programming vulnerability to send more data than a buffer can handle, potentially crashing the system.

    d. **Smurf Attack**: The attacker sends Internet Control Message Protocol broadcast packets to a number of hosts with a spoofed source Internet Protocol (IP) address that belongs to the target machine. The recipients of these spoofed packets will then respond, and the targeted host will be flooded with those responses.

- **Distributed Denial-of-Service (DDoS) Attacks**: A distributed denial-of-service (DDoS) attack occurs when multiple machines are operating together to attack one target. DDoS attackers often leverage the use of a botnet—a group of hijacked internet-connected devices to carry out large-scale attacks. Attackers take advantage of security vulnerabilities or device weaknesses to control numerous devices using command and control software. Once in control, an attacker can command their botnet to conduct DDoS on a target. In this case, the infected devices are also victims of the attack.

    Botnets—made up of compromised devices—may also be rented out to other potential attackers. Often, the botnet is made available to "attack-for-hire" services, which allow unskilled users to launch DDoS attacks.

    DDoS allows for exponentially more requests to be sent to the target, therefore increasing the attack power. It also increases the difficulty of attribution, as the true source of the attack is harder to identify.

    DDoS attacks have increased in magnitude as more and more devices come online through the Internet of Things (IoT) (see Securing the Internet of Things). IoT devices often use default passwords and do not have sound security postures, making them vulnerable to compromise and exploitation. Infection of IoT devices often goes unnoticed by users, and an attacker could easily compromise hundreds of thousands of these devices to conduct a high-scale attack without the device owners' knowledge.

- **Zero-Day Exploits**: Targeting previously unknown software or hardware vulnerabilities before they are patched. A zero-day exploit is a cyberattack vector that takes advantage of an unknown or unaddressed security flaw in computer software, hardware, or firmware. "Zero day" refers to the fact that the software or device vendor has zero days to fix the flaw because malicious actors can already use it to access vulnerable systems.

    Zero-day is sometimes written as 0-day. The words vulnerability, exploit, and attack are typically used alongside zero-day, and it's helpful to understand the difference:

a. **A zero-day vulnerability** is a software vulnerability discovered by attackers before the vendor has become aware of it. Because the vendors are unaware, no patch exists for zero-day vulnerabilities, making attacks likely to succeed.

  b. **A zero-day exploits** the method hackers use to attack systems with a previously unidentified vulnerability.

  c. **A zero-day attack** is the use of a zero-day exploit to cause damage to or steal data from a system affected by a vulnerability.

- **Emerging Threats**: IoT security, cloud security vulnerabilities, and AI-powered cyber threats.

2. Vulnerabilities: Weaknesses That Can Be Exploited

Vulnerabilities are security gaps in systems, applications, or infrastructure that attackers can exploit. These include

- **Software Bugs**: Coding flaws that introduce security loopholes for attackers to exploit
- **Weak Passwords**: Easily guessable passwords that allow unauthorized access
- **Unpatched Systems**: Failing to apply critical security updates, leaving systems vulnerable to known exploits
- **Misconfigured Systems**: Incorrect system settings that expose organizations to unnecessary risks
- **Human Error**: Unintentional mistakes by users or administrators that create security gaps

3. Risks: The Consequences of Cyber Threats

Risks are the potential outcomes of successful cyberattacks, depending on likelihood and impact. These include

- **Data Loss:** Unauthorized access, theft, or destruction of sensitive information
- **Financial Loss:** Monetary damage from fraud, extortion, operational disruptions, and ransomware
- **Reputational Damage:** Loss of trust in an organization due to security incidents
- **Disruption of Operations:** System outages affecting business continuity, production, or customer service

Navigating the Evolving Threat Landscape

Understanding the threat landscape is key to building a resilient security strategy. Organizations must

- Stay informed on emerging cyber threats.
- Continuously assess risks and vulnerabilities.
- Implement proactive security measures to mitigate risks.
- Prepare and train teams for rapid incident response.
- Adapt and evolve security strategies to counter new attack techniques.

By integrating cyber threat intelligence, security frameworks, and adaptive defense mechanisms, organizations can enhance their resilience against evolving cyber threats and secure their critical assets.

Key Takeaways

- **Ever-Evolving Threat Landscape:** The core message is that the threat landscape in cybersecurity is constantly changing and growing. This means new threats, attack methods, and vulnerabilities are always emerging.

- **Need for Continuous Adaptation**: Because the threats change so rapidly, organizations and individuals must continuously adapt their security measures to stay protected. Static security strategies are no longer effective.

- **Importance of Vigilance**: Vigilance is crucial. Staying informed about the latest threats and vulnerabilities is essential for maintaining a strong security posture.

- **Proactive Security Measures**: The text emphasizes the need for proactive security measures. Don't just react to attacks; anticipate and prepare for them.

- **Key Threat Categories**: The text highlights two major categories of cyber threats:
  - **Malware**: Including various types like viruses, worms, trojans, and ransomware.
  - **Social Engineering**: Such as phishing, spear phishing, and whaling attacks.

- **Components of the Threat Landscape**: The text defines the threat landscape as encompassing malicious actors, attack methods, and vulnerabilities. **Goal: Navigating the Digital World with Confidence**: By understanding the threat landscape and implementing appropriate security measures, individuals and organizations can operate more safely and confidently in the digital realm.

PART II

The Role of the Executive Leaders (CXO), CISO, and Board of Directors

The Apex of Cybersecurity Leadership. This section delves into the crucial responsibilities and collaborative dynamic of an organization's highest-level leadership in managing cybersecurity risk. It highlights how these key players—from the Chief Executive Officer (CEO) and other C-suite executives (CXOs) to the Chief Information Security Officer (CISO) and the Board of Directors—are no longer just spectators but are active participants in shaping a robust security posture.

We will explore the specific duties of each role: the CISO as the technical and strategic security expert; the CXOs as champions of security across business operations; and the Board of Directors as the ultimate overseers of risk and governance. The section emphasizes the critical importance of a cohesive, top-down approach to cybersecurity, where communication and accountability flow seamlessly to protect the organization's assets, reputation, and long-term viability in an increasingly digital world.

CHAPTER 4

The Role of CXO/ Executive Leaders

Executive leaders play a critical role in cybersecurity by setting the strategic direction, allocating resources, fostering a security-conscious culture within the organization, making critical decisions during incidents, and ensuring cybersecurity aligns with overall business objectives, effectively acting as the driving force behind a robust cybersecurity posture.

The Role of Executive Leaders in Secure Digital Transformation

Providing data security and secure information access is a growing challenge for organizations today. Over the past 30 years, many companies have relied on hub-and-spoke networks, where each branch is connected to a central data center via a private network.

This model was effective when

- The data center served as the core for applications and storage.
- Employees primarily worked from office locations.

However, application transformation has changed how businesses operate, with most applications now residing in cloud-based environments, such as

- Software as a Service (SaaS) solutions
- Public cloud platforms like Microsoft Azure and AWS

CHAPTER 4   THE ROLE OF CXO/EXECUTIVE LEADERS

The New Digital Landscape and Security Challenges

- **Data Is Everywhere**: Sensitive data is now distributed across multiple environments, requiring new security strategies.
- **Workforce Mobility**: Employees and contractors work remotely, making traditional security models insufficient.

The Role of Executive Leadership in Driving Change

Secure digital transformation is not a single initiative—it is an ongoing process that requires a shift in mindset and culture.

Key Responsibilities for Leaders

- **Set the Security Vision**: Executive leadership must drive security initiatives from the top down.
- **Overcome Resistance to Change**: Many employees prefer familiar processes, but leaders must embrace and advocate for transformation.
- **Invest in Modern Security Solutions**: Implement:
  - Zero Trust Architectures
  - Cloud-native security frameworks
  - Adaptive access controls
- **Align Security with Business Strategy**: Security should function as a business enabler, ensuring both compliance and resilience.

By leading security-driven digital transformation, executive teams can ensure their organizations

- Adapt to new cybersecurity threats.
- Leverage innovation securely.
- Remain resilient in an evolving digital landscape.

CHAPTER 5

The Role of the Board of Directors

The board of directors plays a crucial role in cybersecurity by overseeing the organization's cybersecurity strategy, ensuring appropriate risk management practices are in place, understanding the potential impact of cyber threats on the business, and allocating necessary resources to mitigate those risks, effectively acting as the highest level of governance for cybersecurity within the company; they are responsible for ensuring the organization is adequately prepared to handle cyber incidents and comply with relevant regulations.

The Role of Board Members in Managing Cyber Risk

Boards play a critical role in safeguarding organizations against cyber threats. As technology advances, cyber risk oversight must continuously evolve. Security vulnerabilities expose companies to regulatory, legal, financial, and reputational threats—all of which require proactive governance. Somewhere right now, cybercriminals are strategizing their next attack. Their targets may include intellectual property, customer data, competitive intelligence, or financial assets for fraud, blackmail, or extortion.

By prioritizing cyber risk oversight, board members can ensure transparent reporting on operational and financial impacts, strengthening their understanding of the organization's risk exposure in today's digital landscape.

CHAPTER 5   THE ROLE OF THE BOARD OF DIRECTORS

Why Is This Important?

- **Cyber Risk Is a Business Risk**: A single cyberattack can devastate an organization, leading to brand damage, regulatory penalties, financial loss, and shareholder devaluation in the millions—or even billions—of dollars.
- **Cybercriminals Evolve Rapidly**: Attackers continuously refine their techniques, tactics, and strategies. Many organizations struggle to keep pace with this evolving threat landscape.

Exploiting Weaknesses: Threat actors probe organizations for vulnerabilities, such as

- Untrained employees susceptible to phishing and social engineering
- Exposed assets with weak security configurations
- Unpatched software and unprotected sensitive data
- Unmanaged devices (e.g., laptops, servers, mobile phones)
- Lack of physical security controls that allow unauthorized access

Case Example: In the 2023 MGM Resorts ransomware attack, cybercriminals manipulated a helpdesk employee into resetting a privileged account, giving attackers access to sensitive data and systems. The breach resulted in $100 million in financial losses and weeks of operational disruption.

Key Takeaways

- **Executive Leadership's Crucial Role in Cybersecurity**: CXO-level executives are essential for establishing a strong cybersecurity posture. Their responsibilities include
    - Setting the strategic direction for cybersecurity
    - Allocating necessary resources
    - Cultivating a security-conscious culture within the organization

- Making critical decisions during cybersecurity incidents
- Aligning cybersecurity with overall business objectives
- Essentially, driving and championing cybersecurity efforts

- **Challenges of Secure Digital Transformation**: Traditional network models (hub-and-spoke) with centralized data centers are no longer sufficient due to application transformation. This older model was effective when
    - Data centers were the primary location for applications and storage.
    - Employees mainly worked from physical office locations.

- **Shift to Cloud-Based Environments**: Modern applications have largely moved to cloud-based environments, including
    - Software as a Service (SaaS) solutions.
    - Public cloud platforms like Microsoft Azure and AWS. This shift presents new security challenges.

CHAPTER 6

The CISO Role and Responsibilities

A Chief Information Security Officer (CISO) isn't just the head of cybersecurity—they're the business's last line of defense against cyber threats. The CISO is responsible for defining and executing an organization's security strategy, mitigating risks, and ensuring regulatory compliance. But the role extends beyond just protecting data—it's about aligning security with business goals, enabling growth, and maintaining trust.

A great CISO doesn't just identify vulnerabilities; they drive resilience. This means building a security-first culture where every employee understands their role in cybersecurity. It requires bridging the gap between security and business operations to ensure security enables, not hinders, innovation. A CISO must stay ahead of threats, whether from external attackers, internal risks, or evolving compliance landscapes.

The CISO isn't just a security executive; they are a business leader who protects not just systems but the organization's reputation, finances, and future. If cybersecurity isn't built into the strategy from day one, it becomes an emergency on day two.

Defining the CISO Role

In today's rapidly evolving digital landscape, cybersecurity threats are more sophisticated and persistent than ever. To effectively mitigate risks and safeguard critical assets, organizations appoint a Chief Information Security Officer (CISO). The CISO plays a strategic and operational role in securing an organization's digital environment while ensuring business continuity in the face of cyber threats.

This chapter explores the key responsibilities, daily tasks, and strategic importance of a modern CISO.

CHAPTER 6   THE CISO ROLE AND RESPONSIBILITIES

Key Responsibilities of a CISO

The CISO serves as the top security executive, leading an organization's cyber defense strategy. Their role is a blend of advisory, operational, and strategic responsibilities, requiring them to effectively communicate with boards, executives, employees, regulators, and customers, many of whom lack technical backgrounds.

Their primary responsibility is to develop and implement a robust cybersecurity strategy aligned with business objectives. This includes

- **Leading and Managing the Security Team**: The CISO directs security analysts, engineers, architects, and penetration testers, ensuring the team is skilled, well-equipped, and prepared to combat evolving threats.

- **Developing and Implementing Security Policies**: Responsible for enforcing security frameworks, policies, and compliance standards related to data protection, access control, and incident response.

- **Risk Assessment and Management**: Conducts regular risk assessments to identify security gaps, prioritizing vulnerabilities based on their potential impact and exploitability.

- **Incident Response and Crisis Management**: Leads efforts to contain data breaches, ransomware attacks, and cyber incidents, coordinating with internal teams and external regulators.

- **Regulatory Compliance and Governance**: Ensures compliance with GDPR, HIPAA, PCI DSS, and SEC cybersecurity disclosure rules, maintaining regulatory alignment.

- **Security Awareness Training**: Oversees cybersecurity education programs, training employees to recognize phishing, insider threats, and social engineering attacks.

- **Budget and Resource Allocation**: Manages cybersecurity spending, balancing cost-effectiveness and risk mitigation.

- **Stakeholder Communication**: Translates cyber risk into business impact, ensuring executives and board members understand security risks and investment priorities.

Example: In 2023, a major US healthcare provider suffered a ransomware attack that encrypted patient data. The CISO's swift response, including activating the incident response team and coordinating with federal agencies, limited downtime and prevented the loss of millions in potential fines.

A Typical Workday for a CISO

A CISO operates under constant pressure, balancing technical expertise, strategic vision, and leadership while managing crises in real time. They are the architects of cybersecurity resilience, responsible for safeguarding the confidentiality, integrity, and availability of critical systems. Their success isn't just measured by preventing breaches—it's about enabling the business to move forward securely.

A typical day includes

- **Morning Briefing**: Starts with a security team update to review incidents, analyze new vulnerabilities, and prioritize urgent issues.
- **Strategic Planning**: Works with IT, legal, and compliance teams to refine cybersecurity strategies, aligning them with business objectives.
- **Policy Development**: Creates and enforces policies on password security, access control, data encryption, and security monitoring.
- **Security Team Leadership**: Leads and mentors the cybersecurity team, ensuring continuous skill development and incident readiness.
- **Incident Response and Mitigation**: If an attack occurs, the CISO leads containment efforts, working with law enforcement, legal, and compliance teams.
- **Security Awareness Training**: Ensures employees receive regular cybersecurity training, reducing the risk of human-error breaches.
- **Networking and Threat Intelligence**: Attends industry events, collaborates with peer CISOs, government agencies, and security vendors to stay ahead of emerging threats.
- **Executive Reporting**: Prepares risk assessments and cybersecurity updates for the board, executive team, and regulators.

Example: Following the 2021 Colonial Pipeline cyberattack, the CISO of a global energy company led a proactive review of their security infrastructure, upgraded their incident response plan, and implemented Zero Trust to prevent a similar breach.

Beyond the Daily Grind: Strategic Initiatives

- **Proactive Threat Hunting**: CISOs actively track and mitigate cyber risks before they escalate, using
  - Threat intelligence platforms
  - Behavioral analytics
  - Penetration testing and red teaming exercises
- **Building a Security-First Culture**: Creates a company-wide cybersecurity mindset, ensuring all employees recognize their role in protecting digital assets.
- **Continuous Learning and Adaptation**: With cyber threats evolving rapidly, CISOs must stay ahead by understanding
  - Emerging threats (AI-driven attacks, deepfakes, supply chain vulnerabilities)
  - New regulations (SEC cybersecurity disclosure rules, NIST standards)
  - Best practices in Zero Trust, SASE, and cloud security frameworks

Example: To counteract phishing attacks, a major financial institution rolled out company-wide phishing simulations and training under the guidance of its CISO. This reduced successful phishing attempts by 70% over a year.

Closing Thoughts: Why the CISO Role Is Crucial

The CISO is more than a cybersecurity expert—they are a key business leader responsible for securing digital transformation, operational resilience, and regulatory compliance. Their ability to translate technical risks into business priorities makes them indispensable in today's cyber threat landscape.

Key Takeaways

CISOs bridge the gap between cybersecurity, business strategy, and regulatory compliance. Their leadership shapes an organization's resilience against cyberattacks. Investing in a strong CISO is crucial for navigating the evolving threat landscape.

Example: Companies like JPMorgan Chase, Amazon, and Microsoft have elevated their CISOs to executive leadership, recognizing cybersecurity as a core business function rather than an IT issue.

Strategic Cybersecurity Planning and Governance

Strategic Planning: A Road Map for Organizational Growth

Strategic planning is a structured and disciplined approach to defining an organization's long-term vision and determining the most effective path to success. It aligns goals, strategies, and execution to ensure sustained growth and competitive advantage.

Key Elements of Strategic Planning

1. **Vision**: A bold and inspiring statement defining the organization's desired future state

2. **Mission**: The core purpose that drives the organization's existence and long-term impact

3. **Values**: Fundamental principles and ethics that shape decision-making and company culture

4. **SWOT Analysis**: A comprehensive evaluation of

    - Strengths: Internal advantages that differentiate the organization

    - Weaknesses: Areas of improvement that could hinder progress

    - Opportunities: External factors that create pathways for expansion

    - Threats: Market risks, competition, and potential obstacles

5. **Goals and Objectives**: Well-defined SMART (Specific, Measurable, Achievable, Relevant, Time-bound) milestones for progress

6. **Strategies**: Action-oriented initiatives designed to achieve goals efficiently and effectively

7. **Implementation Plan**: A detailed execution framework with clear steps, resources, and deadlines

8. **Monitoring and Evaluation**: Ongoing assessment of progress, key performance indicators (KPIs), and necessary adjustments to ensure continuous improvement

Strategic Planning in Action

Example: Amazon's long-term strategic planning revolutionized retail by transitioning from an online bookstore to a tech-driven global enterprise. By focusing on customer obsession, rapid innovation, and operational efficiency, Amazon expanded into cloud computing, AI, logistics, and streaming services, securing its position as an industry leader.

Takeaway: Organizations that embrace strategic planning are better equipped to anticipate challenges, capitalize on opportunities, and sustain long-term success in an evolving marketplace.

Governance

Governance is a structured system of rules, practices, and processes that directs and controls an organization. It ensures accountability, ethical conduct, and risk management, all while safeguarding the interests of stakeholders.

Key Aspects of Governance

- **Leadership**: Providing strategic oversight, direction, and executive accountability

- **Accountability**: Holding individuals and entities responsible for decisions and actions

- **Risk Management**: Identifying, assessing, and mitigating financial, operational, and cybersecurity risks

- **Control**: Implementing internal controls, compliance measures, and performance benchmarks
- **Transparency**: Ensuring open, honest communication with stakeholders at all levels
- **Ethical Behavior**: Upholding high ethical standards and corporate responsibility

Relationship Between Strategic Planning and Governance

- Strategic planning sets the road map, while governance ensures the journey is disciplined and ethical.
- Governance creates the framework within which strategic goals are developed and executed.
- Effective governance guides risk-informed decision-making, ensuring accountability in achieving strategic objectives.
- Strategic planning defines where the organization is headed, while governance ensures responsible execution, compliance, and ethical leadership throughout the process.

Risk Management and Compliance: Safeguarding Organizational Integrity

Risk management is the process of identifying, assessing, and controlling threats that could impact an organization's capital, earnings, and operations. Compliance ensures adherence to laws, regulations, and industry standards, reducing legal and financial risks.

Key Elements of Risk Management

- **Identification**: Recognizing potential threats, including financial, operational, reputational, and legal risks
- **Assessment**: Evaluating the likelihood and potential impact of each risk

- **Control**: Implementing risk mitigation strategies such as avoidance, mitigation, transfer, or acceptance
- **Monitoring**: Continuously tracking and reviewing risk management controls to ensure effectiveness

Key Aspects of Compliance

- **Identification**: Determining which laws, regulations, and standards apply to the organization
- **Interpretation**: Understanding and correctly applying compliance requirements
- **Implementation**: Developing policies, procedures, and controls to ensure adherence
- **Monitoring**: Regularly reviewing and updating compliance measures to reflect regulatory changes
- **Enforcement**: Taking corrective action to address noncompliance issues and mitigate risks

Relationship Between Risk Management and Compliance

- Compliance is a subset of risk management—failing to comply creates significant risks.
- Noncompliance risks include
  - **Legal and Financial Penalties**: Fines, lawsuits, and reputational damage
  - **Operational Disruptions**: Business interruptions, customer loss, and brand damage
- Risk management focuses on all potential threats, while compliance addresses risks related to regulatory adherence.
- Effective risk management programs integrate compliance to ensure a holistic approach to governance.

By managing both risk and compliance, organizations can

- **Enhance Resilience**: Withstand unexpected challenges.
- **Strengthen Reputation**: Build trust with stakeholders.
- **Increase Profitability**: Minimize financial losses and maximize opportunities.
- **Ensure Sustainability**: Operate responsibly and ethically.

Security Operations and Incident Response

Security operations involve continuous monitoring, threat detection, and risk mitigation to protect an organization's security posture. Incident response focuses on coordinated actions to contain and recover from security breaches.

Key Aspects of Security Operations

- **Monitoring**: Continuously analyzing networks, systems, and applications for threats
- **Threat Hunting**: Actively searching for hidden or undetected cyber threats
- **Vulnerability Management**: Identifying, assessing, and patching security weaknesses
- **Access Control**: Managing user privileges and restricting unauthorized access
- **Security Information and Event Management (SIEM)**: Collecting and analyzing security logs for threat detection

Key Phases of Incident Response

- **Preparation**: Developing incident response plans, training personnel, and establishing communication protocols
- **Detection and Analysis**: Identifying and evaluating security incidents
- **Containment**: Isolating the threat to prevent further damage

- **Eradication**: Eliminating the root cause of the incident
- **Recovery**: Restoring systems, data, and normal business operations
- **Lessons Learned**: Conducting post-incident analysis to improve future defenses

Integration of Security Operations and Incident Response

- Security operations provide proactive defense by identifying and mitigating threats before they escalate.
- Incident response ensures rapid containment when a breach occurs, minimizing business impact.
- Together, they form a comprehensive cybersecurity strategy that safeguards an organization's digital assets and operational resilience.

Defend against threats and effectively respond to incidents when they occur.

Technology and Architecture in Cybersecurity

Cybersecurity technology encompasses tools, systems, and techniques designed to protect networks, systems, and data from cyber threats. Architecture defines how these technologies integrate to create a cohesive security framework

Key Cybersecurity Technologies

- **Endpoint Security**: Antivirus, firewalls, IDS/IPS, EDR solutions
- **Network Security**: Firewalls, VPNs, routers, network segmentation
- **Cloud Security**: CASB, CWPP, DLP solutions
- **Identity and Access Management (IAM)**: MFA, SSO, RBAC
- **Data Security**: Encryption, DLP, tokenization, data masking
- **Security Information and Event Management (SIEM)**: Security log analysis and correlation
- **Threat Intelligence Platforms**: Real-time cyber threat analysis

Cybersecurity Architecture

- **Defense in Depth**: Layered security measures to strengthen defenses
- **Zero Trust Model**: Continuous verification of users and devices
- **Security Zones**: Segmentation into restricted, private, and public zones
- **Network Segmentation**: Isolating systems to minimize attack surface
- **Integration**: Seamless collaboration between security tools and frameworks

Takeaway: Cybersecurity technology provides the tools, while architecture ensures a structured and effective defense strategy.

People and Culture in Cybersecurity

A cybersecurity culture is more than just securing entry points to a building, implementing multifactor authentication, or enforcing least privilege access. It is a mindset—an organization-wide commitment where every individual plays a role in protecting the enterprise. A strong security culture is not just a defensive measure; it is an enabler of trust and resilience. It reduces risk, safeguards critical assets, and saves enterprises millions by mitigating data corruption, revenue loss, regulatory fines, and reputational damage.

Before the advent of personal computers (PCs) and the internet, cybersecurity was relatively straightforward. Systems were centralized—green-screen terminals connected to mainframes housed in secure locations. The primary security concern was ensuring that unauthorized individuals couldn't physically access the building. Even if someone obtained credentials, they needed to be physically present to breach the system.

However, the landscape changed with the rise of PCs and, later, the internet. Cyber threats are now borderless, and attackers can operate from anywhere in the world. Security is no longer just about physical enforcement; it requires an enterprise-wide security culture. Every employee, from frontline staff to executives, must understand their role in cybersecurity. The human element remains the most vulnerable link, making continuous education and awareness programs essential.

At the executive level, fostering a cybersecurity culture is about leadership, accountability, and embedding security into the DNA of an organization. We must shift from viewing cybersecurity as a compliance requirement to recognizing it as a business imperative—one that protects not just data but the very foundation of trust with our customers, partners, and stakeholders.

Key Cybersecurity Roles

- **Security Analysts**: Monitor logs and detect threats.
- **Security Engineers**: Design and maintain security systems.
- **Security Architects**: Define security frameworks.
- **Security Managers**: Oversee security policies and teams.
- **Penetration Testers**: Identify and exploit vulnerabilities.
- **Incident Responders**: Handle cyberattacks and breaches.
- **Compliance Officers**: Ensure regulatory adherence.

People drive cybersecurity success. Their knowledge and vigilance are crucial to security.

Building a Strong Cybersecurity Culture

A security culture constitutes more than just cyber awareness. It must:

Incorporate a broader corporate culture of day-to-day actions, encouraging employees to make thoughtful decisions that align with security policies.

- Require the workforce to know the security risk and the processes for avoiding that risk.
- Build and enforce an operating process of tasks that keeps the enterprise safe.
- A security culture includes a healthy combination of knowledge and follow-through of daily work tasks.

Cybersecurity isn't just about firewalls and threat detection—it starts with culture. A strong security culture is the best investment any organization can make. Intuitively, we all know that training employees to recognize threats, curb risky behaviors, and follow basic security practices delivers the highest return on investment (ROI). But here's the challenge—how do we quantify that ROI? How do we convince leadership to invest in something they can't immediately measure?

The reality is this: the chances of an employee accidentally starting a fire in the office are significantly lower than them unintentionally opening the door to a cyberattack. Yet, we conduct fire drills without question. Why? Because we recognize the risk. Cybersecurity awareness should be no different. It's not a one-time training; it's a continuous, ingrained part of how we operate.

As cybersecurity professionals, our job isn't just to implement controls—it's to advocate, to educate, and to shift mindsets. Whether it's the executive team, HR, or the employee next to you, everyone plays a role in protecting the enterprise. And when a cyber incident happens, one question will echo through the boardroom: "How did this happen?" The answer almost always ties back to human behavior.

So, we need to be relentless. We need to integrate cybersecurity into the DNA of the organization. That means making it part of everyday conversations, tying it to business objectives, and ensuring leadership understands that security isn't an IT issue—it's a business imperative.

If we want to build a true security culture, we don't just follow best practices—we lead the charge:

- **Security Awareness**: Educating employees on cyber risks
- **Accountability**: Making individuals responsible for security actions
- **Collaboration**: Encouraging interdepartmental cooperation
- **Continuous Improvement**: Adapting to evolving cyber threats
- **Transparency**: Open discussions about security concerns

A strong security culture fosters secure behaviors and proactive risk management.
Red, Blue, and Purple Teams in Cybersecurity
Security teams conduct attack and defense simulations to improve cyber resilience. In cybersecurity, "Red," "Blue," and "Purple" teams represent different roles within an organization's security testing, with Red teams simulating attacks, Blue teams defending against them, and Purple teams acting as a bridge by facilitating collaboration between the two, combining offensive and defensive strategies to improve overall security posture.

RED TEAM

Focus:
Think and behave like a threat actor to better prepare businesses for true threats

Tasks
- Simulate attack techniques
- Host lengthy intrusion campaigns
- Identify vulnerabilities within systems and networks

BLUE TEAM

Focus:
Handle business cyber-security tasks, including detection, prevention, and response

Tasks
- Manage everyday security operations
- Monitor networks and systems
- Triage alerts

PURPLE TEAM

Focus:
Red and blue teams combine the data they both gather over time and make it actionable.

Tasks
- Analyze vulnerability data
- improve overall recommendationss for security ops team
- Document best practices and change

- **Red Team (Attackers):** Simulates real-world attacks to find vulnerabilities
- **Blue Team (Defenders):** Monitors, detects, and mitigates threats
- **Purple Team (Collaboration):** Bridges Red and Blue teams to improve security defenses

Purple teaming enhances detection, response, and security strategy effectiveness.

Security Operations and Incident Response

Security operations focus on preventing cyber threats, while incident response ensures effective remediation after an attack.

Security Operations

- **Monitoring**: Continuous network and system threat detection
- **Threat Hunting**: Identifying hidden cyber risks
- **Vulnerability Management**: Identifying and patching weaknesses
- **Access Control**: Restricting unauthorized system access
- **SIEM**: Analyzing security logs to detect anomalies

Incident Response Life Cycle

- **Preparation**: Creating incident response plans and training teams
- **Detection and Analysis**: Identifying and assessing security threats
- **Containment**: Isolating the threat to minimize impact
- **Eradication**: Removing malicious actors and vulnerabilities
- **Recovery**: Restoring affected systems and data
- **Lessons Learned**: Reviewing incidents to strengthen future defenses

Proactive security operations and a solid incident response plan reduce cyber risk impact.

Communication and Advocacy in Cybersecurity

Communication and advocacy in cybersecurity refers to the practice of effectively conveying cybersecurity risks and best practices to various audiences, including employees, executives, and the public, by actively promoting security measures and influencing policy decisions to enhance overall cyber resilience, often requiring strong interpersonal skills and the ability to tailor messages to different stakeholders. Effective communication ensures clarity in policies, risk awareness, and incident response.

Internal Cybersecurity Communication

- **Security Policies and Best Practices**: Educating employees on cyber hygiene
- **Threat Intelligence Sharing**: Keeping teams informed of potential threats
- **Security Awareness Training**: Conducting phishing simulations and workshops
- **Incident Reporting Protocols**: Ensuring rapid response to security breaches

External Cybersecurity Communication

- **Customer and Partner Transparency**: Notifying stakeholders of security breaches
- **Law Enforcement Collaboration**: Working with authorities on cybercrime investigations
- **Public and Media Engagement**: Raising cybersecurity awareness

Clear and timely communication is essential to a strong security culture.

Cybersecurity Advocacy: Strengthening Digital Security

Advocacy focuses on raising awareness, influencing policies, and improving security practices.

- **Policy Advocacy**: Promoting effective cybersecurity laws and frameworks
- **Public Awareness**: Educating individuals on cyber risks and protection
- **Industry Collaboration**: Sharing security best practices across organizations

Advocacy fosters a stronger, more secure digital environment.

Final Takeaways

- Technology and architecture build cybersecurity defenses through integrated security frameworks.
- People and culture are the backbone of cybersecurity—awareness, training, and accountability are key.
- Red, Blue, and Purple teams strengthen security through adversarial simulations.
- Security operations ensure proactive defense, while incident response ensures swift recovery.
- Communication and advocacy promote cybersecurity awareness, transparency, and policy improvements.

Cybersecurity is a collective effort—leveraging technology, people, and culture creates a secure digital environment.

CIO's Role in Championing Cybersecurity with CISO and CXO

Cybersecurity is no longer just an IT concern—it's a business-critical function. This shift places the Chief Information Officer (CIO) at the forefront, working alongside the Chief Information Security Officer (CISO) and other CXOs to embed security into the organization's DNA. The CIO's ability to bridge technology and business strategy makes them the driving force behind a unified, enterprise-wide cybersecurity approach. Their leadership determines whether security is an afterthought or a strategic enabler of growth and resilience.

Beyond Technology: Cybersecurity As a Business Enabler

Traditionally, the CIO's focus has been on technology infrastructure and innovation. While these remain crucial, the modern CIO must also recognize that robust cybersecurity is not just a cost center but a fundamental enabler of business growth and resilience. A security breach can cripple operations, damage reputation, and erode customer trust, leading to significant financial losses. Therefore, the CIO must champion cybersecurity as a strategic investment, not simply an expense.

CHAPTER 6   THE CISO ROLE AND RESPONSIBILITIES

The CIO-CISO Partnership: A Symbiotic Relationship

The CIO and CISO share a crucial symbiotic relationship. While the CISO possesses the deep technical expertise in security threats and vulnerabilities, the CIO understands the broader business context, including risk appetite, resource allocation, and strategic objectives. A strong partnership between these two roles is essential for developing and implementing a comprehensive cybersecurity strategy that aligns with business goals.

IT and cybersecurity are both sides of the same coin. One cannot exist without the other, and a collaborative partnership is necessary for mutual success. The collaborative relationship between the Chief Information Officer (CIO) and the Chief Information Security Officer (CISO) is crucial for an organization's overall success and resilience in today's digital landscape. While the CIO focuses on leveraging technology to drive business innovation, efficiency, and growth, overseeing the entire IT infrastructure, and aligning IT strategy with business goals, the CISO is dedicated to safeguarding the organization's information assets from cyber threats, managing security risks, and ensuring compliance. Their joint efforts are essential for developing a holistic cybersecurity strategy that balances business objectives with robust security measures. This often involves shared responsibilities in risk management, vendor security, incident response planning, and promoting a company-wide culture of security awareness. Effective communication, mutual respect, a shared understanding of risks and priorities, and a unified voice when reporting to the board are key to a successful CIO-CISO partnership.

CHAPTER 6   THE CISO ROLE AND RESPONSIBILITIES

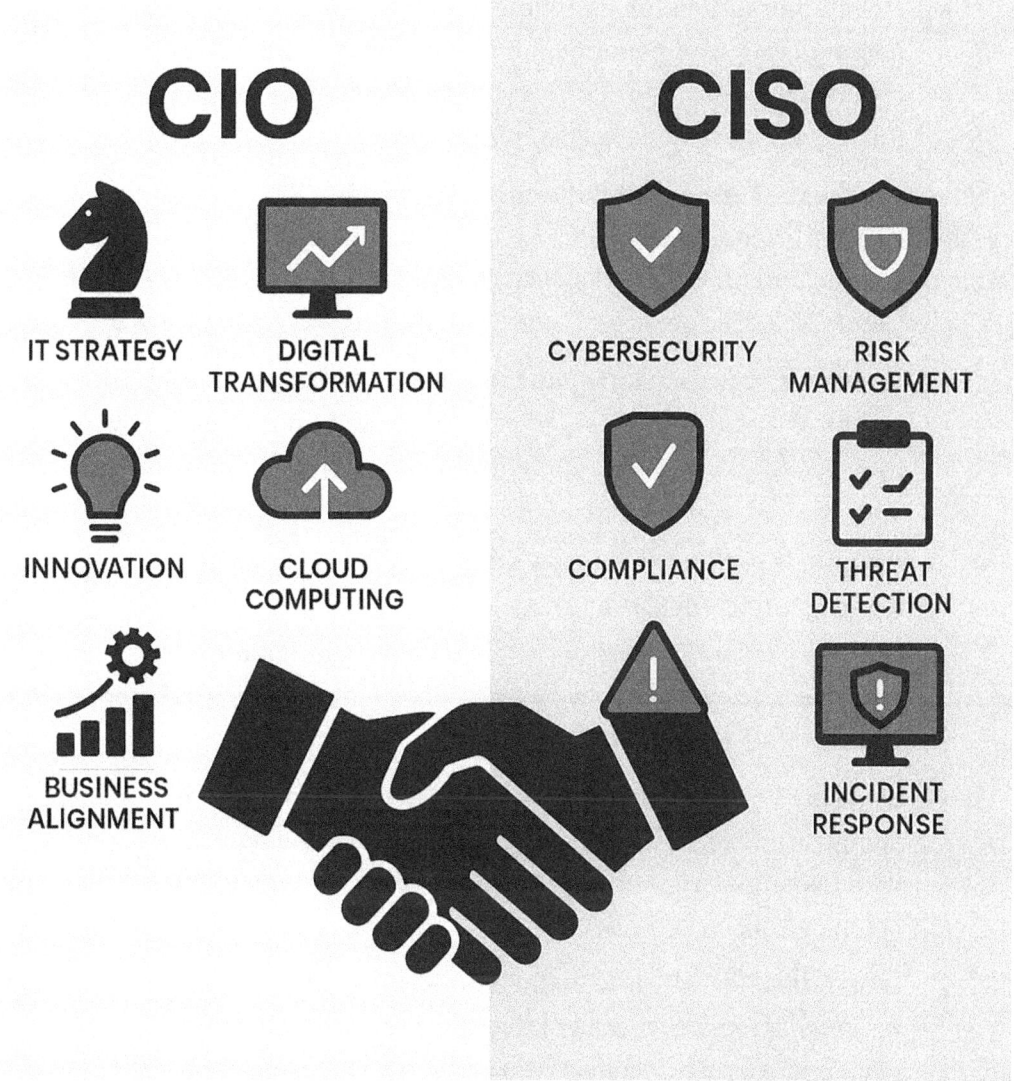

This collaboration should include

- **Jointly Defining Cybersecurity Strategy**: The CIO and CISO should work together to develop a cybersecurity road map that addresses the organization's specific risks and supports its overall business strategy.

- **Shared Responsibility for Risk Management**: Both roles should share responsibility for identifying, assessing, and mitigating cybersecurity risks.

- **Open Communication and Information Sharing**: Regular communication and information sharing between the CIO and CISO are crucial for staying ahead of evolving threats and ensuring that security initiatives are effectively implemented.

Engaging the CXO Suite: A Collaborative Approach

The CIO's role extends beyond the CISO partnership. They must effectively communicate the importance of cybersecurity to the entire C-suite, including the CEO, CFO, COO, and CMO. This involves

- **Framing Cybersecurity in Business Terms**: Instead of focusing on technical jargon, the CIO should articulate the business impact of cybersecurity risks, such as potential financial losses, reputational damage, and regulatory penalties.

- **Building a Culture of Security Awareness**: The CIO should work with other CXOs to foster a culture of security awareness throughout the organization. This includes providing regular training to employees on cybersecurity best practices and promoting a shared responsibility for security.

- **Securing Budget and Resources**: The CIO must advocate for adequate budget and resources for cybersecurity initiatives, demonstrating the return on investment through reduced risk and enhanced business resilience.

- **Integrating Security into Business Decisions**: The CIO should ensure that security considerations are integrated into all business decisions, from new product development to mergers and acquisitions.

The CIO As a Transformational Leader

In conclusion, the CIO's role in cybersecurity has evolved from a technical focus to a leadership imperative. By forging strong partnerships with the CISO and other CXOs, the CIO can champion a holistic, business-aligned approach to cybersecurity. This includes communicating the business value of security, fostering a culture of awareness, and securing the necessary resources. In doing so, the CIO becomes a transformational leader, enabling the organization to navigate the digital age with confidence and resilience.

Key Takeaways

In today's digital-first world, the **Chief Information Security Officer (CISO)** is more than a technical expert—they're a strategic business leader. The CISO leads cybersecurity efforts while aligning them with organizational goals, enabling innovation, protecting reputation, and ensuring compliance. Alongside the CIO and other CXOs, the CISO plays a vital role in building a security-first culture that reduces risk and enhances resilience.

Key Responsibilities and Strategic Priorities:

- **Lead and Manage** security teams, policies, and response capabilities.
- **Align cybersecurity** with business goals and risk appetite.
- **Drive incident response** and regulatory compliance efforts.
- **Foster a security culture** through employee training and awareness.
- **Translate technical risk** into business impact for executives and boards.

Core Security Pillars

- **Strategic Planning and Governance**: Tie cybersecurity strategy to long-term business vision, enforced through disciplined governance and KPIs.
- **Risk Management and Compliance**: Identify and mitigate threats while maintaining adherence to regulations like GDPR, HIPAA, and SEC rules.
- **Security Operations and Incident Response**: Monitor continuously, hunt threats proactively, and respond swiftly to reduce incident impact.
- **Technology and Architecture**: Implement layered defenses (Zero Trust, segmentation, SIEM, encryption) for a cohesive security framework.

- **People and Culture**: Empower every employee to act as a security advocate—because the strongest defenses begin with awareness.
- **Communication and Advocacy**: Clearly communicate risks and solutions across all levels, influence cyber policy, and build trust.

Executive Alignment

- **CIO + CISO collaboration** is essential. Together, they embed security into strategy, secure resources, and ensure cybersecurity is seen as a **business enabler**, not just an IT function.

CHAPTER 7

Leadership and Communication

In cybersecurity, leadership and communication are intricately linked, where effective leaders must excel at clearly conveying complex technical information to diverse stakeholders, building a security culture within the organization, and fostering open communication to proactively identify and mitigate cyber threats; essentially, strong communication is critical for successful cybersecurity leadership, enabling the implementation of robust security strategies and timely response to incidents.

Building and Leading a High-Performing Security Team

A strong security team is the backbone of an organization's cybersecurity strategy. Effective leadership, strategic hiring, and a culture of collaboration are essential to building and sustaining a high-performing security team.

Building a High-Performing Security Team

Recruitment and Hiring

- **Attracting Top Talent**: Actively sourcing skilled professionals such as threat intelligence analysts, penetration testers, security engineers, and incident responders through networking, cybersecurity conferences, and online recruitment platforms

- **Skills Assessment**: Evaluating technical expertise through hands-on security assessments, coding challenges, and real-world threat scenarios
- **Cultural Fit**: Ensuring candidates align with the organization's values, security-first mindset, and work ethic

Team Composition

- **Diverse Skillsets**: Assembling a team with a broad range of cybersecurity competencies to address multiple security challenges
- **Clear Roles and Responsibilities**: Defining individual responsibilities to eliminate overlap and ensure accountability

Leading a High-Performing Security Team

Leadership and Mentorship

- **Empowering Team Members**: Providing guidance, coaching, and career development opportunities
- **Fostering an Inclusive Environment**: Creating a space where team members feel valued and motivated to contribute

Communication and Collaboration

- **Open Communication Channels**: Establishing clear reporting mechanisms for security incidents and threat intelligence sharing
- **Cross-Departmental Collaboration**: Encouraging cooperation between the security team and IT, legal, compliance, and executive leadership

Motivation and Recognition

- **Acknowledging Contributions**: Recognizing and rewarding exceptional performance, innovation, and problem-solving
- **Providing Growth Opportunities**: Offering professional development through certifications, workshops, and hands-on training

- **Creating a Dynamic Work Environment**: Keeping team members engaged by exposing them to emerging technologies and real-world security challenges

Performance Management

- **Setting Clear Expectations**: Defining measurable goals and key performance indicators (KPIs)
- **Regular Feedback and Performance Reviews**: Conducting consistent evaluations to track progress and address challenges
- **Addressing Performance Issues**: Offering constructive feedback and tailored development plans to enhance skills and effectiveness

Key Considerations for Success

- **Continuous Improvement**: Regularly assessing and refining security operations and response strategies
- **Adaptability**: Staying ahead of evolving cyber threats and emerging security technologies
- **Building Trust and Relationships**: Strengthening interdepartmental collaboration to enhance overall security posture

Takeaway: A high-performing security team is not just about technical skills—it thrives on leadership, culture, adaptability, and collaboration. Investing in people, fostering innovation, and driving continuous learning are critical for success in today's cybersecurity landscape.

Communicating Security Risks and Strategies to Executives and the Board

Cybersecurity isn't just a technical issue—it's a business priority. Effective communication ensures that security stays at the forefront of organizational strategy. A CISO who can translate cyber risks into business impact will gain executive buy-in and drive real action. Without clear, business-aligned insights, cybersecurity becomes an afterthought rather than a core function.

Strong communication bridges the gap between technical teams and leadership. It transforms security from a compliance requirement into a strategic advantage. The ability to articulate risks, justify investments, and align security initiatives with business objectives determines whether cybersecurity is seen as a cost center or a business enabler. If security leaders don't own the narrative, someone else will—and it won't be in their favor.

Key Aspects of Effective Communication

Tailoring the Message

- Executive Level
- Focus on the business impact of security risks.
- Translate technical jargon into financial, reputational, and operational consequences.
  - Highlight ROI on cybersecurity investments.
- Board Level
  - Provide a high-level security overview aligned with strategic goals.
  - Emphasize compliance requirements and security control effectiveness.
  - Demonstrate the financial and regulatory risks of security gaps.

Key Metrics and Reporting

- **Track and Present KPIs**: Measure the effectiveness of security controls and risk mitigation strategies.
- **Data-Driven Insights**: Use real-world examples of cyber incidents and response effectiveness.
- **Data Visualization**: Utilize dashboards, charts, and reports to simplify complex cybersecurity information.

Example: Instead of reporting "X vulnerabilities detected," reframe it as "Our security measures prevented Y potential breaches, avoiding a projected $Z in losses."

Building Strong Relationships

- **Regular Engagement**: Proactively update executives and board members on security initiatives.
- **Availability**: Be accessible to answer questions, provide insights, and clarify concerns.
- **Trust Building**: Establish credibility through consistent, transparent communication.

Example: Hosting quarterly cybersecurity briefings fosters an ongoing dialogue between security leaders and executives.

Risk Assessment and Prioritization

- **Identify Critical Threats**: Conduct regular risk assessments to prioritize the most significant security risks.
- **Quantify Business Impact**: Communicate how security risks directly affect business objectives.
- **Align Risk Mitigation Strategies**: Present solutions that fit within the organization's risk tolerance.

Example: Instead of saying "Our firewall needs an upgrade," state, "Upgrading our firewall will reduce attack risk by 40%, preventing potential revenue losses of $X million."

Security Awareness for Executives and Boards

- **Educate on Emerging Threats**: Ensure decision-makers understand evolving cyber risks.
- **Promote a Security-First Mindset**: Embed cybersecurity into the organization's strategic discussions.

Example: Conducting executive-level cybersecurity training helps leaders make informed risk-based decisions.

Why Effective Communication Matters

- **Clear Communication Gains Executive Buy-In**: Ensures budget allocation and resource support for cybersecurity initiatives
- **Informed Decision-Making**: Helps leaders understand risks and prioritize investments
- **Building Trust and Confidence**: Strengthens the relationship between security teams and senior leadership

Takeaway: A strong security posture starts with leadership engagement. Aligning cybersecurity with business objectives ensures long-term protection, resilience, and strategic success.

Stakeholder Management and Collaboration

Stakeholder management in cybersecurity involves identifying, understanding, and maintaining relationships with individuals or entities impacted by or influencing cybersecurity efforts.

Collaboration involves working alongside organizations, agencies, and experts to strengthen cybersecurity resilience and address shared challenges.

Key Aspects of Stakeholder Management

- **Identification**: Determine key stakeholders, including
    - Employees
    - Customers
    - Suppliers
    - Business partners

- Regulators
- Shareholders
- The general public
- **Analysis**: Understand the needs, expectations, and concerns of each stakeholder group.
- **Engagement**: Actively communicate and involve stakeholders in cybersecurity discussions, policies, and decision-making.
- **Communication**: Relay security risks, mitigation strategies, and incident responses effectively to stakeholders.
- **Relationship Management**: Build trust, transparency, and cooperation among stakeholders to ensure alignment on security goals.

Key Aspects of Collaboration in Cybersecurity

- Information Sharing
    - Exchange threat intelligence, best practices, and incident data with trusted partners.
    - Leverage global security intelligence networks to stay ahead of emerging threats.
- Joint Initiatives
    - Participate in threat-hunting exercises, penetration testing, and security awareness programs with other organizations.
- Industry Partnerships
    - Work with cybersecurity industry groups, private organizations, and regulatory bodies to address sector-wide security risks.
- Public–Private Partnerships
    - Collaborate with government agencies, law enforcement, and cyber task forces to enhance national cybersecurity resilience.

Importance of Stakeholder Management and Collaboration

- **Improved Security Posture**: Understanding and addressing stakeholder needs results in stronger cybersecurity policies and preparedness.

- **Enhanced Resilience**: Collaboration strengthens defenses against large-scale cyber threats.

- **Increased Trust and Confidence**: Transparent communication builds credibility and stakeholder confidence.

- **Better Decision-Making**: Involving stakeholders ensures informed cybersecurity investments and risk assessments.

- **Long-Term Success**: A well-integrated approach to stakeholder management and collaboration supports ongoing security improvements.

Stakeholder engagement ensures alignment with business goals, while collaboration strengthens cybersecurity across industries. Both are essential for a comprehensive, adaptive security strategy.

Crisis Communication and Incident Response Communication

Crisis communication focuses on how an organization communicates with its stakeholders during critical security events, such as data breaches, cyberattacks, or other major security incidents.

Incident response communication refers specifically to communication activities during a cybersecurity incident, such as a ransomware attack, malware infection, or system breach.

Key Aspects of Crisis Communication

- Proactive Planning
  - Develop and maintain a crisis communication plan outlining roles, responsibilities, and communication protocols.
- Key Messages
  - Craft clear, concise, and consistent messages for different audiences, including employees, customers, investors, regulators, and the media.
- Communication Channels
  - Utilize appropriate communication platforms, such as press releases, website updates, social media, and internal employee briefings.
- Spokesperson Training
  - Train designated spokespeople on how to communicate professionally, accurately, and confidently during a crisis.
- Monitoring and Response
  - Monitor news coverage and social media to identify misinformation and negative sentiment.
  - Respond quickly and appropriately to maintain trust and transparency.

Key Aspects of Incident Response Communication

- Internal Communication
  - Keep employees, IT teams, security teams, and legal departments informed about the incident and the steps being taken.
- External Communication
  - Notify customers, regulators, partners, and law enforcement as appropriate and necessary.

- Technical Communication
  - Provide detailed technical insights to cybersecurity teams involved in containment, mitigation, and recovery.
- Legal and Regulatory Communication
  - Ensure compliance by reporting incidents to relevant authorities based on regulatory requirements (e.g., GDPR, HIPAA, SEC disclosures).

Why Crisis and Incident Response Communication Matter in Cybersecurity

- Mitigating Damage
  - Effective communication minimizes panic, confusion, and misinformation during security incidents.
- Maintaining Reputation
  - Transparent and timely updates protect brand reputation and stakeholder confidence.
- Ensuring Compliance
  - Helps organizations adhere to legal and regulatory disclosure requirements, avoiding penalties and lawsuits.
- Facilitating Recovery
  - Clear and structured communication enables a faster and more effective recovery process.

Both crisis communication and incident response communication are critical in ensuring organizations can navigate, respond to, and recover from cybersecurity incidents efficiently.

Key Takeaways

Strong leadership and clear communication are foundational to building and sustaining a high-performing cybersecurity team. Security leaders must not only convey technical risks in business terms but also foster a collaborative culture that empowers their teams, drives continuous improvement, and ensures accountability. Hiring the right mix of talent, supporting their growth, and cultivating cross-functional trust are essential to long-term cyber resilience.

- **Communicate Effectively**: Translate cybersecurity risks into business language for stakeholders.
- **Lead with Vision**: Create a security-first culture through transparency, mentorship, and inclusion.
- **Build the Right Team**: Hire diverse, skilled professionals who align with the organization's culture and security goals.
- **Define Roles Clearly**: Avoid overlap by assigning specific responsibilities and ensuring accountability.
- **Empower and Motivate**: Recognize achievements, offer development opportunities, and keep the team engaged.
- **Monitor Performance**: Set KPIs, provide feedback regularly, and address issues proactively.
- **Stay Adaptive**: Continuously refine tools, skills, and processes to address evolving threats.
- **Foster Collaboration**: Build strong relationships with IT, legal, compliance, and executive teams to enhance the security posture.

CHAPTER 8

CISO Skills and Competencies

A CISO (Chief Information Security Officer) requires a combination of technical cybersecurity knowledge, strong leadership skills, excellent communication abilities, business acumen, risk management expertise, and the ability to translate complex security concepts into understandable terms for executives, making effective risk mitigation a key competency; essentially, a CISO needs to understand both the technical aspects of security and how to align security strategies with overall business goals.

The CISO role requires a unique blend of technical expertise, leadership skills, business acumen, and personal qualities. Developing these skills enables CISOs to effectively lead their organizations through an increasingly complex cybersecurity landscape.

Technical Expertise

- Cybersecurity Fundamentals
    - Strong understanding of threat modeling, vulnerability management, incident response, cryptography, and access control
- Cloud Security
    - Deep knowledge of cloud security principles, including IaaS, PaaS, SaaS, and the shared responsibility model
- Network Security
    - Expertise in network security protocols, firewalls, intrusion detection systems (IDS), and intrusion prevention systems (IPS)

- Data Security
  - Proficiency in encryption, data loss prevention (DLP), and data classification to protect sensitive information
- Threat Intelligence
  - Ability to analyze threat intelligence feeds and understand the latest cyber threats and attack vectors
- Emerging Technologies
  - Knowledge of AI/ML, blockchain, and IoT security implications, as well as their impact on cybersecurity strategies

Business Acumen

- Business Understanding
  - Deep comprehension of the organization's business objectives, operations, and risk tolerance
- Financial Management
  - Ability to manage cybersecurity budgets effectively and demonstrate the return on investment (ROI) of security initiatives
- Compliance
  - Knowledge of regulatory frameworks and industry standards such as GDPR, HIPAA, PCI DSS, and NIST

Communication and Interpersonal Skills

- Communication and Collaboration
  - Strong ability to communicate effectively with executives, technical teams, and legal/compliance departments

- Adaptability
  - Ability to adjust to evolving threats, industry trends, and new security technologies
- Continuous Learning
  - Commitment to staying updated on cybersecurity threats, best practices, and technological advancements

Leadership and Management Skills

- Strategic Leadership
  - Capability to develop and implement a cybersecurity strategy aligned with business objectives
- Risk Management
  - Ability to identify, assess, and mitigate cybersecurity risks across the enterprise
- Team Leadership
  - Competency in mentoring, managing, and developing high-performing cybersecurity teams

Negotiation and Influencing Skills

- Negotiation and Influence
  - Proficiency in securing executive buy-in, negotiating with vendors, and advocating for cybersecurity investments

Ethical Considerations and Decision-Making

- Strong Ethical Principles
  - Commitment to high ethical standards and integrity in all cybersecurity practices

CHAPTER 8   CISO SKILLS AND COMPETENCIES

- Problem-Solving and Analytical Skills
  - Ability to analyze complex security issues, identify root causes, and develop effective solutions
- Decision-Making
  - Capability to make sound and timely decisions in high-pressure situations

The infographic below illustrates the multifaceted role of a Chief Information Security Officer (CISO), segmented into four interconnected responsibilities: Strategist, Advisor, Technologist, and Guardian. Each role is visually represented as a puzzle piece, emphasizing how these functions interlock to form a comprehensive security leadership profile. The Strategist (25%) aligns business and cyber risk strategies, fostering innovation and value-driven decision-making. The Advisor (22%) focuses on engaging with the business to educate and influence cyber risk-related activities. The Technologist (19%) is responsible for building capabilities that support organizational objectives. The Guardian (31%) plays the most time-intensive role, safeguarding business assets by understanding the threat landscape and enhancing the effectiveness of the cyber risk program. This model underscores the CISO's evolving role as both a business enabler and a security leader.

CHAPTER 8 CISO SKILLS AND COMPETENCIES

Strategist
25%
Drives business and cyber risk strategy alignment, fosters innovation, manages to metrics and risk through value-based decisions.

Advisor
23%
Engages with the business, educates, advises, and influences activities wit cyber risk

Technologist
19%
Leads security programs and operations, builds organizational capabilities

Guardian
33%
Protects business assets, understands the the threat landscape, increases enterprise resilience to cyber risk exposure

CISO

PART III

Cybersecurity Frameworks and Standards

This section provides a comprehensive overview of essential frameworks and standards that guide organizations in building and maintaining robust cybersecurity programs. It's an indispensable resource for anyone looking to understand the foundational principles and practical applications of cybersecurity governance.

CHAPTER 9

The CISO in the Modern World

In the modern world, a CISO (Chief Information Security Officer) is not just a technical expert but a strategic business leader primarily responsible for identifying, assessing, and mitigating cyber risks across an organization, often by collaborating with various departments to cultivate a culture of cybersecurity awareness while aligning security strategies with overall business objectives, particularly in the face of evolving threats like AI, quantum computing, and complex digital landscapes.

The CISO role has become increasingly critical in today's digital world. To be successful, CISOs must be strategic leaders, risk managers, business enablers, and security advocates. They must also be able to adapt to the ever-changing threat landscape and navigate the complexities of the modern business environment.

The Evolving Role of the CISO

The CISO (Chief Information Security Officer) in the modern world has evolved significantly. Here's a look at their key functions and challenges:

CHAPTER 9   THE CISO IN THE MODERN WORLD

Evolving Role of the CISO

- **From Technician to Strategist**: CISOs are no longer just technical experts. They now play a strategic role in the organization, advising on business decisions with a focus on security implications.

- **Risk Management Leader**: CISOs are responsible for identifying, assessing, and mitigating cyber risks across the entire organization. This includes understanding the business context and aligning security strategies with overall business objectives.

- **Business Enabler**: Instead of simply saying "no" to new technologies, CISOs must find ways to enable innovation while maintaining a strong security posture. This involves collaborating with business units to identify and implement secure solutions that support business growth.

- **Culture Champion**: CISOs play a critical role in fostering a security-conscious culture within the organization. This includes educating employees about security best practices, promoting a culture of security awareness, and encouraging responsible security behavior.

- **Compliance Advocate**: CISOs must ensure compliance with relevant security regulations and industry standards, such as GDPR, HIPAA, and PCI DSS.

Key Challenges Facing CISOs

- **The Evolving Threat Landscape**: The threat landscape is constantly evolving, with new threats and vulnerabilities emerging every day. CISOs must stay ahead of these threats and adapt their security strategies accordingly.

- **The Rise of Remote Work**: The shift to remote work has increased the attack surface for organizations. CISOs must ensure that remote employees have access to secure devices and networks and that sensitive data is protected.

- **The Cloud and Digital Transformation**: The increasing reliance on cloud computing and digital technologies presents both opportunities and challenges for CISOs. They must ensure that cloud environments are secure and that data is protected in the cloud.

- **Talent Shortage**: There is a significant shortage of skilled cybersecurity professionals. CISOs must find ways to attract and retain top talent.

- **Budget Constraints**: Cybersecurity budgets are often limited, forcing CISOs to make difficult decisions about how to best allocate resources.

Emerging Trends and Technologies Impacting the CISO Role

There are several emerging trends and technologies that are significantly impacting the CISO role:

1. Artificial Intelligence (AI) and Machine Learning (ML)

    - **Enhanced Threat Detection**: AI/ML algorithms can analyze massive datasets to identify subtle patterns and anomalies that might be missed by human analysts. This leads to faster detection of threats, including zero-day attacks and advanced persistent threats (APTs).

    - **Automated Response**: AI/ML can automate routine security tasks, such as quarantining infected systems, blocking malicious IP addresses, and initiating remediation actions.

    - **Predictive Analytics**: AI/ML can be used to predict future cyberattacks based on historical data and current trends, allowing organizations to proactively implement preventative measures.

2. Zero Trust Security

    - **Shifting Security Paradigm**: The traditional "castle-and-moat" approach is being replaced by a zero trust model, where trust is not implicitly granted.

    - **Focus on Least Privilege**: Emphasis on granting users only the minimum necessary access to perform their job duties.

    - **Continuous Verification**: Continuous authentication and authorization are crucial in a zero trust environment.

3. Cloud Security

    - **Cloud Migration and Adoption**: The increasing reliance on cloud computing presents both opportunities and challenges for CISOs.

- **Shared Responsibility Model**: Understanding and managing the shared responsibility model between the organization and the cloud provider is critical.

- **Cloud Security Posture Management (CSPM)**: Tools and technologies for continuously monitoring and assessing the security posture of cloud environments.

4. DevSecOps

    - **Integrating Security into the Development Life Cycle**: Shifting security left, integrating security considerations into the entire software development life cycle

    - **Automation and Orchestration**: Automating security tasks throughout the development and deployment process

5. Internet of Things (IoT) Security

    - **Securing a Growing Number of Devices**: The proliferation of IoT devices increases the attack surface and presents new security challenges.

    - **Addressing Device Vulnerabilities**: Ensuring the security of IoT devices and the data they collect.

6. Cybersecurity Mesh

    - **Decentralized Security Architecture**: A distributed approach to security that connects and coordinates security controls across different domains and environments

    - **Improved Collaboration and Information Sharing**: Facilitates better collaboration and information sharing among different security teams and organizations

7. Quantum Computing

    - **Potential Impact on Cryptography**: Quantum computing could potentially break current encryption methods, requiring new cryptographic solutions.

    - **Preparing for the Future**: CISOs need to be aware of the potential impact of quantum computing and plan for the future.

These trends and technologies are significantly impacting the CISO role, requiring them to develop new skills, adapt their strategies, and embrace a more proactive and holistic approach to cybersecurity.

The Future of Cybersecurity Leadership

The future of cybersecurity leaders will require a blend of technical expertise, business acumen, and strong leadership skills. They will need to be adaptable, innovative, and ethical to effectively address the challenges of the evolving threat landscape.

The future of cybersecurity leaders will be shaped by several key trends:

1. Increased Focus on Business Acumen

    - **Strategic Alignment**: CISOs will need to become even more deeply integrated into the business, aligning security strategies with overall business goals and risk tolerance.

    - **Value Demonstration**: CISOs will need to demonstrate the value of their security investments to the business, showing how security initiatives contribute to the bottom line.

2. Embrace of Emerging Technologies

    - **AI and ML**: CISOs will need to leverage AI and ML to improve threat detection, automate responses, and gain deeper insights into security threats.

    - **Cloud Security**: With the increasing reliance on cloud computing, CISOs must develop expertise in cloud security best practices and the shared responsibility model.

    - **Zero Trust Security**: Adopting a zero trust security model, where trust is not implicitly granted, will be crucial for modern organizations.

3. Leadership and Communication

    - **Building a Security Culture**: CISOs will need to foster a security-conscious culture within the organization, encouraging employees to be vigilant and report suspicious activity.

- **Communication and Collaboration**: Effective communication and collaboration with other departments, such as IT, HR, and legal, will be essential.

Talent Development: CISOs will need to focus on developing and retaining top cybersecurity talent, including investing in training and upskilling programs.

4. Proactive and Predictive Security

    - **Threat Intelligence**: CISOs will need to leverage threat intelligence to proactively identify and mitigate emerging threats.

    - **Risk-Based Approach**: Adopting a risk-based approach to security, focusing on the most critical assets and threats.

    - **Continuous Improvement**: Continuously evaluating and improving security controls and processes to stay ahead of the evolving threat landscape.

5. Ethical Considerations

    - **Data Privacy and Ethics**: CISOs will need to navigate the ethical implications of data collection, use, and protection.

    - **Transparency and Accountability**: Building and maintaining trust requires transparency and accountability in security practices.

Key Metrics, KPIs, and Reporting

In cybersecurity, key performance indicators (KPIs) and key metrics are crucial for evaluating the effectiveness of security measures, identifying potential vulnerabilities, and improving overall risk management. They help organizations assess how well their cybersecurity programs are functioning and ensure they meet strategic objectives.

Table 9-1 shows an overview of key metrics and KPIs in cybersecurity, Table 9-2 lists KPIs in cybersecurity, and Table 9-3 shows reporting in cybersecurity.

CHAPTER 9   THE CISO IN THE MODERN WORLD

Table 9-1. Key Metrics in Cybersecurity

Metrics Types	What It Measures	Why It Matters
• Incident Detection Time (IDT)	The time it takes from the moment a cybersecurity incident occurs until it is detected.	The quicker the detection, the faster the response, minimizing damage.
• Incident Response Time (IRT)	Time taken from detection to containment and resolution of the incident.	A shorter response time leads to better mitigation and less impact on the organization.
• Mean Time to Detect (MTTD)	Average time to identify a threat or security breach.	A lower MTTD indicates better threat detection capabilities.
• Mean Time to Resolve (MTTR)	Average time to resolve a security incident after detection.	Reducing MTTR is key to minimizing the impact of breaches.
• Percentage of Patching Compliance	The proportion of systems that are up-to-date with the latest security patches.	Delayed patches often lead to vulnerabilities. Ensuring timely patching minimizes exposure to known threats.
• Vulnerability Remediation Rate	The speed at which identified vulnerabilities are fixed.	Faster remediation of vulnerabilities reduces the window of opportunity for attackers.
• Number of Detected Vulnerabilities	The number of security vulnerabilities discovered in a given period.	This gives insight into how secure the system is and whether resources should be allocated for improvement.
• False Positive Rate (FPR)	The percentage of security alerts that turn out to be false alarms.	Lower FPR ensures that resources are focused on genuine threats, reducing alert fatigue.
• Security Audit Findings	The number and severity of issues found during security audits.	Regular audits identify gaps and ensure that security policies are being followed.
• Data Loss Prevention (DLP) Incidents	The number of incidents where sensitive data is at risk or exposed.	Protecting data is a critical component of cybersecurity; minimizing DLP incidents prevents data breaches.

Table 9-2. KPIs in Cybersecurity

Metrics Types	What It Measures	Why It Matters
Cybersecurity Awareness and Training Completion Rate	The percentage of employees who have completed mandatory cybersecurity training.	Ensuring that employees are aware of security best practices reduces the risk of human error, which is a major cause of breaches.
Phishing Simulation Success Rate	The percentage of employees who successfully identify phishing emails in simulated exercises.	Regular testing of employee awareness of phishing can reduce susceptibility to this common attack vector.
Security Incident Frequency	The frequency of security incidents over a set period	A high frequency indicates that the security posture might need to be reviewed and improved.
Cost per Incident	The cost incurred to contain and mitigate a single security incident.	This helps in determining the financial impact of breaches and aids in budgeting for future defense strategies.
Percentage of Encrypted Data	The proportion of sensitive data that is encrypted, both at rest and in transit.	Encrypting data helps prevent unauthorized access and data breaches, which is vital for safeguarding privacy and compliance.
Security Coverage Rate	The percentage of critical assets that are covered by security solutions like firewalls, antivirus, and intrusion detection systems.	Higher security coverage reduces the risk of vulnerabilities going undetected in key assets.
Security Budget Compliance	The percentage of the allocated cybersecurity budget that is actually spent as planned.	Staying within the allocated budget ensures proper investment in defense systems, tools, and training.

(*continued*)

Table 9-2. (*continued*)

Metrics Types	What It Measures	Why It Matters
Third-Party Vendor Risk	The risk posed by third-party vendors or service providers to the organization's cybersecurity.	Vendors can be an attack vector, so assessing and managing third-party risks helps prevent supply chain attacks.
Security Maturity Level	The current maturity level of the organization's cybersecurity program.	Higher maturity indicates stronger overall security posture, reducing vulnerabilities.
Return on Investment (ROI) in Security Tools	The return on investment from cybersecurity tools and technologies.	Effective tools should save time, reduce breaches, and lower long-term costs, making ROI a critical metric.

Table 9-3. *Reporting in Cybersecurity*

Executive Dashboards	Visual summaries for top-level management that highlight key cybersecurity KPIs, incidents, trends, and risk levels. These help executives make informed decisions quickly.
Incident Reports	Detailed reports generated after security incidents, outlining the attack's scope, impact, resolution, and lessons learned. These help in analyzing root causes and improving future responses.
Compliance Reports	Periodic reports to ensure adherence to regulatory standards like GDPR, HIPAA, or PCI DSS. These reports are essential for demonstrating legal compliance and risk mitigation.
Risk Assessment Reports	Provide a comprehensive overview of the organization's threat landscape, including vulnerability assessments, threat analysis, and risk mitigation strategies.
Audit Logs	These logs track user activities and system events. Regular reporting from audit logs provides insights into potential threats or anomalies.
Security Posture Reports	Reflects the current status of the organization's overall security posture. It highlights the effectiveness of policies, procedures, and tools in place to protect the system.

CHAPTER 9   THE CISO IN THE MODERN WORLD

Key Takeaways

The role of a **Chief Information Security Officer (CISO)** has dramatically evolved, transforming from a purely technical position into a crucial **strategic business leadership** function. Modern CISOs are primarily responsible for identifying, assessing, and mitigating cyber risks across an organization, aligning security strategies with overall business objectives, and fostering a culture of cybersecurity awareness amid an increasingly complex and evolving threat landscape. They are essential for navigating challenges posed by new technologies like AI and quantum computing, as well as shifts toward remote work and extensive cloud adoption.

Here are the key takeaways regarding the CISO in the modern world:

- **Strategic Business Partner**: CISOs are no longer just technical experts; they are **strategic leaders** advising on business decisions with a focus on security implications and enabling innovation.

- **Comprehensive Risk Management**: Their core responsibility is to **identify, assess, and mitigate cyber risks** across the entire organization, ensuring security strategies align with business goals.

- **Culture Champion**: CISOs play a critical role in **fostering a security-conscious culture** within the organization through education and promoting best practices.

- **Compliance Advocate**: They ensure adherence to crucial security regulations and industry standards like **GDPR, HIPAA, and PCI DSS**.

- **Navigating Evolving Threats**: CISOs must constantly adapt to a **dynamic threat landscape**, including challenges from remote work, cloud adoption, and a persistent cybersecurity **talent shortage**.

- **Impact of Emerging Technologies**: Key trends significantly impacting the CISO role include **artificial intelligence (AI) and machine learning (ML)** for threat detection, the shift to **Zero Trust Security**, securing **cloud environments** (understanding the shared responsibility model), integrating security into development through **DevSecOps**, and addressing **IoT security**.

- **Future-Proofing**: CISOs need to be aware of the potential impact of **quantum computing** on current cryptography and prepare for future cryptographic solutions.

- **Key Metrics for Success**: Effective CISOs utilize **key performance indicators (KPIs)** and metrics such as incident detection time (IDT), incident response time (IRT), mean time to detect (MTTD), mean time to resolve (MTTR), and patching compliance to measure and improve security posture.

- **Leadership Qualities**: The future of cybersecurity leadership demands a blend of technical expertise, **business acumen, strong communication skills, and ethical considerations** regarding data privacy and transparency.

CHAPTER 10

Key Cybersecurity Frameworks

"Cybersecurity frameworks and standards aren't just checklists—they're the foundation of a resilient security strategy." These structured guidelines help organizations identify, assess, and manage risks while safeguarding critical digital assets. Simply put, aligning security practices with industry frameworks doesn't just reduce the risk of a breach—it ensures that cybersecurity is embedded into the business, not treated as an afterthought.

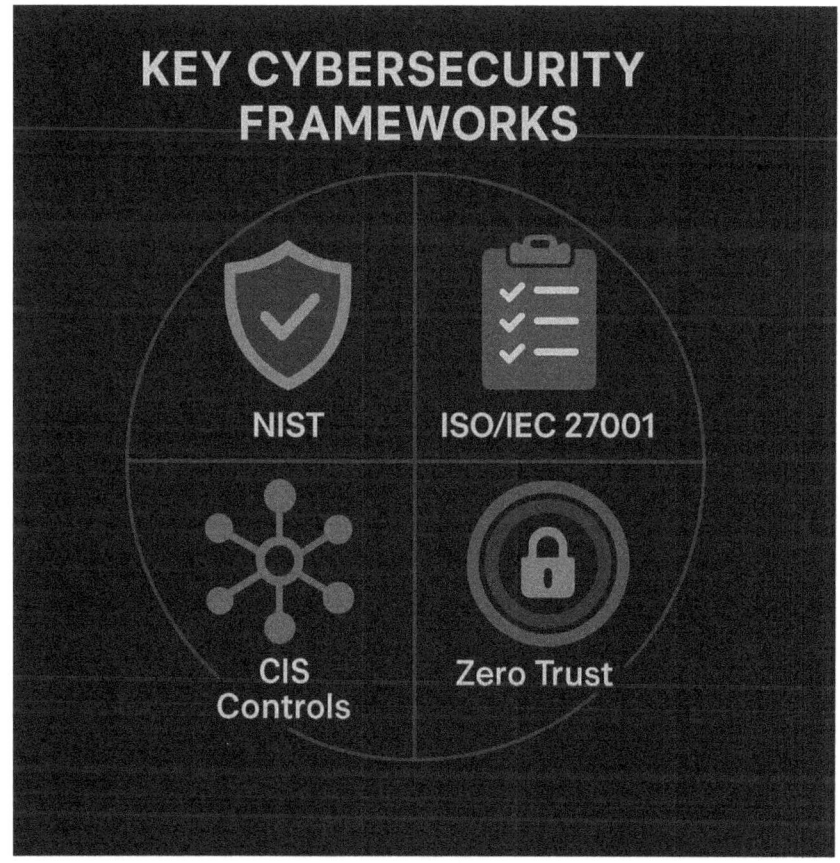

© GS Jha 2025
GS. Jha, *Securing the Enterprise*, https://doi.org/10.1007/979-8-8688-1654-3_10

The right framework—whether NIST, ISO 27001, or CIS—provides a road map to resilience. It's not about compliance for compliance's sake; it's about proactively mitigating threats, improving response capabilities, and building trust with customers, regulators, and stakeholders.

If security isn't built into your organization's DNA today, a breach will force it there tomorrow.

The Cybersecurity Framework (CSF) is a structured set of best practices and guidelines that assist organizations in enhancing information security and managing cyber risks effectively. It provides a proactive approach to assessing, monitoring, and mitigating existing and emerging threats. By implementing CSF, organizations can strengthen security measures and protect their data, infrastructure, and information systems from cyber threats.

NIST Cybersecurity Framework

As shown in the diagram below, the NIST Cybersecurity Framework (CSF) is a set of guidelines developed by the National Institute of Standards and Technology (NIST) to help organizations manage and reduce cybersecurity risks. It provides a flexible and voluntary framework for improving critical infrastructure cybersecurity, but it is widely adopted across various industries due to its practical and adaptable approach.

CHAPTER 10   KEY CYBERSECURITY FRAMEWORKS

Based on the NIST Cybersecurity Framework

The NIST CSF provides a structured and flexible approach to managing cybersecurity risk. By following the core functions and incorporating the recommended best practices, organizations can significantly enhance their cybersecurity posture and improve their overall resilience to cyber threats.

Key Components and Functions of the NIST CSF

1. Core
   - The Core is a set of cybersecurity activities, outcomes, and references organized into three parts:

CHAPTER 10 KEY CYBERSECURITY FRAMEWORKS

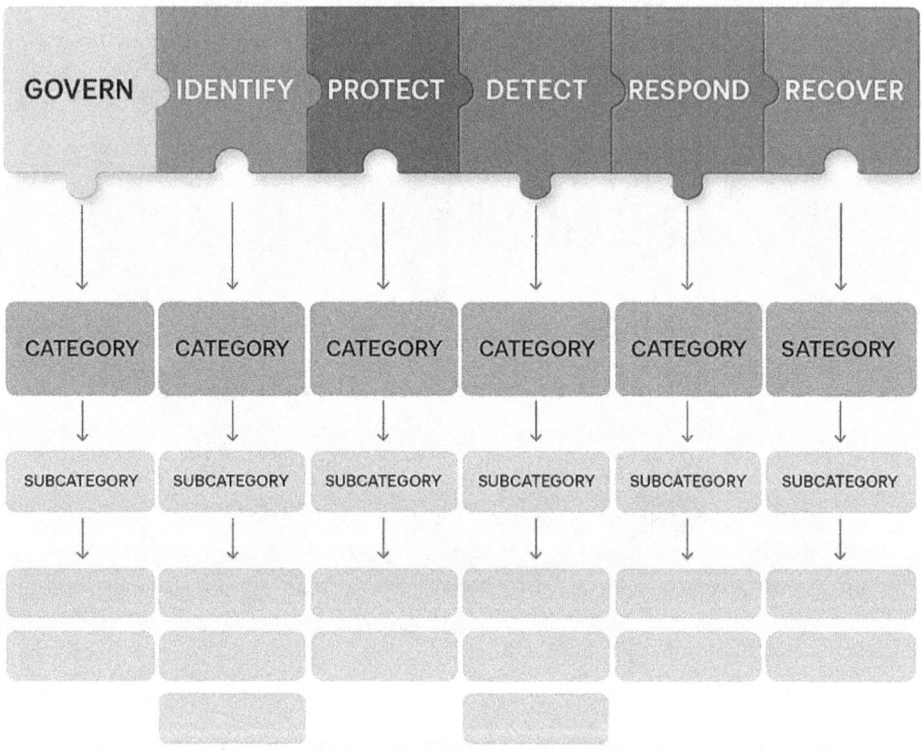

- **Functions**: High-level categories of cybersecurity tasks (Identify, Protect, Detect, Respond, Recover)
- **Categories**: Subdivisions of the functions that group related outcomes
- **Subcategories**: Specific outcomes or technical and management activities

Example: The "Identify" function includes categories like Asset Management and Risk Assessment.

2. Implementation Tiers
   - These tiers describe the degree to which an organization's cybersecurity practices align with the Framework, ranging from Tier 1 (Partial) to Tier 4 (Adaptive). They help organizations understand their current cybersecurity posture and set goals for improvement.

3. Profiles
   - Profiles are customized alignments of the Framework Core to an organization's specific needs, risk appetite, and resources. They help organizations prioritize actions to reduce cybersecurity risks.

The Six Functions of the NIST CSF

As shown below, the CSF core functions—Govern, Identify, Protect, Detect, Respond, and Recover—organize cybersecurity outcomes at their highest level.

CHAPTER 10   KEY CYBERSECURITY FRAMEWORKS

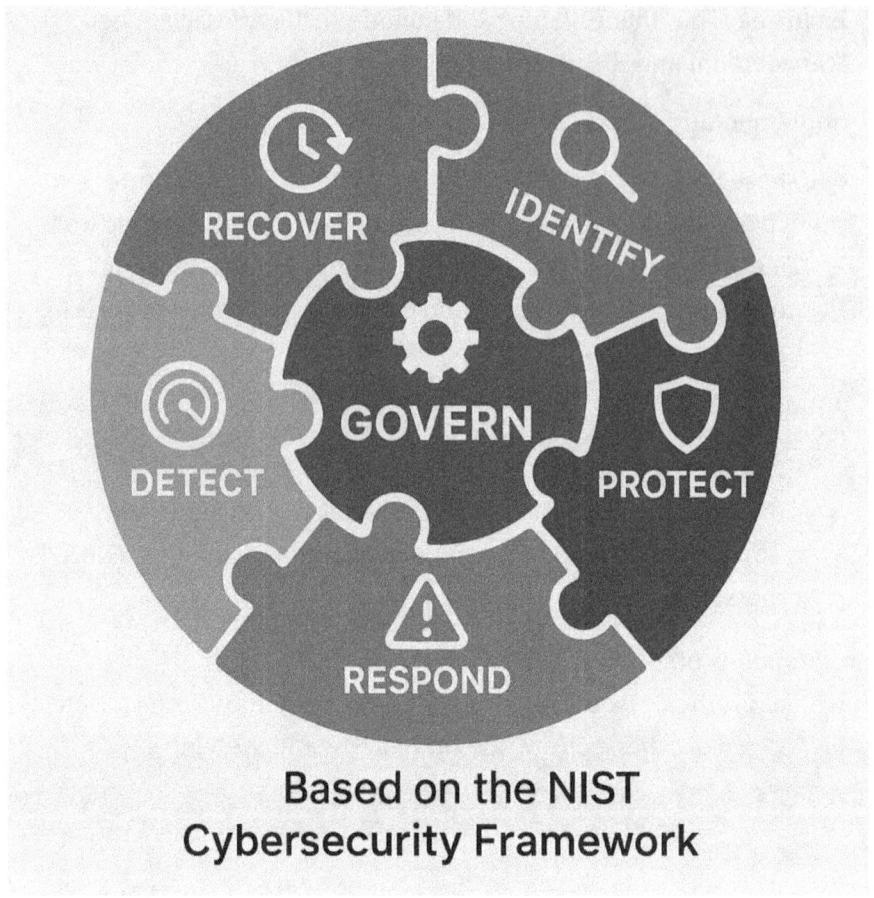

Based on the NIST Cybersecurity Framework

1. **Govern (GV)**: The organization's cybersecurity risk management strategy, expectations, and policy are established, communicated, and monitored. The Govern function provides outcomes to inform what an organization may do to achieve and prioritize the outcomes of the other five functions in the context of its mission and stakeholder expectations. Governance activities are critical for incorporating cybersecurity into an organization's broader enterprise risk management (ERM) strategy. Govern addresses an understanding of organizational context; the establishment of cybersecurity strategy and cybersecurity supply chain risk management; roles, responsibilities, and authorities; policy; and the oversight of cybersecurity strategy.

2. **Identify (ID)**: Develop an understanding of the organization's business environment and assets, as well as the potential threats and vulnerabilities. The organization's current cybersecurity risks are understood. Understanding the organization's assets (e.g., data, hardware, software, systems, facilities, services, people), suppliers, and related cybersecurity risks enables an organization to prioritize its efforts consistent with its risk management strategy and the mission needs identified under Govern. This function also includes the identification of improvement opportunities—as described in the NIST Cybersecurity Framework (CSF) 2.0, NIST CSWP 29, February 26, 2024—for the organization's policies, plans, processes, procedures, and practices that support cybersecurity risk management to inform efforts under all six functions.

3. **Protect (PR)**: Develop and implement appropriate safeguards to protect critical systems and assets. Safeguards to manage the organization's cybersecurity risks are used. Once assets and risks are identified and prioritized, Protect supports the ability to secure those assets to prevent or lower the likelihood and impact of adverse cybersecurity events, as well as to increase the likelihood and impact of taking advantage of opportunities. Outcomes covered by this function include identity management, authentication, and access control; awareness and training; data security; platform security (i.e., securing the hardware, software, and services of physical and virtual platforms); and the resilience of technology infrastructure.

4. **Detect (DE)**: Develop and implement the appropriate activities to identify the occurrence of a cybersecurity event. Possible cybersecurity attacks and compromises are found and analyzed. Detect enables the timely discovery and analysis of anomalies, indicators of compromise, and other potentially adverse events that may indicate that cybersecurity attacks and incidents are occurring. This function supports successful incident response and recovery activities.

5. **Respond (RS)**: Develop and implement the appropriate activities to take action regarding a cybersecurity event. Actions regarding a detected cybersecurity incident are taken. Respond supports the ability to contain the effects of cybersecurity incidents. Outcomes within this function cover incident management, analysis, mitigation, reporting, and communication.

6. **Recover (RC)**: Develop and implement the appropriate activities to maintain plans for resilience and to restore any capabilities or services that were impaired due to a cybersecurity event. Develop and implement the appropriate activities to maintain plans for resilience and to restore any capabilities or services that were impaired due to a cybersecurity event. Assets and operations affected by a cybersecurity incident are restored. Recover supports the timely restoration of normal operations to reduce the effects of cybersecurity incidents and enable appropriate communication during recovery efforts.

Purpose

The NIST CSF is designed to

- Help organizations understand, manage, and reduce cybersecurity risks.

- Provide a common language for addressing cybersecurity risks.

- Enable organizations to align cybersecurity efforts with business objectives and regulatory requirements.

ISO 27001

ISO/IEC 27001, also known as ISO 27001, is a security standard that outlines the suggested requirements for building, monitoring, and improving an Information Security Management System (ISMS). An ISMS is a set of policies for protecting and managing an enterprise's sensitive information, e.g., financial data, intellectual property, customer details, and employee records.

ISO 27001 is a voluntary standard employed by service providers to secure customer information. It requires an independent and accredited body to formally audit an organization to ensure compliance.

As shown below, the ISO 27001 is an internationally recognized standard for establishing, implementing, maintaining, and continually improving an Information Security Management System (ISMS). ISO 27001 provides a structured and systematic approach to managing information security, helping organizations protect their valuable assets and build a more secure and resilient business environment.

COBIT

COBIT (Control Objectives for Information and Related Technologies) is a globally accepted framework for governing and managing enterprise IT. COBIT provides a holistic framework for managing enterprise IT, helping organizations ensure that IT is a valuable asset that supports and enables business success. At its core, the COBIT framework is a compass that enables organizations to navigate the intricate waters of IT governance, risk management, and compliance. The ultimate goal of COBIT is to ensure that IT operations are in alignment with business objectives while mitigating risks, enhancing value delivery, and ensuring compliance. This multidimensional approach serves as a bridge, connecting the often technical realm of IT with the strategic goals of the organization.

Developed by ISACA, COBIT 5 offers organizations a structured approach to aligning IT strategies with business goals, managing risks, optimizing resources, and ensuring accountability.

The following seven-step framework explores the core principles, key concepts, and real-world implications of COBIT 5, unveiling how this framework empowers businesses to make informed decisions, enhance operational efficiency, and foster a culture of excellence in IT governance. As we delve into the depths of COBIT 5, we gain valuable insights into its application, benefits, and significance in the modern technological era.

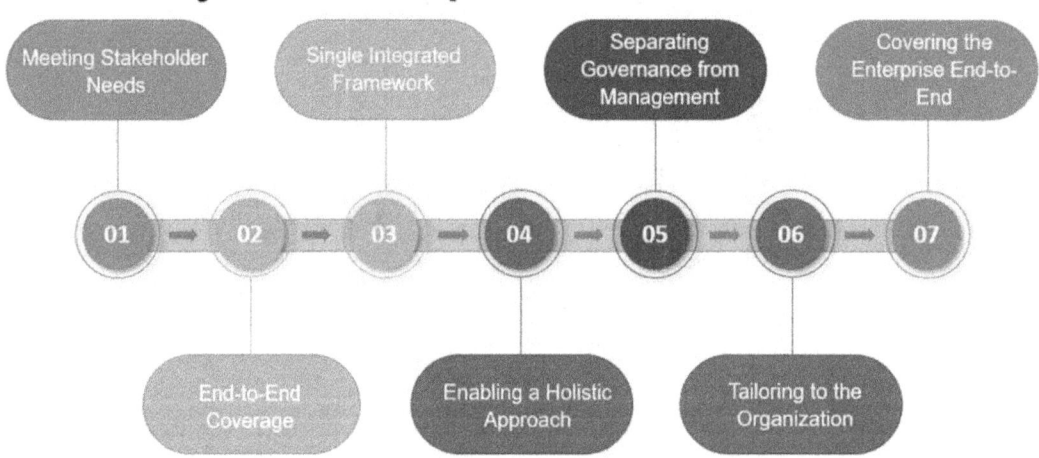

Image source: isaca.org

CIS Controls

The CIS Controls, short for CIS Critical Security Controls, are a prioritized set of cybersecurity best practices developed by the Center for Internet Security (CIS). They offer a focused and actionable approach to defending against common and dangerous cyberattacks, helping organizations improve their overall security posture.

CHAPTER 10   KEY CYBERSECURITY FRAMEWORKS

As shown below, CIS Controls are a prioritized set of actions for cybersecurity that form a defense-in-depth set of specific and actionable best practices to mitigate the most common cyberattacks. The CIS Controls provide a practical and effective road map for organizations to improve their cybersecurity defenses and protect themselves from the ever-evolving threat landscape.

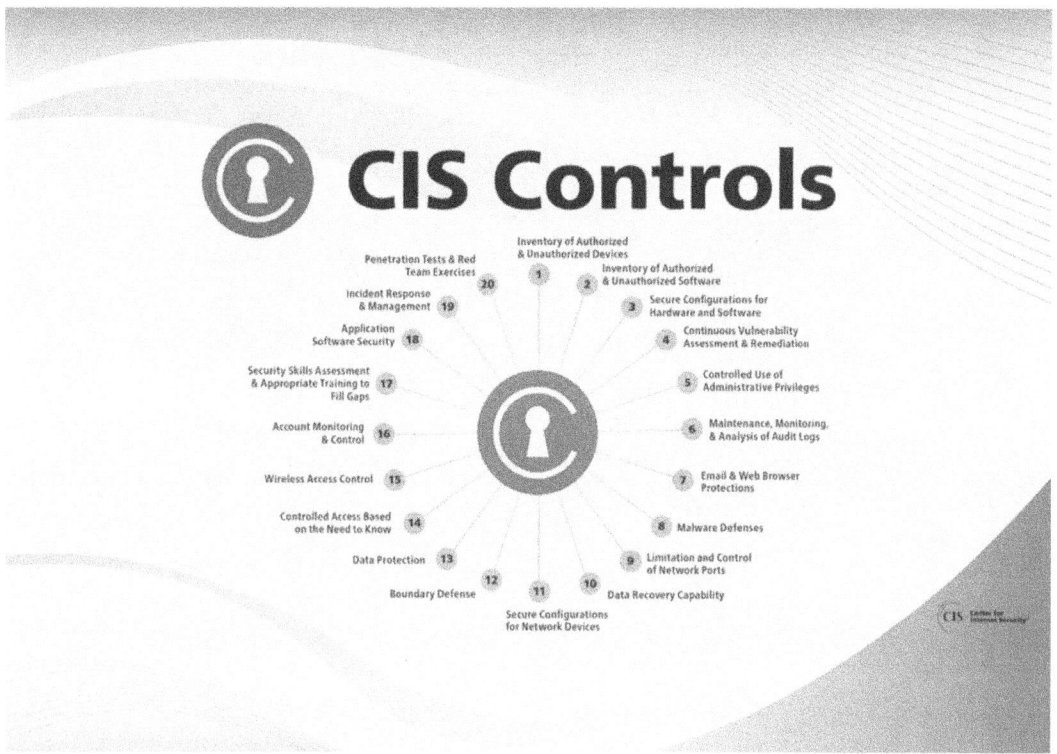

Image source: Center for Internet Security

CIS Controls version 8 was released in May 2021. This version introduced updates to align with cloud computing, mobile environments, and changing attacker tactics, according to the SANS Institute. CIS Controls version 8 significantly restructured and consolidated the controls compared to version 7.

As shown below, there are now 18 controls instead of 20, with a focus on addressing modern technologies like cloud and mobile. Key changes include enhanced clarity, streamlined implementation, and improved mapping to other frameworks like NIST CSF.

CHAPTER 10 KEY CYBERSECURITY FRAMEWORKS

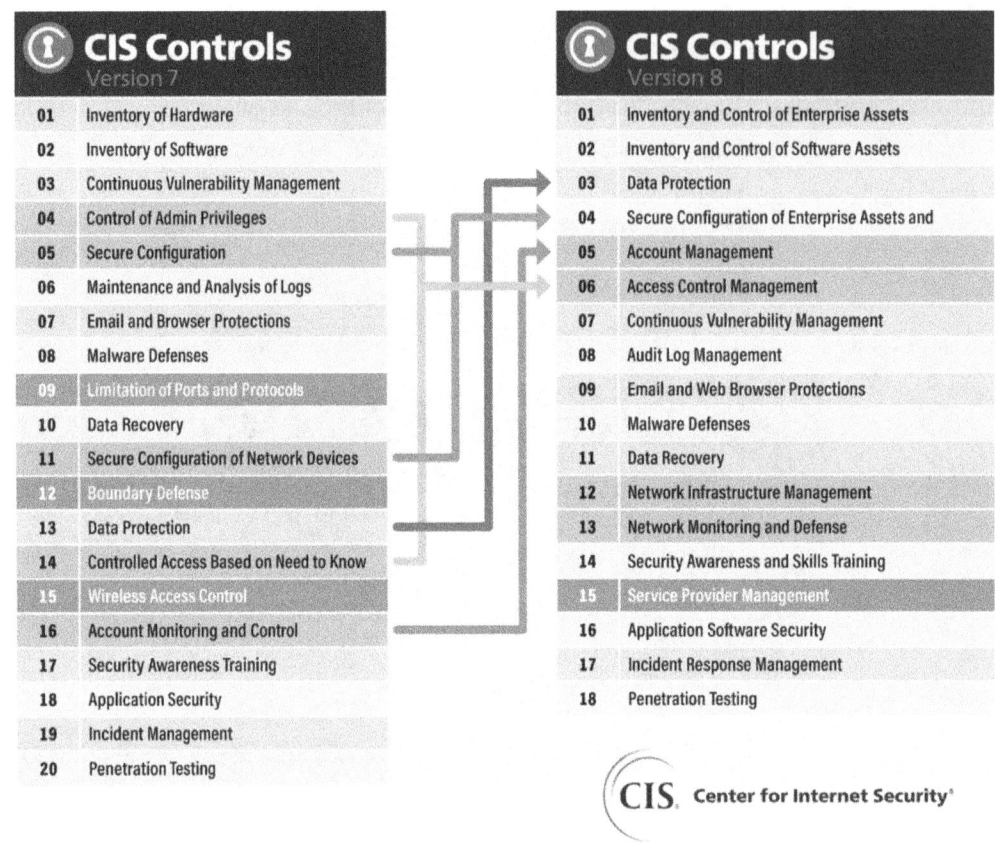

Image source: Center for Internet Security

MITRE ATT&CK

The MITRE ATT&CK framework is a comprehensive knowledge base that documents adversary tactics, techniques, and procedures (TTPs) based on real-world observations. Developed and maintained by Mitre Corp., a not-for-profit security research organization, ATT&CK serves as a globally recognized resource for cybersecurity professionals across the private sector, government, and security communities.

The ATT&CK matrix maps techniques used by cyber adversaries to achieve specific objectives, categorized as tactics in a structured sequence. These tactics progress linearly, from initial reconnaissance to data exfiltration or system impact.

CHAPTER 10   KEY CYBERSECURITY FRAMEWORKS

The Enterprise ATT&CK matrix includes tactics applicable across Windows, macOS, Linux, Azure AD, Office 365, Google Workspace, SaaS, IaaS, networks, and containers, categorizing adversary actions into the following phases:

1. **Reconnaissance**: Gathering information to plan future adversary operations.

   - **Example**: An attacker scans public-facing web servers for outdated software versions that may contain vulnerabilities.

   - **Example**: A cybercriminal harvests employee email addresses from LinkedIn to craft a spear phishing attack.

2. **Resource Development**: Establishing resources to support operations.

   - **Example**: A threat actor registers a domain resembling a legitimate company to send phishing emails.

   - **Example**: Attackers purchase or compromise cloud servers to host malware distribution campaigns.

3. **Initial Access**: Trying to get into your network.

   - **Example**: A hacker sends a spear phishing email containing a malicious link or attachment to an unsuspecting employee.

   - **Example**: An adversary exploits a web application vulnerability (e.g., SQL injection) to gain unauthorized access to a database.

4. **Execution**: Running malicious code on a target system.

   - **Example**: A remote access Trojan (RAT) executes a backdoor script once a user opens an infected email attachment.

   - **Example**: A macro-enabled Office document runs PowerShell commands when opened, downloading malware.

5. **Persistence**: Maintaining long-term access to a compromised system.

   - **Example**: An attacker modifies system registry keys to ensure their malware runs every time the computer restarts.

   - **Example**: A cybercriminal creates a hidden user account to regain access after an initial compromise.

6. **Privilege Escalation**: Gaining higher-level permissions to execute more impactful attacks.

    - **Example**: A hacker exploits an unpatched privilege escalation vulnerability to gain administrator-level access.

    - **Example**: A malicious insider finds an insecure admin password stored in a configuration file.

7. **Defense Evasion**: Avoiding detection by security systems.

    - **Example**: Attackers use fileless malware, executing malicious code directly in memory to bypass antivirus solutions.

    - **Example**: A Trojan masquerades as a legitimate software update, avoiding suspicion from endpoint security tools.

8. **Credential Access**: Stealing account names and passwords.

    - **Example**: A hacker installs a keylogger to capture a victim's keystrokes, including passwords.

    - **Example**: Cybercriminals dump hashed passwords from a compromised domain controller to crack them offline.

9. **Discovery**: Learning about the target environment to expand access.

    - **Example**: Attackers run network scans to identify open ports and connected devices.

    - **Example**: A cyber adversary queries Active Directory to map out user roles and privileges.

10. **Lateral Movement**: Moving deeper into the network to reach valuable data.

    - **Example**: Attackers use stolen credentials to access shared network drives on another system.

    - **Example**: A hacker leverages Remote Desktop Protocol (RDP) to pivot between compromised machines.

11. **Collection**: Gathering data of interest to achieve an attack goal.

    - **Example**: An attacker accesses cloud storage accounts (e.g., Google Drive, Dropbox) to search for sensitive documents.
    - **Example**: A Trojan monitors keystrokes and screenshots to gather confidential information.

12. **Command and Control (C2)**: Communicating with compromised systems to issue commands.

    - **Example**: Malware disguises C2 traffic as normal HTTPS web browsing to blend into everyday traffic.
    - **Example**: Attackers use DNS tunneling to covertly send data to an external server without detection.

13. **Exfiltration**: Stealing data from a target system.

    - **Example**: A hacker compresses and encrypts stolen documents, then uploads them to a third-party cloud storage service.
    - **Example**: Cybercriminals exfiltrate sensitive financial data via an encrypted email channel to evade detection.

14. **Impact**: Manipulating, interrupting, or destroying systems and data.

    - **Example**: A ransomware attack encrypts critical business files and demands a payment for decryption.
    - **Example**: A nation-state actor wipes all data from infected servers, causing operational disruption.

The MITRE ATT&CK framework provides an essential road map for cybersecurity teams to detect, analyze, and mitigate these tactics, helping organizations strengthen their defenses against real-world cyber threats.

Within each tactic of the MITRE ATT&CK matrix, there are adversary techniques, which describe the actual activity carried out by the adversary. Some techniques have sub-techniques that explain how an adversary carries out a specific technique in greater detail. The full ATT&CK Matrix for Enterprise from the MITRE ATT&CK Navigator is represented below:

CHAPTER 10   KEY CYBERSECURITY FRAMEWORKS

Image source: attack.mitre.org

Unified Kill Chain

The Cyber Kill Chain by Lockheed Martin (CKC) was traditionally regarded as the industry standard threat model for defending against advanced cyberattacks. Despite (or because of) its prominent status, the CKC has been widely criticized. The most damaging criticisms argue that the CKC is perimeter- and malware-focused. A more comprehensive model is required to deal with advanced cyberattacks beyond the organizational perimeter and beyond malware attacks. The term "kill chain" describes an end-to-end process, or the entire chain of events, that is required to perform a successful attack. Once an attack is understood and deconstructed into discrete phases, it allows defenders to map potential countermeasures against each one of these phases. Kill chain and other attack life cycle models can thus help defenders understand and defend against the increasingly complex attacks that they are facing. Advanced cyberattacks typically extend beyond exploiting one vulnerability in an internet-connected system. Depending on the security posture of the target, attacks may require attackers to forge an attack path through the internal network of the victim, in which multiple correlated vulnerabilities are exploited before critical assets can be targeted and objectives can be achieved.

The Unified Kill Chain offers a substantiated basis for strategically realigning defensive capabilities and cybersecurity investments within organizations, in the areas of prevention, detection, response, and intelligence. The Unified Kill Chain allows for a structured analysis and comparison of threat intelligence regarding the tactical modus operandi of attackers. In the area of prevention, the Unified Kill Chain can be used to map countermeasures to the discrete phases of an attack. Detection can be prioritized based on the insights into the ordered arrangement of the attack phases. In emergency response situations, the Unified Kill Chain aids investigators in triage and modeling likely attack paths. The model also specifically allows for the improvement of the predictive value of Red Team threat emulations, which aim to test the security posture of organizations in these areas.

#	The Unified Kill Chain	
1	Reconnaissance	Researching, identifying and selecting targets using active or passive reconnaissance.
2	Weaponization	Preparatory activities aimed at setting up the infrastructure required for the attack.
3	Delivery	Techniques resulting in the transmission of a weaponized object to the targeted environment.
4	Social Engineering	Techniques aimed at the manipulation of people to perform unsafe actions.
5	Exploitation	Techniques to exploit vulnerabilities in systems that may, amongst others, result in code execution.
6	Persistence	Any access, action or change to a system that gives an attacker persistent presence on the system.
7	Defense Evasion	Techniques an attacker may specifically use for evading detection or avoiding other defenses.
8	Command & Control	Techniques that allow attackers to communicate with controlled systems within a target network.
9	Pivoting	Tunneling traffic through a controlled system to other systems that are not directly accessible.
10	Discovery	Techniques that allow an attacker to gain knowledge about a system and its network environment.
11	Privilege Escalation	The result of techniques that provide an attacker with higher permissions on a system or network.
12	Execution	Techniques that result in execution of attacker-controlled code on a local or remote system.
13	Credential Access	Techniques resulting in the access of, or control over, system, service or domain credentials.
14	Lateral Movement	Techniques that enable an adversary to horizontally access and control other remote systems.
15	Collection	Techniques used to identify and gather data from a target network prior to exfiltration.
16	Exfiltration	Techniques that result or aid in an attacker removing data from a target network.
17	Impact	Techniques aimed at manipulating, interrupting or destroying the target system or data.
18	Objectives	Socio-technical objectives of an attack that are intended to achieve a strategic goal.

Image source: Lockheed Martin

MITRE ATT&CK vs. the Cyber Kill Chain

The Lockheed Martin Cyber Kill Chain is another well-known framework for understanding adversary behavior in a cyberattack. The seven steps of the Cyber Kill Chain enhance visibility into an attack and enrich an analyst's understanding of an adversary's tactics, techniques, and procedures.

CHAPTER 10   KEY CYBERSECURITY FRAMEWORKS

The Kill Chain model contains the following stages, presented in sequence:

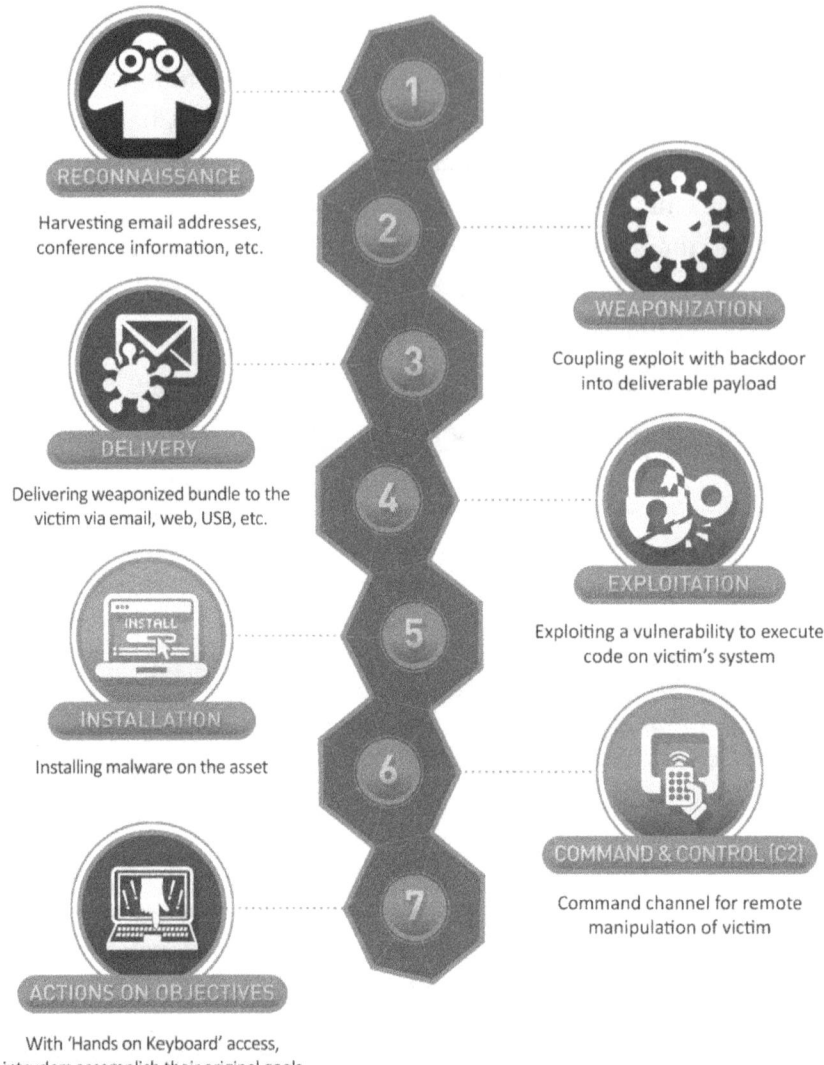

Image source: Lockheed Martin

- **Reconnaissance**: This is the information-gathering phase where the attacker silently gathers as much data as possible about their target. Think of it as a scout mission before an invasion. The goal is to identify weaknesses, understand the target's infrastructure, and find points of entry.

- **Passive Reconnaissance**: This involves collecting publicly available information without directly interacting with the target. Examples include

  - **Open Source Intelligence (OSINT)**: Searching public records, social media (LinkedIn, Facebook, X/Twitter for employee information, company structure), news articles, corporate websites, and financial reports.

  - **Domain Name System (DNS) Lookups**: Gathering information about domain registrations, mail servers, and name servers.

  - **Public Email Addresses**: Harvesting email addresses of employees or executives for phishing campaigns.

  - **Conference Information**: Looking for employee attendance at conferences, which might reveal interests, technologies used, or even travel plans.

  - **Job Postings**: These can reveal the technologies, software, and operating systems an organization uses, providing clues about potential vulnerabilities.

- **Active Reconnaissance**: This involves directly interacting with the target's systems, though often in a subtle way to avoid detection. Examples include

  - **Port Scanning**: Identifying open ports and services running on target systems

  - **Network Mapping**: Discovering network topology and device types

  - **Vulnerability Scanning (Light)**: Identifying potential weaknesses in systems without actively exploiting them yet

- **Why It's Crucial**: The more information an attacker has, the more tailored and effective their subsequent attack stages can be. A well-executed reconnaissance phase can significantly increase the chances of a successful breach.

- **Weaponization**: In this stage, the attacker takes the information gathered during reconnaissance and uses it to create a deliverable exploit. This is where the "weapon" is forged.

  - **Exploit Selection**: The attacker identifies a specific vulnerability in the target's software, operating system, or applications that they can exploit. This could be a zero-day (unknown vulnerability) or a known vulnerability for which a patch hasn't been applied.

  - **Backdoor Development/Selection**: A backdoor is a hidden method of bypassing normal authentication or encryption to gain remote access to a computer. The attacker selects or develops a backdoor that will provide persistent access.

  - **Payload Creation**: The exploit and the backdoor are combined into a single, deliverable payload. This payload is designed to be executed on the victim's system and perform specific malicious actions. Common payload types include

    - **Malware**: Viruses, worms, Trojans, ransomware, spyware.

    - **Remote Access Trojans (RATs)**: Provide attackers with full control over the compromised system.

    - **Keyloggers**: Record keystrokes to steal credentials.

  - **Encoding/Obfuscation**: Attackers often encode or obfuscate the payload to evade detection by antivirus software and intrusion detection systems. This makes the malicious code harder to identify.

- **Delivery**: This stage involves transmitting the weaponized bundle to the victim. This is the point where the attacker's creation is sent on its way to the target.

  - **Email**: This is a very common delivery method, often involving

    - **Phishing**: Deceptive emails designed to trick users into opening malicious attachments or clicking on malicious links

- **Spear Phishing**: Highly targeted phishing attacks aimed at specific individuals, often impersonating trusted sources
- **Whaling**: Phishing attacks targeting high-level executives
- **Web**: Delivering the payload through
  - **Malicious Websites**: Websites hosting drive-by downloads (where malware is downloaded automatically when a user visits the site)
  - **Compromised Legitimate Websites**: Legitimate websites that have been infected and now serve malware
  - **Malvertising**: Malicious advertisements injected into legitimate ad networks
- **USB/Removable Media**: Leaving infected USB drives in public places, hoping a curious employee will plug it into a work computer.
- **Direct Network Access**: If the attacker already has some level of access or is targeting a specific internal system, they might directly push the payload over the network.
- **Supply Chain Attacks**: Injecting malware into legitimate software updates or products distributed by a trusted vendor.

- **Exploitation:** This is the critical phase where the weaponized bundle successfully leverages a vulnerability to execute code on the victim's system. This is often the "moment of truth" for the attacker.
  - **Vulnerability Trigger**: The delivery mechanism successfully triggers a flaw in the target's software, operating system, or hardware. Examples include
    - **Software Bugs**: Buffer overflows, format string bugs, unhandled exceptions
    - **Misconfigurations**: Default passwords, open ports, lax security settings
    - **User Error**: A user clicking on a malicious link, opening an infected attachment, or enabling macros in a document

- **Code Execution**: Once the vulnerability is exploited, the attacker gains the ability to run their malicious code (the payload) on the victim's system. This could involve privilege escalation to gain higher-level access.

- **Ephemeral Access**: The initial exploitation might only provide temporary or limited access. The subsequent installation phase aims to establish more persistent control.

• **Installation**: After successful exploitation, the attacker's next step is to establish a persistent presence on the compromised system by installing malware. This ensures they can regain access even if the initial exploit is patched or the system is rebooted.

- **Persistence Mechanisms**: Malware employs various techniques to ensure it can restart with the system or maintain access:

- **Registry Keys**: Adding entries to the Windows Registry to launch at startup

- **Scheduled Tasks:** Creating scheduled tasks to execute the malware at specific times or intervals

- **Startup Folders**: Placing executable files in system startup folders

- **Rootkits**: Hiding the presence of the malware and its activities from the operating system and security tools

- **Backdoors/Web Shells**: Creating hidden access points for future entry

- **Covering Tracks**: The attacker might attempt to delete logs, modify timestamps, or use other techniques to obscure their actions and prevent detection.

- **Establishing Foothold**: This phase solidifies the attacker's control over the compromised system, turning it into a beachhead for further operations.

- **Command and Control (C2)**: Once the malware is installed, it establishes a communication channel with the attacker's control server. This allows the attacker to remotely manipulate the compromised system.
  - **Communication Channels**: C2 channels can use various protocols to blend in with legitimate network traffic:
    - **HTTP/HTTPS**: Commonly used, making it difficult to distinguish from normal web browser.
    - **DNS**: Malicious traffic can be hidden within DNS queries.
    - **ICMP**: Using ping requests for covert communication.
    - **Custom Protocols**: More sophisticated attackers might develop unique protocols to avoid detection.
  - **Remote Manipulation**: Through the C2 channel, the attacker can
    - **Issue Commands**: Send instructions to the malware (e.g., download more tools, exfiltrate data, launch further attacks).
    - **Receive Data**: Get status updates from the malware or receive exfiltrated data.
    - **Update Malware**: Push new versions or modules to the installed malware.
  - **Evasion Techniques**: Attackers often use techniques to make C2 detection harder:
    - **Domain Fronting**: Hiding the true destination of C2 traffic behind legitimate content delivery networks
    - **Fast Flux DNS**: Rapidly changing IP addresses associated with a domain name to evade blacklisting
    - **Encrypted Traffic**: Encrypting C2 communications to prevent deep packet inspection

- **Actions on Objectives:** This is the final and most critical stage, where the intruders use their "hands on keyboards" access to achieve their original goals. This is why the entire attack was launched in the first place.

- **Original Goals (Motivations):** The objectives vary widely depending on the attacker's motivation:

  - **Data Exfiltration:** Stealing sensitive information (customer data, intellectual property, financial records, PII, government secrets). This is common in espionage and financial crime.

  - **Disruption/Destruction:** Damaging systems, deleting data, or disabling critical infrastructure (e.g., ransomware attacks, wiper malware, attacks on industrial control systems).

  - **Financial Gain:** Ransomware, cryptocurrency mining, stealing financial credentials, direct money transfers.

  - **Espionage:** Gaining access to classified information or intelligence for state-sponsored actors.

  - **Reputation Damage:** Defacing websites and leaking sensitive information to damage a company's image.

  - **Lateral Movement:** Moving further into the network to access more valuable assets, gain higher privileges, or compromise additional systems.

  - **Persistence and Future Access:** Establishing multiple backdoors and hidden access points to ensure long-term access to the network.

- **Post-exploitation Tools:** Attackers use a variety of tools to achieve their objectives:

  - **Credential Dumping Tools:** Mimikatz to extract passwords from memory

  - **Network Scanners:** To map internal networks

  - **File Transfer Tools:** To exfiltrate data

  - **Privilege Escalation Tools:** To gain administrative access

- **Impact**: This phase is where the real damage or compromise occurs, leading to financial losses, data breaches, operational disruptions, or reputational harm for the victim.

By understanding each stage of the Cyber Kill Chain, organizations can develop more effective defensive strategies and implement security controls at each phase to disrupt an attacker's progress.

The Lockheed Martin Cyber Kill Chain provides a structured approach to understanding and responding to cyberattacks. However, it differs from the MITRE ATT&CK framework in two key ways:

- **Depth and Detail**: MITRE ATT&CK provides a much more detailed breakdown of how each stage of an attack is carried out. It includes a comprehensive list of tactics, techniques, and sub-techniques used by adversaries. Additionally, it is continuously updated with industry input, ensuring defenders have the latest intelligence to refine their defenses.

- **Cloud-Native Attacks**: The Cyber Kill Chain primarily focuses on traditional attack methods, assuming adversaries deliver a malicious payload to an on-premises environment. In contrast, MITRE ATT&CK factors in the modern tactics used in cloud-native attacks, such as identity-based compromises, API exploitation, and misconfigurations.

Both frameworks offer valuable insights into adversary behavior, but MITRE ATT&CK's granular approach and continuous updates make it particularly effective for adapting to evolving threats in hybrid and cloud environments.

OWASP (The Open Worldwide Application Security Project)

The OWASP is a nonprofit organization focused on improving software security. OWASP plays a crucial role in improving the security of web applications worldwide by providing valuable resources and fostering a community of security professionals.

What Is OWASP Top 10?

The OWASP Top 10 is published every four years and is based on data from the previous four years. The list is not structured around how severe each vulnerability is. Instead, it compiles vulnerabilities based on how common they are, so you can prevent the most common risks to sensitive data exposure. The OWASP Top 10 is a starting point for organizations to improve their software security.

OWASP Top 10 Vulnerabilities Overview

1. Broken Access Control
2. Cryptographic Failures
3. Injections
4. Insecure Design
5. Security Misconfigurations
6. Vulnerable and Outdated Components
7. Identification and Authentication Failures
8. Software and Data Integrity Failures
9. Security Logging and Monitoring Failures
10. Server-Side Request Forgery (SSRF)

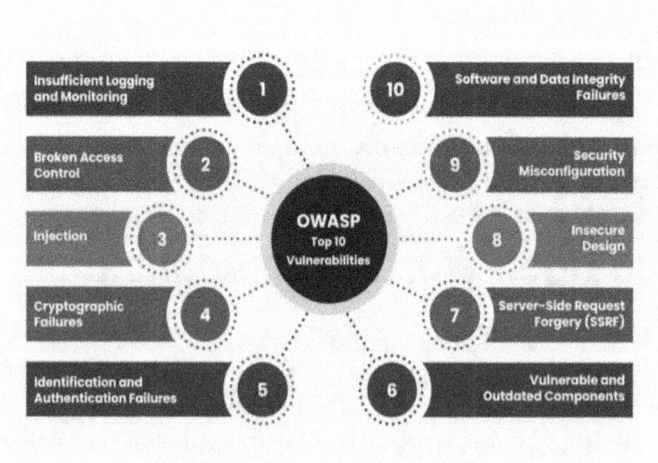

Image source: Open Source OWASP

Breaking Down the OWASP Top 10 Vulnerabilities

As the world of web application security continues to evolve, the OWASP Top 10 threats provides a robust framework for developers and security professionals to identify and mitigate the most common attacks.

Here are the OWASP Top 10 vulnerabilities and tips on how to prevent them.

1. Broken Access Control

    In a nutshell, broken access control means that an attacker can access resources or data they should not have access to. This can be done in many ways, but typically by exploiting flaws in how the system controls access to those resources. 61% of all breaches involve broken access control.

    There are many ways to exploit broken access control, but the result is always the same: the attacker gains access to data or resources they should not have access to.

    - **Preventing Broken Access Control**

        Access control is a security measure that protects resources from unauthorized access. There are many different ways to achieve this, but one common method is to use a whitelist.

        A whitelist is a list of authorized users who are allowed to access a particular resource.

        This list can be maintained manually or generated automatically based on user credentials.

        A whitelist can be implemented by creating a list of approved websites or IP addresses and then comparing any incoming requests against that list. If the request is not on the list, it will be blocked.

        One way to create a whitelist on AWS is through an IAM policy that allows access only to the specific IP addresses or CIDR ranges that you wish to allow access to and configuring your security groups to only allow traffic from those IP addresses or CIDR ranges.

2. Cryptographic Failures

   Insecure communications constitute a significant problem on the internet today.

   Unencrypted or weakly encrypted communications can be intercepted and read by anyone with the right tools. This can lead to the disclosure of sensitive information, like passwords, financial data, and personal information.

   In 2023 alone, there were well over 8 billion records breached, and the average cost of a data breach sits at around $4.54 million.

   - **Preventing Cryptographic Failures**
   - When data is sent over the internet using HTTPS, it is encrypted using a cryptographic algorithm, which makes it difficult for attackers to read or tamper with the data.
   - To implement HTTPS in Nginx, you will need to purchase and install an SSL certificate. Once you have your certificate, you will need to edit your Nginx configuration file to enable SSL.

   The specific directives you need to edit will depend on your configuration, but they will typically be something like

   ```
   ssl_certificate /path/to/your/certificate.crt;
   ssl_certificate_key /path/to/your/certificate.key;
   ```

   After you have edited your configuration file, you will need to restart Nginx for the changes to take effect.

3. Injections

   Injection attacks are among the most prevalent web security risks. They occur when applications fail to properly validate user input before processing it in SQL queries or other operations.

   This vulnerability enables attackers to manipulate database queries, leading to unauthorized access, data corruption, or even full system compromise. In severe cases, it can expose sensitive information such as passwords, financial records, or personal user data.

There are multiple forms of SQL injection attacks, but all rely on exploiting weak input handling mechanisms, making proper validation and security measures essential to prevent breaches.

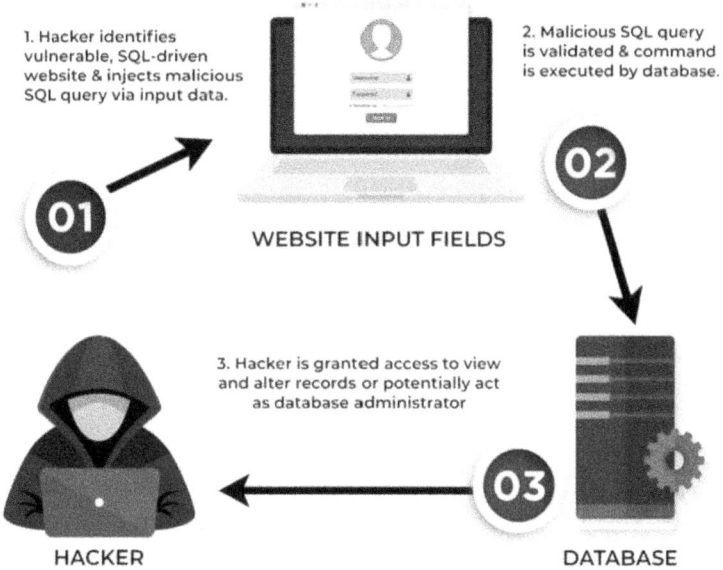

- **Preventing Injections**

    - Cross-site scripting (XSS) attacks occur when a malicious user injects code into a web page that is then executed by other users who visit the page. This can lead to the theft of sensitive information or the execution of unwanted code on the user's machine.

    - Sanitizing user input is important because it helps to prevent XSS attacks.

    There are a few ways to sanitize user input in React, Vue, and Angular:

    - **In React**: Use the DOMPurify library to sanitize user input. DOMPurify will parse and sanitize HTML, making it safe to render on your page.

- **In Vue**: Use the v-html directive to render HTML safely. The v-html directive will ensure that any HTML code passed to it is properly encoded and escaped, making it safe to render.

- **In Angular**: Use the DomSanitizer service to sanitize user input. DomSanitizer will help you prevent XSS attacks by sanitizing untrusted values that are passed into your application.

4. Insecure Design

   Insecure design refers to security flaws introduced during the software development's design phase. Design flaws can lead to a wide range of security vulnerabilities, including

   - **Injection Flaws**: User input is not properly sanitized before it's used by the application. The malicious code is injected and then executed by the application, leading to data loss or corruption, Denial of Service (DoS) attacks, or arbitrary code execution.

   - **Cross-Site Scripting (XSS) Flaws**: XSS flaws occur when user input is not correctly escaped or sanitized before it's displayed by the application. Attackers inject malicious code executed by unsuspecting users who visit the compromised page.

   - **Broken Authentication and Session Management**: These occur when authentication and session management mechanisms are not correctly implemented. Attackers can access sensitive data, hijack user sessions, or perform other malicious actions.

   - **Insecure Communications**: Insecure communications refer to the use of insecure protocols or encryption algorithms that allow attackers to eavesdrop on communications or tamper with data.

   Preventing Insecure Design

   One way to prevent cross-site scripting is to implement a content security policy (CSP).

   A CSP is a list of directives that specify what resources are allowed to be loaded on a page.

These directives can be used to restrict the sources of content that can be loaded on a page and can be implemented in the <meta> tag of an HTML document or in the HTTP headers of a server.

Here is an example of a content security policy implemented in the <meta> tag of an HTML document:

<meta http-equiv="Content-Security-Policy" content="default-src 'self'; img-src https://example.com;">

This policy allows content from the same origin (self) to be loaded by default and will allow images from https://example.com to be loaded.

Here is an example of a content security policy implemented in the HTTP headers of a server:

>   Content-Security-Policy: default-src 'self'; img-src https://example.com;

>   This policy will have the same effect as the policy above.

5. Security Misconfigurations

    Security misconfiguration is a broad category of issues that can arise when an application or server is not configured correctly.

    Incorrectly configured systems are more vulnerable to attacks, allow unauthorized access to sensitive data, and provide misleading information to users.

    All too often, systems are not adequately configured because administrators don't have the time or knowledge to do so correctly, which leaves systems open to attack. Sometimes, administrators are aware of how important proper configuration is, but corporate policies and other restrictions may prevent them from ensuring it.

    Common security misconfiguration issues include

    - Leaving the default administrator account active and using weak passwords
    - Not disabling directory listing

- Not requiring SSL/TLS for sensitive communications
- Not properly restricting access to files and directories
- Not properly securing database passwords and other sensitive data

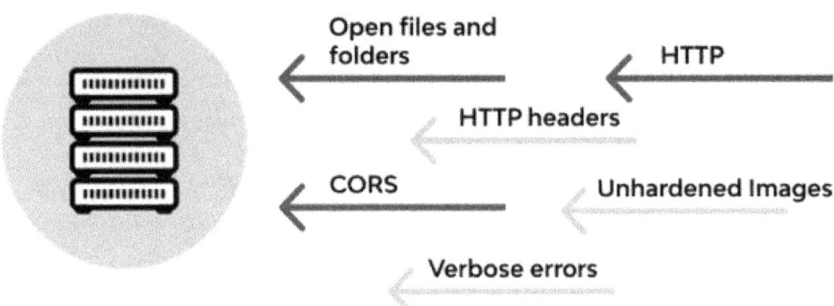

Preventing Security Misconfigurations

One way to make SSL/TLS compulsory is to use a web server that requires it for all connections. For example, the Apache web server can be configured to require SSL/TLS by adding the following directive to the server configuration:

SSLRequireSSL

Another way to make SSL/TLS compulsory is to use a load balancer or proxy server that supports SSL/TLS and requires it for all connections.

For example, the Nginx web server can be configured as a proxy server to require SSL/TLS by adding the following directive to the server configuration:

proxy_ssl_session_reuse on;
proxy_ssl_protocols TLSv1 TLSv1.1 TLSv1.2;
proxy_ssl_ciphers HIGH:!aNULL:!MD5;

6. Vulnerable and Outdated Components

   Vulnerable and outdated components are often the Achilles' heel of an organization's security posture. A vulnerable component is one with known security flaws that can be exploited to gain unauthorized access or cause other harm.

   An outdated component is one for which security patches or updates are no longer available from the vendor, making it more susceptible to attack.

   Preventing Vulnerable and Outdated Components

   Preventing vulnerable and outdated components is not complicated—which is all the more reason to do it.

   The best ways to prevent vulnerable and outdated components include

   - Removing all unused components
   - Monitoring components for vulnerabilities
   - Limiting access to components
   - Regularly auditing components

7. Identification and Authentication Failures

   An identification and authentication failure occurs when a system fails to correctly identify and/or authenticate a user.

   This can happen for various reasons, but typically it is due to

   - Weak or easy-to-guess passwords
   - Lack of strong password policies
   - Lack of two-factor authentication

   Organizations are vulnerable to approximately $1.76 million in business costs when a Zero Trust authentication system is not implemented.

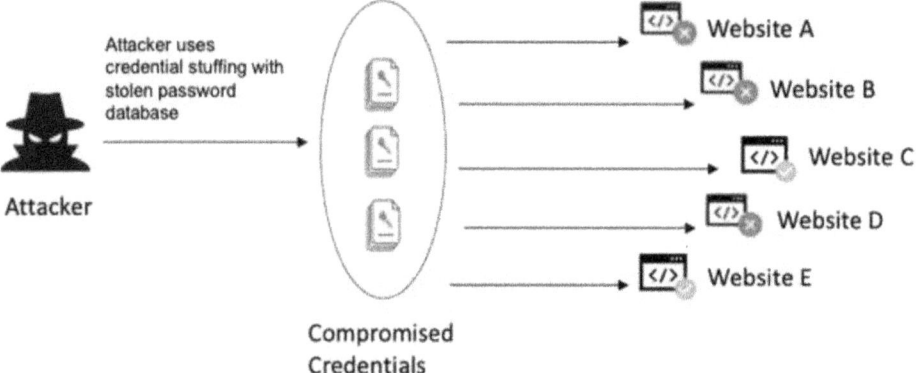

Preventing Identification and Authentication Failures

There are many ways to implement two-factor authentication (2FA) with AWS. One way to do it is to use AWS identity and access management (IAM) with multifactor authentication (MFA).

IAM is a web service that helps you securely control access to AWS resources.

MFA adds an extra layer of security by requiring a second factor, such as a code from a hardware device or a mobile app, in addition to your username and password.

To set up an MFA, you first need to create an IAM user and then attach an MFA device to that user. You can use any type of MFA device that is compatible with AWS, such as a hardware device or virtual device.

Once you have an IAM user with an MFA device attached, you can enable MFA for that user. To do this, you need to create an IAM policy that requires MFA. You can then attach this policy to the IAM user.

Here is an example of an IAM policy that requires MFA:

```
{
  "Version": "2022-11-11",
  "Statement": [
    {
      "Sid": "Allow access only with MFA",
      "Effect": "Deny",
      "Action": "*",
      "Resource": "*",
      "Condition": {
        "Bool": {
          "aws:MultiFactorAuthPresent": "false"
        }
      }
    }
  ]
}
```

This policy denies all access to all resources unless the user has an MFA device attached.

After you have created this policy, you must attach it to the IAM user. You can do this via the AWS Management Console or the AWS Command Line Interface (CLI).

Once the policy is attached, the user must use MFA when accessing AWS resources.

8. Software and Data Integrity Failures

Data integrity failures are a type of security vulnerability that can occur when data is modified or destroyed without authorization. This can happen either through malicious attacks or accidental mistakes.

Software and data integrity failures can have serious consequences, such as financial losses or the exposure of confidential information.

There are several ways to protect data from integrity failures.

One is to use cryptographic methods, such as digital signatures or hashes, to verify that data has not been changed.

Another is to store data in multiple locations so that if one copy is destroyed, others can be used to reconstruct it. Back up data regularly so that a copy is always available in case of an integrity failure.

Preventing Software and Data Integrity Failures

In order to prevent software and data integrity failures, make sure to

- Regularly back up data and software
- Keep software and data secure
- Ensure data and software integrity
- Monitor systems for changes
- Detect and respond to changes quickly

9. Security Logging and Monitoring Failures

    In the world of information security, logging and monitoring failures are all too common.

    Log data integrity failures can lead to data loss or corruption, while monitoring failures allow attackers to operate undetected.

    Security logging is tracking events that occur on a computer or network. This data can be used to identify attacks, monitor system activity, and track user behavior. However, if this data is not secured correctly, attackers can compromise it.

    Failures can have severe consequences for an organization. The average life cycle of a breach is 200 days, which, on average, translates to $4.45 million in costs.

Security Logging and Monitoring Failures Attack Example

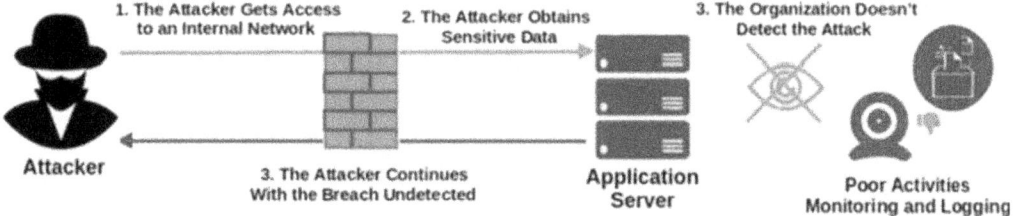

Preventing Security Logging and Monitoring Failures

To prevent security logging and monitoring failures, a company can

- Ensure that all logging and monitoring tools are correctly configured and tested

- Establish clear and concise logging and monitoring policies and procedures

- Educate all staff on the proper handling of sensitive information

- Regularly review logs and monitor activity for unusual or suspicious activity

- Investigate and resolve any issues identified through logging and monitoring

10. Server-Side Request Forgery (SSRF)

Server-side request forgery (SSRF) is an attack in which the attacker tricks a server into requesting on their behalf.

SSRF can be performed by specifying a malicious URL in a parameter or embedding an HTTP request in an XML document. If the server does not properly validate the request, it will send the request to the attacker-specified URL.

SSRF can be used to attack internal systems that are generally not accessible from the outside. For example, an attacker could use SSRF to access a server's internal network or read sensitive files on the server.

Preventing Server-Side Request Forgery (SSRF)

Preventing a server-side request forgery includes several steps:

- Ensure that user input is validated and sanitized
- Restrict user access to only the resources that they need
- Implement a whitelist approach to input validation
- Monitor server access logs for suspicious activity
- Keep all server software up-to-date with the latest security patches

Protect Your Applications Against OWASP Top 10 Threats

Malicious users never rest, and neither should your security postures. To guard against attacks exploiting OWASP Top 10 vulnerabilities, try using tools like OWASP ZAP to run dynamic scans against your applications to look for holes. Or, to quickly implement ZAP alongside other application security tools like SAST, SCA, secrets detection, and others, consider Jit to protect your applications against OWASP Top 10 vulnerabilities while causing no friction to your software engineering team.

Key Takeaways

Cybersecurity frameworks are no longer mere checklists; they are the bedrock of a resilient security strategy, providing structured guidelines to identify, assess, and manage risks while safeguarding critical digital assets. By embedding security practices into an organization's core operations, frameworks like NIST, ISO 27001, and CIS help proactively mitigate threats, enhance response capabilities, and build trust with stakeholders, ultimately preventing breaches rather than reacting to them.

Understanding and implementing these frameworks provides a robust foundation for an organization's cybersecurity resilience.

- **NIST Cybersecurity Framework (CSF)**: A flexible, voluntary framework to manage cyber risks, built on six core functions: **Govern, Identify, Protect, Detect, Respond, and Recover**. It includes **implementation tiers** and **profiles** for customization.

- **ISO 27001**: An international standard for establishing and maintaining an **Information Security Management System (ISMS)** to protect sensitive information.

- **COBIT**: A framework for **governing and managing enterprise IT**, aligning IT strategies with business goals and risk management.

- **CIS Controls**: A prioritized set of **actionable best practices** to mitigate common cyberattacks.

- **MITRE ATT&CK**: A comprehensive knowledge base of **adversary tactics, techniques, and procedures (TTPs)**, detailing the phases of a cyberattack from reconnaissance to impact. It offers more granularity and cloud-native focus than the Cyber Kill Chain.

- **Unified Kill Chain**: A more comprehensive model than the traditional Cyber Kill Chain, designed for **advanced cyberattacks** beyond perimeter and malware, helping map countermeasures across attack phases.

- **OWASP Top 10**: A frequently updated list of the **most common web application vulnerabilities** (e.g., broken access control, cryptographic failures, injections), providing guidance on prevention.

- **Metrics and KPIs**: Key indicators like **incident detection/response time, vulnerability remediation rate, and security awareness training completion** are crucial for evaluating security effectiveness and demonstrating ROI.

CHAPTER 11

Compliance and Regulations

Cybersecurity regulatory compliance is the process of following laws, regulations, and standards to protect an organization's digital systems and information. It's important for protecting against cyber threats, such as unauthorized access, breaches, and disruption.

Cybersecurity compliance and governance are intertwined concepts that focus on establishing and maintaining a secure and reliable cybersecurity posture within an organization.

- **Compliance**: Adhering to external laws, regulations, and industry standards related to cybersecurity. This often involves demonstrating that specific security controls and measures are in place to protect sensitive data.

- **Governance**: The framework of rules, policies, and processes that guide how an organization manages its cybersecurity risks. It ensures that cybersecurity decisions are aligned with business objectives and that appropriate resources are allocated to security initiatives.

Key Aspects

1. Cybersecurity Governance

    Cybersecurity governance refers to the framework of policies, processes, and structures that an organization implements to direct and control its cybersecurity activities to achieve business objectives and manage risk effectively. It's not just about technology but about aligning security with the overall business strategy. This includes establishing clear roles and responsibilities for cybersecurity leadership, defining risk appetite, ensuring compliance with relevant laws and regulations (like GDPR and CCPA), allocating resources, and overseeing the effectiveness of security controls. Effective cybersecurity governance provides the strategic direction and oversight necessary to protect an organization's information assets, maintain business continuity, and build trust with customers and stakeholders in an increasingly complex threat landscape.

- **Establishing Policies and Procedures**: Creating and enforcing clear policies and procedures related to data security, access control, incident response, and other key areas

- **Risk Management Framework**: Implementing a robust risk management framework to identify, assess, and mitigate cybersecurity risks

- **Accountability and Oversight**: Defining roles and responsibilities for cybersecurity within the organization and establishing oversight mechanisms to ensure compliance

- **Resource Allocation**: Allocating appropriate resources (budget, personnel, technology) to support cybersecurity initiatives

2. Cybersecurity Compliance

Cybersecurity compliance is the adherence to a defined set of laws, regulations, standards, and frameworks designed to protect an organization's information systems and data from cyber threats. This isn't just about avoiding hefty fines and legal repercussions (like those under GDPR or HIPAA); it's a strategic imperative that builds customer trust, enhances an organization's security posture, and proactively manages risks. By implementing controls such as data encryption, access management, incident response plans, and regular employee training, organizations not only meet regulatory obligations but also strengthen their defenses against evolving cyberattacks, ultimately safeguarding sensitive information and maintaining operational integrity.

- **Identifying Applicable Regulations**: Determining which laws, regulations, and industry standards apply to the organization (e.g., GDPR, CCPA, HIPAA, PCI DSS)

- **Conducting Compliance Audits**: Regularly auditing systems and processes to ensure compliance with relevant regulations

- **Maintaining Documentation**: Maintaining adequate documentation to demonstrate compliance with regulatory requirements

- **Responding to Audits and Investigations**: Effectively responding to audits and investigations conducted by regulatory authorities

Benefits

- **Reduced Risk of Data Breaches**: Helps prevent data breaches and other security incidents

- **Improved Reputation**: Builds trust with customers, partners, and stakeholders

- **Enhanced Compliance**: Avoids costly fines and penalties for noncompliance

- **Improved Security Posture**: Strengthens overall security posture and reduces the likelihood of successful attacks

- **Enhanced Business Continuity**: Minimizes disruption to business operations in the event of a security incident

Key Considerations

- **Continuous Monitoring**: Ongoing monitoring and assessment of cybersecurity risks and controls are essential.

- **Adaptability:** The compliance and governance framework must be adaptable to changing threats and regulatory requirements.

- **Integration**: Cybersecurity governance and compliance should be integrated with other organizational processes and objectives.

In essence, cybersecurity compliance and governance are critical for any organization that handles sensitive data. By establishing a strong framework for managing cybersecurity risks and ensuring compliance with relevant regulations, organizations can protect their valuable assets, maintain their reputation, and minimize the impact of potential security incidents.

GDPR (General Data Protection Regulation)

The **General Data Protection Regulation (GDPR)** is a comprehensive data protection law in the European Union (EU) that aims to give individuals more control over their personal data. It is a landmark data privacy law enacted by the European Union (EU) in 2018, aiming to give individuals greater control over their personal data. It has a broad extraterritorial reach, applying not only to organizations located within the EU but also to any organization worldwide that processes the personal data of EU residents. The GDPR establishes core principles like lawfulness, fairness, and transparency, data minimization, purpose limitation, and accountability, requiring organizations to obtain explicit consent for data collection, ensure data accuracy and security, and limit data retention. It also grants individuals significant rights, including the right to access their data, rectify inaccuracies, erase their data ("right to be forgotten"), and data portability. Noncompliance can result in substantial fines, reaching up to €20 million or 4% of a company's annual global turnover, whichever is higher, making robust GDPR compliance a critical concern for businesses operating internationally.

CHAPTER 11 COMPLIANCE AND REGULATIONS

Key Principles of GDPR

- **Lawfulness, Fairness, and Transparency**: Data processing must be lawful, fair, and transparent to the data subject.

- **Purpose Limitation**: Data must be collected for specified, explicit, and legitimate purposes and not processed further in a manner incompatible with those purposes.

- **Data Minimization**: Only the data necessary for the specific purposes should be collected.

- **Accuracy**: Data must be accurate and kept up-to-date.

- **Storage Limitation**: Data should not be stored for longer than is necessary for the purposes for which it was collected.

- **Integrity and Confidentiality**: Data must be processed in a manner that ensures appropriate security, including protection against unauthorized or unlawful processing and accidental loss, destruction, or damage.
- **Accountability**: The data controller is responsible for and can demonstrate compliance with the GDPR.

Key Rights of Individuals

- **Right to Access**: Individuals have the right to access their personal data and obtain confirmation on whether or not their personal data is being processed.
- **Right to Rectification**: Individuals have the right to rectify inaccurate or incomplete personal data.
- **Right to Erasure ("Right to be Forgotten")**: Individuals have the right to request the erasure of their personal data under certain circumstances.
- **Right to Restriction of Processing**: Individuals have the right to restrict the processing of their personal data under certain circumstances.
- **Right to Data Portability**: Individuals have the right to receive their personal data in a structured, commonly used, and machine-readable format and transmit that data to another controller.
- **Right to Object**: Individuals have the right to object to the processing of their personal data, including profiling.
- **Rights Related to Automated Decision-Making**: Individuals have the right not to be subject to a decision based solely on automated processing, including profiling, that produces legal or similarly significant effects.

Impact of GDPR

- **Increased Data Security**: Organizations have implemented stronger security measures to protect personal data.
- **Greater Transparency**: Organizations are more transparent about how they collect, use, and share personal data.

- **Enhanced Individual Control**: Individuals have more control over their personal data and how it is used.

- **Global Impact**: The GDPR has had a global impact, influencing data protection laws in other countries.

Compliance with GDPR

- **Appointing a Data Protection Officer (DPO)**: Organizations that process personal data on a large scale or process special categories of personal data are required to appoint a DPO.

- **Data Protection Impact Assessment (DPIA)**: Organizations must conduct a DPIA for high-risk processing activities.

- **Maintaining Records of Processing Activities**: Organizations must maintain records of their data processing activities.

- **Data Breach Notification**: Organizations must notify the relevant supervisory authority of any personal data breaches without undue delay.

CCPA (California Consumer Privacy Act)

The **California Consumer Privacy Act (CCPA),** enacted in 2018 and effective from January 1, 2020, is a groundbreaking state-level data privacy law in the United States, often compared to Europe's GDPR. It grants California residents significant rights over the personal information businesses collect about them. Key provisions include the right to know what personal information is being collected, the right to request its deletion, and crucially, the right to opt out of the sale or sharing of their personal information. The CCPA applies to for-profit businesses that operate in California and meet certain thresholds related to revenue or the volume of consumer data they process. While it primarily uses an "opt-out" model, requiring businesses to provide mechanisms for consumers to decline data sale, it also imposes obligations for transparency, data security, and nondiscrimination against consumers who exercise their rights. The CCPA was further strengthened by the California Privacy Rights Act (CPRA), which expanded consumer rights and established the California Privacy Protection Agency (CPPA) for enforcement.

Key Provisions

- **Consumer Rights**: The CCPA grants California residents several key rights regarding their personal information:
    - **Right to Know**: Consumers have the right to know what personal information a business collects about them, the categories of sources from which the information is collected, the business purposes for collecting or selling the information, and the categories of third parties with whom the business shares the information.
    - **Right to Delete**: Consumers have the right to request that a business delete their personal information, subject to certain exceptions.
    - **Right to Opt Out of the Sale of Personal Information**: Consumers have the right to opt out of the sale of their personal information.
    - **Right to Nondiscrimination**: Businesses cannot discriminate against consumers for exercising their CCPA rights.
- **Business Obligations**: The CCPA imposes several obligations on businesses that collect personal information from California residents, including
    - **Providing a "Do Not Sell My Personal Information" Link**: Businesses must prominently display a "Do Not Sell My Personal Information" link on their website.
    - **Providing a Clear and Conspicuous Privacy Policy**: The privacy policy must inform consumers about their rights under the CCPA.
    - **Responding to Consumer Requests**: Businesses must respond to consumer requests within a reasonable time frame.

- **Scope:** The CCPA applies to businesses that meet certain thresholds, such as those that

    - Have annual gross revenue of more than $25 million.

    - Collect personal information of 50,000 or more California consumers, households, or devices.

    - Derive 50% or more of their annual revenue from selling California consumers' personal information.

Relationship to CPRA

The **California Privacy Rights Act (CPRA)**, also known as Proposition 24, was passed by California voters in November 2020 and amends and expands upon the CCPA. The CPRA introduces new rights for consumers, such as the right to correct inaccurate personal information and the right to limit the use of sensitive personal information. It also creates a new state agency, the California Privacy Protection Agency (CPPA), to enforce the CCPA and CPRA.

Impact

The CCPA has had a significant impact on how businesses collect, use, and share personal information. It has led to increased transparency and consumer awareness about data privacy issues. It has also prompted many businesses to review and update their privacy practices to comply with the law.

CCPA vs. GDPR

The California Consumer Privacy Act (CCPA) and the General Data Protection Regulation (GDPR) are both comprehensive data privacy laws aimed at giving individuals more control over their personal data, but they differ in scope and approach. As shown below, the GDPR, a European Union law, applies broadly to any organization worldwide that processes the personal data of EU residents and emphasizes an "opt-in" consent model, requiring explicit permission before data collection. Conversely, the CCPA, a California state law, specifically protects the personal information of California residents and primarily operates on an "opt-out" model, meaning businesses can collect data but must provide consumers with the right to prevent its sale. While both grant rights like access and deletion, GDPR is generally considered more stringent with higher potential fines and a broader definition of personal data.

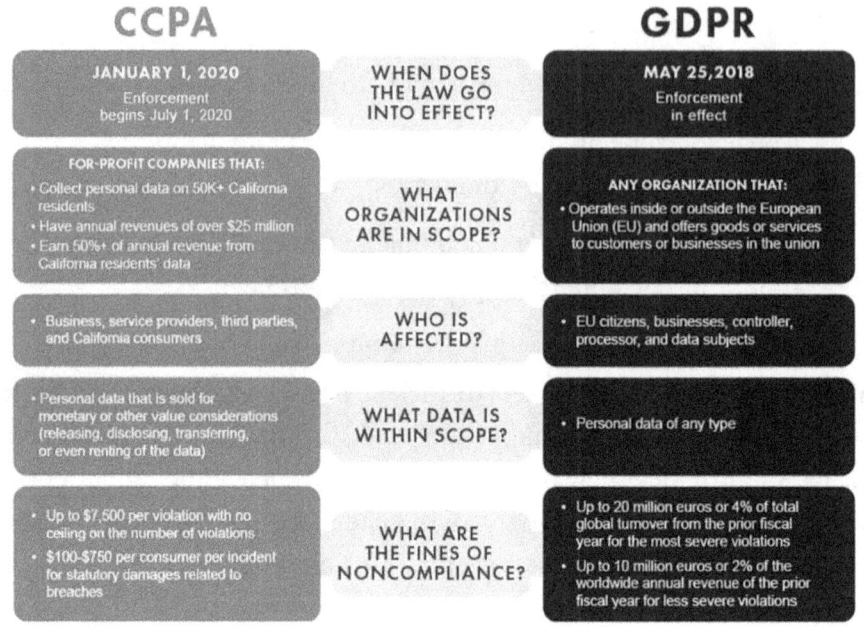

HIPAA (Health Insurance Portability and Accountability Act)

The Health Insurance Portability and Accountability Act of 1996 (HIPAA) is a US law designed to protect sensitive patient health information (PHI). It sets the standard for safeguarding medical records and other personal health data.

CHAPTER 11   COMPLIANCE AND REGULATIONS

Here's a breakdown of key aspects:

What it protects:

- **Protected Health Information (PHI):** This includes any information that can be used to identify an individual and relates to their past, present, or future physical or mental health condition, the provision of healthcare to them, or the payment for that healthcare. Examples include names, addresses, birthdates, Social Security numbers, and medical diagnoses.

Who it applies to:

- **Covered Entities**: These are healthcare providers (doctors, hospitals, clinics), health plans (insurance companies), and healthcare clearinghouses (entities that process healthcare claims electronically).

- **Business Associates**: Organizations that provide services to covered entities and have access to PHI (e.g., billing companies, IT service providers).

Key provisions:

- **Privacy Rule**: Sets standards for how PHI can be used and disclosed. It gives patients' rights regarding their health information, such as the right to access their records and request amendments.

- **Security Rule**: Establishes national standards for safeguarding electronic protected health information (ePHI). This includes technical, physical, and administrative safeguards to protect the confidentiality, integrity, and availability of ePHI.

- **Breach Notification Rule**: Requires covered entities to notify affected individuals and the Department of Health and Human Services (HHS) of certain breaches of unsecured PHI.

Impact

- **Increased Patient Privacy**: HIPAA has significantly improved the privacy and security of patient health information.

- **Improved Healthcare Quality**: By promoting the use of electronic health records, HIPAA has helped to improve the quality and efficiency of healthcare delivery.

- **Reduced Healthcare Fraud and Abuse**: HIPAA has helped to reduce healthcare fraud and abuse by improving the accuracy and integrity of healthcare claims.

CHAPTER 11   COMPLIANCE AND REGULATIONS

SOX (Sarbanes-Oxley Act)

The Sarbanes-Oxley Act of 2002, also known as SOX, is a federal law enacted in the United States to protect investors from fraudulent financial reporting by corporations. It was passed in response to a series of corporate scandals in the early 2000s that involved publicly traded companies such as Enron and WorldCom.

SOX mandates strict reforms to existing securities regulations and imposes tough new penalties on lawbreakers. It created the Public Company Accounting Oversight Board (PCAOB) to oversee public audit companies and promulgate auditing standards to ensure quality reporting and independent auditing.

Key provisions of SOX include

- **Establishing the PCAOB**: An independent, nonprofit organization that oversees the audits of public companies.

- **Increasing Auditor Independence**: Auditors are prohibited from performing certain non-audit services for their audit clients.

- **CEO and CFO Certification**: CEOs and CFOs are required to certify the accuracy of their company's financial statements.

- **Enhanced Financial Disclosures**: Public companies are required to provide more detailed financial information to investors.

- **New Penalties for Securities Fraud**: Increased penalties for securities fraud and other white-collar crimes.

SOX has had a significant impact on corporate governance and financial reporting in the United States. It has helped to restore investor confidence in the accuracy and reliability of financial statements and has led to significant improvements in corporate accountability.

SOX compliance can be complex and costly for public companies. It requires significant resources to implement and maintain the necessary internal controls and procedures. However, it is essential for ensuring the integrity of financial markets and protecting investors.

PCI DSS (Payment Card Industry Data Security Standard)

The Payment Card Industry Data Security Standard (PCI DSS) is a set of security standards designed to protect cardholder data. It was created by the major card brands (Visa, Mastercard, American Express, Discover, and JCB) to increase controls around cardholder data and reduce credit card fraud through increased security measures globally.

Here are some key aspects of PCI DSS:

- **Scope**: Applies to any entity that stores, processes, or transmits cardholder data. This includes merchants, service providers, and any other organization involved in payment card transactions.

- **Requirements**: Outlines 12 key requirements with over 300 sub-requirements covering areas such as
  - **Build and Maintain a Secure Network**: Implementing and maintaining a secure network and systems
  - **Protect Cardholder Data**: Protecting stored cardholder data
  - **Maintain a Vulnerability Management Program**: Regularly scanning and assessing systems for vulnerabilities
  - **Implement Strong Access Control Measures**: Restricting access to cardholder data and systems
  - **Regularly Monitor and Test Networks**: Monitoring networks and systems for malicious activity
  - **Maintain an Information Security Policy**: Developing and maintaining an information security policy
- **Compliance Validation**: Organizations must demonstrate compliance through annual or quarterly assessments, depending on their transaction volume.
- **Benefits**
  - Reduced risk of data breaches and fraud
  - Increased customer trust and confidence
  - Improved brand reputation
  - Enhanced security posture
  - Compliance with industry regulations

In essence, PCI DSS is a critical standard for any organization that handles payment card data. By adhering to the requirements, businesses can significantly reduce their risk of data breaches and protect themselves from the financial and reputational consequences of fraud.

CHAPTER 11   COMPLIANCE AND REGULATIONS

Key Takeaways

Cybersecurity compliance and regulations form the bedrock of a secure digital environment, ensuring organizations not only protect sensitive data but also operate within legal and ethical boundaries. This section distills the essence of various key frameworks and acts, highlighting their purpose and impact on safeguarding information in today's complex landscape

- **Compliance and Governance Are Core**: Cybersecurity isn't just about tech; it's about adhering to external laws (**compliance**) and building internal frameworks (**governance**) to manage risks and align with business goals.

- **Key Regulations**

  - **GDPR**: EU law focusing on individual control over **personal data**, with global impact on data handling, rights (e.g., right to be forgotten), and breach notifications

  - **CCPA/CPRA**: California laws giving consumers rights over their **personal information**, including knowing what's collected, deletion, and opting out of sales

  - **HIPAA**: US law specifically protecting sensitive **patient health information (PHI)** for healthcare entities and their associates via Privacy, Security, and Breach Notification Rules

  - **SOX**: US law safeguarding investors from **financial fraud**, mandating strict financial reporting controls and accountability

  - **PCI DSS**: Industry standard for **protecting payment card data**, outlining security requirements for any entity handling cardholder information

- **Benefits**: Adherence to these frameworks reduces breaches, improves reputation, avoids fines, and strengthens overall security posture.

CHAPTER 12

Implementing and Maintaining a Security Program

A strong security program isn't just about compliance—it's about proactive risk management. It starts with identifying threats, applying the right security controls, and continuously adapting to an evolving threat landscape. Security isn't static; controls must be monitored, tested, and updated to stay ahead of attackers. Employees play a critical role—without ongoing security training and awareness, even the best defenses will fail. Effective programs focus on risk assessments, policy enforcement, technical safeguards, real-time monitoring, and a culture of security that extends beyond IT. Cyber resilience isn't a checklist—it's a mindset.

CHAPTER 12   IMPLEMENTING AND MAINTAINING A SECURITY PROGRAM

As shown above, implementing and maintaining a robust cybersecurity program involves a multilayered approach that includes risk assessment, technology implementation, employee training, and continuous monitoring and improvement. It is a resource-intensive and time-consuming undertaking involving multiple steps in collaboration with cross-functional teams under executive leaders' sponsorship.

Develop a Cybersecurity Strategy

A cybersecurity strategy is a structured plan designed to protect an organization's information systems, networks, and data from cyber threats.

By implementing a comprehensive cybersecurity strategy, organizations can significantly enhance their resilience against cyber threats and protect their valuable assets.

Implement and Monitor Security Controls

Implementing and monitoring security controls is a crucial part of any effective cybersecurity strategy.

By effectively implementing and monitoring security controls, organizations can significantly enhance their cybersecurity posture, reduce their risk of cyberattacks, and protect their valuable data and systems.

Conduct Security Audits and Assessments

Both security audits and assessments are valuable tools for improving an organization's cybersecurity posture. The choice of which to conduct will depend on specific needs, industry regulations, and risk tolerance (see Table 12-1).

Table 12-1. Security Assessment Features

Feature	Security Audit	Security Assessment
Focus	Compliance, standards	Vulnerabilities, risks
Scope	More specific, often limited to certain areas	Broader, encompassing the entire IT environment
Depth	In-depth, detailed examination	Less formal, may be less comprehensive
Methodology	Primarily focused on documentation and controls	Includes technical testing (e.g., vulnerability scans)
Outcome	Compliance report, evidence of adherence	Report with identified vulnerabilities and risks

Continuous improvement and adoption are critical aspects of a successful cybersecurity strategy. Here's why:

- **Cybersecurity Is a Constant Arms Race**: Attackers continuously refine tactics, leveraging zero-day vulnerabilities and advanced persistent threats (APTs).
  - **Example**: The SolarWinds breach (2020) demonstrated how sophisticated nation-state actors compromised supply chains, forcing organizations to adopt stronger monitoring and response mechanisms.
- **New Technologies Emerge**: Innovations like AI-driven automation, IoT devices, and multicloud environments expand attack surfaces and require new security models.
  - **Example**: The rise of deepfake technology has enabled social engineering attacks, requiring companies to integrate AI-powered verification tools to detect fraudulent content.
- **Regulations Change**: Governments and industries regularly update compliance standards, requiring organizations to reassess and modify security controls.
  - **Example**: The introduction of GDPR and CCPA forced companies to implement stringent data protection measures, such as encryption and explicit user consent for data collection.

By fostering a culture of continuous improvement and proactively adopting new security frameworks, organizations can anticipate threats, strengthen defenses, and ensure compliance with evolving regulatory landscapes.

Implementing and Maintaining a Cybersecurity Program

1. Assessment and Planning
   - **Risk Assessment**: Identify and analyze potential threats and vulnerabilities.

- **Framework Selection**: Choose a framework like NIST CSF, ISO 27001, or CIS Controls to guide your program.
- **Strategy Development**: Define clear cybersecurity goals and objectives.
- **Policy and Procedure Creation**: Develop and document security policies, procedures, and standards.

2. Implementation

   - **Technology Deployment**: Implement necessary security controls (firewalls, intrusion detection systems, antivirus, encryption).
   - **Access Control**: Implement strong access control measures (multifactor authentication, role-based access).
   - **Data Security**: Implement data loss prevention (DLP) measures and secure data storage.
   - **Employee Training**: Train employees on cybersecurity awareness, phishing prevention, and safe computing practices.

3. Monitoring and Maintenance

   - **Vulnerability Scanning**: Regularly scan for and address vulnerabilities.
   - **Incident Response Testing**: Conduct drills and simulations to test incident response plans.
   - **Security Information and Event Management (SIEM)**: Implement SIEM to monitor security events and detect threats.
   - **Compliance Audits**: Conduct regular audits to ensure compliance with relevant regulations and standards.
   - **Continuous Improvement**: Regularly review and update the cybersecurity program based on new threats, vulnerabilities, and best practices.

Key Considerations

- **Leadership Commitment**: Gain support and commitment from senior management.
- **Resource Allocation**: Allocate sufficient budget and resources for cybersecurity initiatives.
- **Continuous Improvement**: Cybersecurity is an ongoing process that requires continuous monitoring, evaluation, and improvement.

In essence, implementing and maintaining a robust cybersecurity program involves a multilayered approach that includes risk assessment, technology implementation, employee training, and continuous monitoring and improvement.

Cybersecurity Key Metrics, KPIs, and Reporting

A core aspect of moving to a more mature cybersecurity program is formalizing the ability to measure and report cybersecurity performance. However, measuring cybersecurity is not easy. In fact, at times, it can be near impossible. Especially with an ever-expanding attack surface.

At the same time, security leaders today are under an immense amount of pressure to demonstrate their value beyond just reducing risk. They also need to demonstrate how their security plans align with the overall goals of their organization, which the right metrics can help achieve.

Cybersecurity key metrics and KPIs include incident response time, number of detected vulnerabilities, patch compliance rate, intrusion attempts, security training completion rates, mean time to detect (MTTD), mean time to respond (MTTR), unidentified devices on the network, phishing click-through rates, and data loss prevention effectiveness; these are used to assess the overall health of a cybersecurity program, identify areas for improvement, and demonstrate compliance with regulations by tracking performance against set goals and targets through reporting.

Metrics vs. KPIs

While metrics track specific data points like the number of security incidents, KPIs are broader measures that assess the effectiveness of security practices against business objectives, like overall risk reduction or compliance level.

- **Incident Response Metrics**
  - **MTTD (Mean Time to Detect)**: Average time taken to identify a security incident
  - **MTTR (Mean Time to Respond)**: Average time taken to mitigate a detected security incident
- **Vulnerability Management Metrics**
  - **Patch Compliance Rate**: Percentage of systems with up-to-date security patches
  - **Number of Open Vulnerabilities**: Total number of unpatched vulnerabilities identified
- **User Awareness Metrics**
  - **Phishing Click-Through Rate**: Percentage of users who click on malicious links in phishing emails
  - **Security Training Completion Rate**: Percentage of employees who have completed cybersecurity training
- **Network Monitoring Metrics**
  - **Intrusion Attempts**: Number of detected attempts to access systems unauthorizedly
  - **Unidentified Devices**: Number of unknown devices connected to the network

Reporting Considerations

- **Dashboard Visualization**
  - Present key metrics in a user-friendly dashboard to easily monitor trends and identify anomalies.
- **Regular Reporting**
  - Generate reports on a scheduled basis to keep stakeholders informed about cybersecurity performance.

CHAPTER 12   IMPLEMENTING AND MAINTAINING A SECURITY PROGRAM

- **Contextualization**
  - Explain the significance of metrics by relating them to business impacts and industry benchmark.

Key Takeaways

Cybersecurity is a strategic, ongoing effort—not a project but a continuous, adaptive risk management process.

- Three core phases:
  - **Plan**: Assess risks, choose a framework, define strategy, write policies.
  - **Implement**: Deploy controls, secure data, train employees.
  - **Maintain**: Monitor threats, run audits, update systems, test response plans.
- **Audit vs. Assessment**
  - Audits focus on compliance; assessments identify risks.
- **Continuous improvement is critical** to counter evolving threats, technologies, and regulations.
- **Measure performance** using key metrics and KPIs (e.g., MTTD, MTTR, patch rate, phishing clicks).
- **Reporting matters**—use dashboards and contextual insights to inform stakeholders.
- Success depends on leadership support, sufficient resources, and a culture of security.

PART IV

Advanced Topics

The Advanced Topics explores the evolving landscape of cybersecurity with a focus on advanced concepts that go beyond foundational principles. This section provides an in-depth look at Cloud Security, covering its essential components, the shared responsibility model, and key security controls for protecting data, applications, and infrastructure in cloud environments. It also delves into Security Information and Event Management (SIEM), explaining how these solutions collect and analyze vast amounts of log data to provide a centralized view for real-time threat detection, incident response, and forensic analysis. This part also examines the transformative role of Artificial Intelligence (AI) and Machine Learning (ML), demonstrating how they enable proactive threat mitigation by analyzing data to identify anomalies and predict attacks more accurately and faster than traditional methods. Finally, it highlights the importance of data privacy, supported by a Zero Trust architecture—a crucial framework that assumes no user or system is trustworthy by default, requiring continuous verification for every access request. Together, these topics represent the cutting edge of modern digital defense, equipping readers with the knowledge needed to build and maintain resilient security frameworks.

CHAPTER 13

Cloud Security

Cloud security is more than defense—it's resilience. A combination of policies, procedures, and technologies, it safeguards cloud-based systems from cyber threats while ensuring data integrity, availability, and compliance. As organizations shift to the cloud, security must evolve to detect, respond, and recover from threats in real time, ensuring business continuity even in the face of attacks or breaches.

The "cloud" in cloud computing refers to a vast network of remote servers hosted in data centers all over the world.

Here's a simple breakdown:

- Instead of storing files on your computer's hard drive, you store them on these remote servers.
- You access these files and applications over the internet.

Think of it like this:

- **Traditional Computing**: Like having your own library in your home. You own all the books, but they're only accessible from your home.
- **Cloud Computing**: Like having access to a massive online library. You can borrow any book you want, anytime, from anywhere with an internet connection.

Key Concepts

- **On-Demand Self-Service**: You can access computing resources (like servers, storage, and software) whenever you need them, without needing to request them from IT.
- **Broad Network Access**: You can access cloud services from anywhere with an internet connection.
- **Resource Pooling**: Cloud providers pool computing resources from multiple servers, allowing them to be shared by many users.

- **Rapid Elasticity**: You can quickly scale your resources up or down to meet changing demands.
- **Measured Service**: You only pay for the computing resources you actually use.

Types of Cloud Services

- **IaaS (Infrastructure as a Service)**: Provides fundamental computing resources like servers, storage, and networking (e.g., Amazon EC2, Microsoft Azure Virtual Machines)
- **PaaS (Platform as a Service)**: Provides a platform for developers to build, run, and manage applications (e.g., Google App Engine, Heroku)
- **SaaS (Software as a Service)**: Delivers software applications over the internet (e.g., Google Drive, Salesforce, Zoom)

In essence, cloud computing allows individuals and businesses to access and use computing resources and services over the internet, without the need to manage their own physical infrastructure.

Cloud security refers to the cybersecurity policies, best practices, controls, and technologies used to secure applications, data, and infrastructure in cloud environments.

Here's a breakdown:

- **Focus**: Protecting data, applications, and infrastructure hosted within cloud computing environments.
- **Key Aspects**
  - **Data Protection**: Safeguarding sensitive data from unauthorized access, breaches, and loss
  - **Application Security**: Ensuring the security and integrity of applications running in the cloud
  - **Infrastructure Security**: Protecting the underlying cloud infrastructure (servers, networks, storage) from threats

- **Identity and Access Management (IAM)**: Controlling who has access to cloud resources and what they can do
- **Compliance**: Adhering to relevant security and compliance regulations (e.g., GDPR, HIPAA)
- **Shared Responsibility Model**: Cloud security is a shared responsibility between the cloud provider and the cloud user.
  - **Cloud Provider**: Responsible for securing the underlying infrastructure (e.g., physical data centers, network)
  - **Cloud User**: Responsible for securing the data and applications they store and run in the cloud

Why Is Cloud Security Important?

- **Data Breaches**: Can have significant financial and reputational consequences.
- **Compliance Risks**: Noncompliance with regulations can lead to fines and legal penalties.
- **Business Disruptions**: Security incidents can disrupt business operations and impact productivity.

Key Security Measures

- **Encryption**: Encrypting data both in transit and at rest
- **Firewalls**: Implementing network firewalls to control traffic
- **Intrusion Detection and Prevention Systems (IDPS)**: Monitoring for and preventing malicious activity
- **Regular Security Audits and Penetration Testing**: Identifying and addressing vulnerabilities
- **Employee Training**: Educating employees about security best practices

Cloud security is an ongoing process that requires continuous monitoring, evaluation, and adaptation to address evolving threats.

Cloud Computing Models (IaaS, PaaS, SaaS)

Cloud computing models refer to the different ways in which cloud services are delivered to users. Here are the three primary models as shown below:

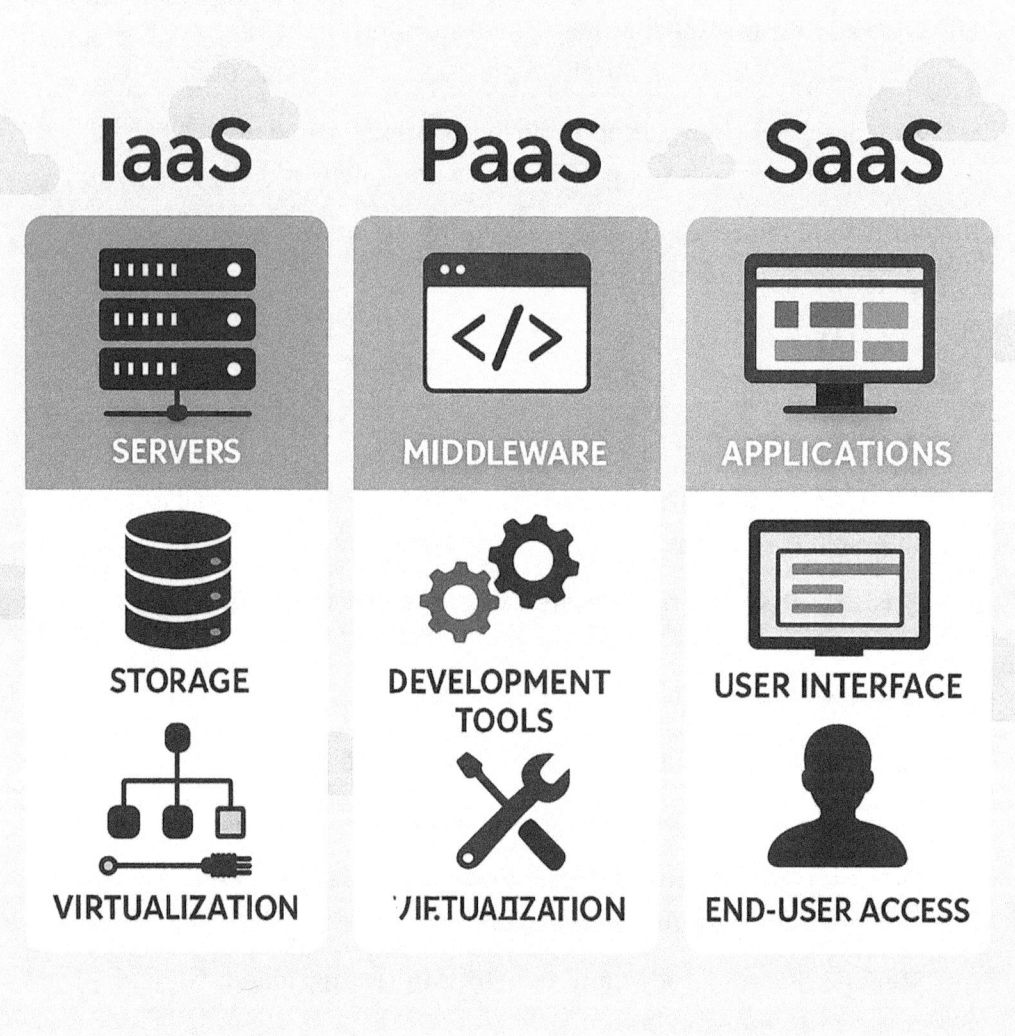

- **Infrastructure as a Service (IaaS)**
    - **What It Is**: Provides fundamental computing resources like servers, storage, and networking.

- **Analogy**: Renting a bare-bones apartment. You get the space, but you're responsible for furnishing, decorating, and maintaining it.
- **Examples**: Amazon EC2, Microsoft Azure Virtual Machines, Google Compute Engine.

- **Platform as a Service (PaaS)**
  - **What It Is**: Provides a platform for developers to build, run, and manage applications. This includes operating systems, programming language execution environments, databases, and web servers.
  - **Analogy**: Renting a furnished apartment. You get the basic necessities, but you still have some flexibility to customize it.
  - **Examples**: Google App Engine, Heroku, AWS Elastic Beanstalk.

- **Software as a Service (SaaS)**
  - **What It Is**: Delivers software applications over the internet. Users access these applications through a web browser or a dedicated client.
  - **Analogy**: Renting a fully furnished and managed apartment. You simply move in and use the space.
  - **Examples**: Google Drive, Salesforce, Zoom, Microsoft Office 365, ServiceNow.

Key Differences Summarized

- **IaaS**: Most control, most responsibility
- **PaaS**: Less control than IaaS, less responsibility than IaaS
- **SaaS**: Least control, least responsibility

These models offer varying levels of control and responsibility for users, allowing organizations to choose the best fit for their specific needs and resources.

CHAPTER 13   CLOUD SECURITY

Security Considerations in the Cloud

Cloud security is essential for safeguarding applications, data, and infrastructure in cloud environments. It involves policies, best practices, controls, and technologies designed to mitigate risks.

Key Cloud Security Considerations

- Data Security

    - **Data Encryption:** Protecting data in transit and at rest to prevent unauthorized access

    - **Data Loss Prevention (DLP):** Implementing safeguards to prevent data leakage

    - **Data Classification:** Categorizing data based on sensitivity to enforce appropriate security measures

- Identity and Access Management (IAM)

    - **Strong Authentication:** Using multifactor authentication (MFA) for added security

    - **Least Privilege:** Restricting access to only necessary resources

    - **Role-Based Access Control (RBAC):** Assigning permissions based on user roles

- Infrastructure Security

    - **Virtual Private Clouds (VPCs):** Isolating network environments for enhanced security

    - **Firewalls and Network Security Groups (NSGs):** Controlling inbound and outbound traffic

    - **Intrusion Detection and Prevention Systems (IDPS):** Identifying and blocking suspicious activity

- Application Security
  - **Secure Development Practices**: Ensuring applications follow secure coding standards
  - **Web Application Firewalls (WAFs)**: Defending against common web-based threats
  - **Container Security**: Protecting containerized applications using vulnerability scanning
- Compliance and Governance
  - **Regulatory Adherence**: Meeting industry standards (e.g., GDPR, HIPAA, PCI DSS)
  - **Regular Security Audits**: Conducting assessments and penetration tests to identify risks
- Shared Responsibility Model
  - **Understanding Responsibilities**: Cloud providers secure infrastructure, while customers must protect data, applications, and configurations.

Key Considerations for Cloud Security

- **Cloud Security Posture Management (CSPM)**: Continuously monitoring cloud environments for misconfigurations
- **Cloud Security Information and Event Management (SIEM)**: Aggregating and analyzing cloud security logs
- **Incident Response Planning**: Preparing for security incidents to minimize disruptions

Why Cloud Security Matters

- **Data Breaches**: Prevents unauthorized access that could lead to financial and reputational damage

- **Compliance Risks**: Avoids regulatory fines and legal consequences
- **Business Continuity**: Ensures operations are not disrupted by cyber threats

Cloud security is a continuous process requiring vigilance, adaptation, and proactive defense mechanisms to counter evolving threats.

Cloud Security Controls and Best Practices

Cloud security controls and best practices are the safeguards and strategies used to protect data, applications, and infrastructure within cloud environments.

Here's a breakdown of key security controls:

- Identity and Access Management (IAM)
  - **Multifactor Authentication (MFA)**: Requires multiple forms of verification (e.g., password + biometrics) for access
  - **Least Privilege**: Granting users only the minimum necessary access to perform their job duties
  - **Role-Based Access Control (RBAC)**: Assigning permissions based on user roles and responsibilities
  - **Identity and Access Management (IAM) Tools**: Utilizing cloud-native IAM services like AWS IAM, Azure Active Directory, or Google Cloud IAM
- Data Security
  - **Data Encryption**: Encrypting data both at rest (when stored) and in transit (while moving)
  - **Data Loss Prevention (DLP)**: Implementing measures to prevent sensitive data from leaving the cloud environment
  - **Data Classification**: Categorizing data based on sensitivity levels to determine appropriate security controls

- Infrastructure Security

    - **Virtual Private Clouds (VPCs)**: Isolating network traffic within a private and secure cloud environment

    - **Network Security Groups (NSGs)**: Controlling network traffic flow to and from cloud resources

    - **Firewalls**: Implementing network firewalls to filter traffic and block unauthorized access

- Application Security

    - **Secure Development Life Cycle (SDLC)**: Integrating security practices throughout the entire application development process

    - **Web Application Firewalls (WAFs)**: Protecting web applications from attacks like SQL injection and cross-site scripting

    - **Container Security**: Securing containerized applications with technologies like image scanning and vulnerability management

- Threat Detection and Response

    - **Intrusion Detection and Prevention Systems (IDPS)**: Monitoring for and preventing malicious activity

    - **Security Information and Event Management (SIEM)**: Collecting and analyzing security logs from cloud resources

    - **Cloud Security Posture Management (CSPM)**: Continuously monitoring and assessing the security posture of cloud environments

Best Practices

- **Embrace the Shared Responsibility Model**: Understand and adhere to the shared security responsibilities between the cloud provider and the user.

- **Implement a Zero Trust Security Model**: Assume no one or nothing is inherently trustworthy.

- **Conduct Regular Security Assessments**: Perform regular penetration tests, vulnerability scans, and security audits.

- **Stay Informed**: Keep up-to-date with the latest cloud security threats and best practices.
- **Employee Training**: Educate employees about cloud security best practices and the importance of security awareness.

Key Considerations

- **Compliance**: Ensure compliance with relevant security and regulatory standards (e.g., GDPR, HIPAA, PCI DSS).
- **Continuous Monitoring**: Continuously monitor cloud environments for threats and vulnerabilities.
- **Incident Response Planning**: Develop and test incident response plans to minimize the impact of security breaches.

By implementing these security controls and following best practices, organizations can significantly enhance the security of their cloud environments and protect their valuable data and applications.

Key Takeaways

Cloud security is vital for safeguarding digital assets in the increasingly popular cloud computing environment, ensuring resilience, data integrity, and compliance. It involves a strategic blend of policies, procedures, and technologies to protect applications, data, and infrastructure hosted on remote servers, demanding a clear understanding of the shared responsibility model between cloud providers and users.

Cloud computing uses remote servers accessible via the internet, offering on-demand self-service, broad network access, resource pooling, rapid elasticity, and measured service.

- **Types of Cloud Services**
    - **IaaS (Infrastructure as a Service)**: Provides basic computing resources (servers, storage)—highest user control
    - **PaaS (Platform as a Service)**: Offers a platform for development and deployment (OS, databases)—moderate user control
    - **SaaS (Software as a Service)**: Delivers ready-to-use software applications over the internet—least user control

- **Defining Cloud Security**: It encompasses policies, best practices, controls, and technologies to protect **data, applications, and infrastructure** within cloud environments.

- **Shared Responsibility Model**: A crucial concept where the **cloud provider secures the "cloud itself"** (underlying infrastructure), while the **user is responsible for security "in the cloud"** (data, applications, configuration, identity, and access).

- **Why Cloud Security Matters**: It's essential for preventing **data breaches**, mitigating **compliance risks**, ensuring **business continuity**, and protecting against financial and reputational damage.

- **Key Security Measures and Controls**

  - **Identity and Access Management (IAM)**: Implementing MFA, least privilege, and role-based access control (RBAC)

  - **Data Security**: Utilizing encryption (at rest and in transit), data loss prevention (DLP), and data classification

  - **Infrastructure Security**: Employing virtual private clouds (VPCs), network security groups (NSGs), and firewalls

  - **Application Security**: Integrating secure development life cycle (SDLC) practices, web application firewalls (WAFs), and container security

  - **Threat Detection and Response**: Using intrusion detection/prevention systems (IDPS), Security Information and Event Management (SIEM), and cloud security posture management (CSPM)

- **Best Practices for Cloud Security**

  - Thoroughly **understand the shared responsibility model**.

  - Implement a **Zero Trust security model** (never trust, always verify).

  - Conduct **regular security assessments** (audits, penetration tests).

- **Stay informed** about evolving threats and best practices.
- Provide **employee training** on cloud security awareness.

• **Continuous Process**: Cloud security is not a one-time setup but an **ongoing process** requiring continuous monitoring, evaluation, and adaptation to evolving threats and regulatory requirements.

CHAPTER 14

Security Information and Event Management (SIEM)

Security Information and Event Management (SIEM) refers to a cybersecurity solution that collects and analyzes log data from various sources across an organization's IT infrastructure, allowing security teams to identify, prioritize, and respond to potential security threats in real time by correlating events and detecting unusual patterns that might indicate a breach, essentially providing a centralized view of security events to improve threat detection and response capabilities.

CHAPTER 14   SECURITY INFORMATION AND EVENT MANAGEMENT (SIEM)

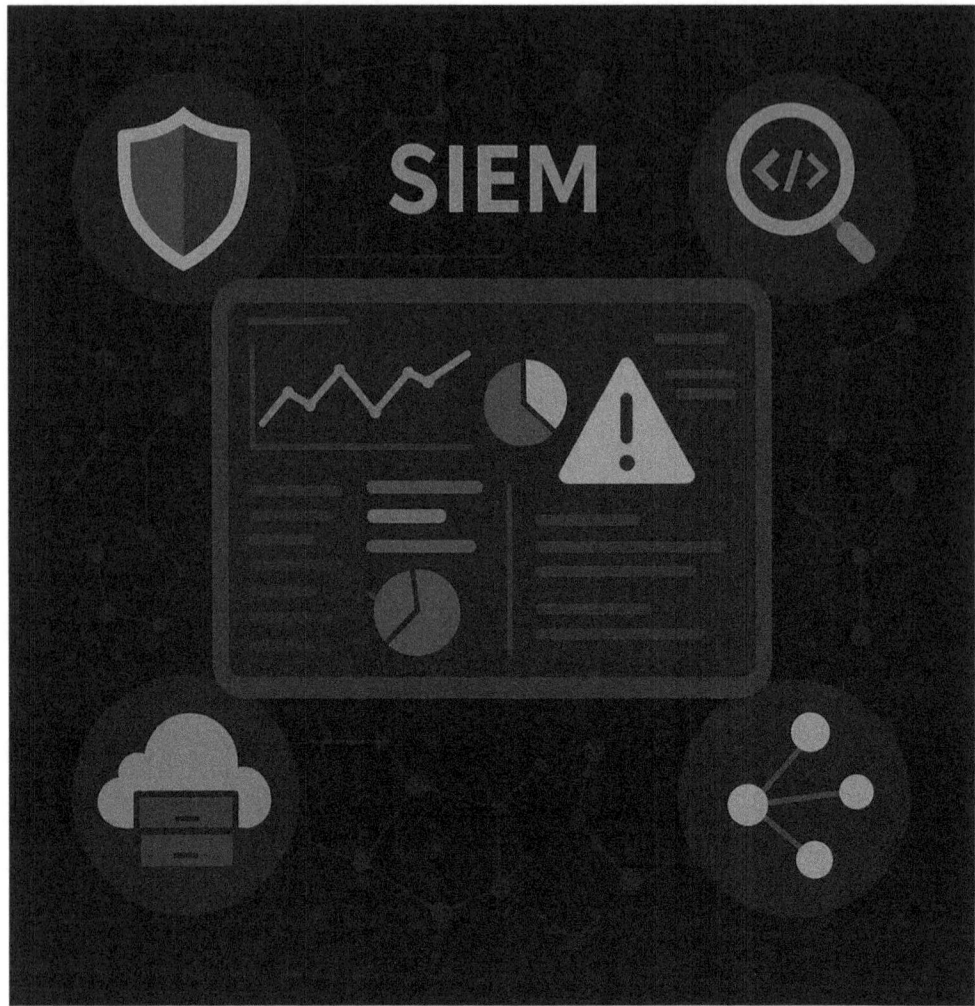

Security Information and Event Management (SIEM) is a cybersecurity solution that helps organizations detect and respond to security threats.

SIEM Fundamentals

The SIEM acts as a central hub for security monitoring and response, providing organizations with critical insights into their security posture and enabling them to proactively defend against cyber threats.

Here's a breakdown of what it does:

- **Collects Security Data**: Gathers security logs and events from various sources across an IT environment, including firewalls, servers, network devices, applications, and cloud platforms

- **Correlates Events**: Analyzes the collected data to identify patterns and relationships between events, such as unusual user activity, suspicious login attempts, or malicious code execution

- **Detects Threats**: Uses advanced analytics and machine learning to detect threats like malware, ransomware, and insider threats

- **Generates Alerts**: Notifies security teams of potential threats in real time

- **Facilitates Incident Response**: Provides tools and workflows to help security teams investigate and respond to security incidents

- **Provides Compliance Reporting**: Helps organizations meet compliance requirements by generating reports on security events and activities

Key Benefits of SIEM

- **Improved Threat Detection**: Proactively identifies and responds to security threats

- **Reduced Security Risks**: Minimizes the impact of security breaches

- **Enhanced Security Posture**: Improves overall security posture and compliance

- **Faster Incident Response**: Speeds up the investigation and resolution of security incidents

- **Cost Savings**: Reduces the cost of security incidents and improves operational efficiency

CHAPTER 14   SECURITY INFORMATION AND EVENT MANAGEMENT (SIEM)

Implementing and Managing a SIEM Solution

Implementing and managing a SIEM solution is an ongoing process that requires careful planning, ongoing monitoring, and continuous improvement. By following these steps, organizations can effectively leverage SIEM to enhance their security posture, improve threat detection capabilities, and accelerate incident response.

1. Planning and Assessment

    - **Define Objectives**: Clearly outline your goals for implementing SIEM. What threats are you trying to detect? Do you have compliance requirements?

    - **Data Source Inventory**: Identify all potential data sources (firewalls, servers, endpoints, cloud services, etc.) that will feed into the SIEM.

    - **Threat Modeling**: Conduct a threat modeling exercise to identify potential attack vectors and prioritize data sources accordingly.

    - **Compliance Requirements**: Understand and document any relevant compliance regulations (e.g., GDPR, HIPAA, PCI DSS).

    - **Budget and Resource Allocation**: Determine the budget for the SIEM solution (hardware, software, personnel), and allocate resources for implementation and ongoing management.

2. SIEM Selection and Deployment

    - **Choose a SIEM Solution**: Evaluate different SIEM vendors (e.g., Splunk, Elastic, IBM QRadar) based on features, pricing, scalability, and integration capabilities.

    - **Deployment Strategy**: Determine the deployment model (on-premises, cloud-based, hybrid), and plan the implementation process.

    - **Data Ingestion**: Configure data sources, and ensure data is being collected effectively and efficiently.

    - **Normalization and Enrichment**: Transform raw data into a consistent format, and enrich it with additional context (e.g., user identity, asset information).

3. Configuration and Tuning

    - **Develop Correlation Rules**: Create rules to identify suspicious patterns and anomalies in the data.

    - **Configure Alerts**: Set up alerts for critical events, and define escalation procedures.

    - **Fine-Tune Performance**: Optimize data processing and query performance to ensure efficient operation.

    - **Test and Validate**: Conduct rigorous testing to ensure the SIEM is detecting threats accurately and generating appropriate alerts.

4. Ongoing Management and Maintenance

    - **Regular Monitoring**: Continuously monitor SIEM performance, review alerts, and investigate incidents.

    - **Security Content Management (SCM)**: Update and maintain threat intelligence feeds and correlation rules.

    - **Performance Tuning**: Regularly review and optimize SIEM performance to ensure scalability and efficiency.

    - **User Training**: Train security analysts on how to use the SIEM effectively.

    - **Compliance Audits**: Conduct regular audits to ensure compliance with relevant regulations.

Key considerations include

- **Data Volume**: SIEMs can generate large volumes of data. Ensure you have sufficient storage and processing capacity.

- **False Positives**: Minimize false positive alerts to reduce alert fatigue and improve analyst efficiency.

- **Integration**: Integrate the SIEM with other security tools (e.g., endpoint detection and response, vulnerability scanners) for a holistic view of security posture.

- **Security**: Protect the SIEM system itself from unauthorized access and tampering.

CHAPTER 14   SECURITY INFORMATION AND EVENT MANAGEMENT (SIEM)

Threat Detection and Response with SIEM

SIEM plays a vital role in detecting, analyzing, and responding to security threats in real time. By leveraging its full capabilities, organizations can strengthen their security posture, reduce incident response time, and proactively mitigate cyber risks. The following is a detailed breakdown of how SIEM enhances threat detection and response.

Threat Detection

Anomaly Detection: SIEM continuously monitors system logs, user activity, and network traffic to detect unusual behavior that may indicate a security threat.

- User Behavior Analytics (UBA)
  - Identifies deviations from normal user activity, such as
    - A user logging in at an unusual time or from an unexpected location
    - Large, unexplained data transfers that could indicate data theft
    - Unauthorized attempts to access confidential information
  - **Example**: If an employee who typically accesses HR files suddenly starts downloading finance reports, SIEM triggers an alert.
- Network Traffic Analysis
  - Detects unusual network activity, including
    - High volumes of outbound traffic suggesting data exfiltration
    - Internal lateral movement indicating an attacker navigating through systems
    - Signs of command and control (C2) activity from a compromised endpoint
  - **Example**: SIEM flags a surge in traffic from a server communicating with an unfamiliar domain, indicating a potential malware infection.

- Log Correlation and Analysis

  - Cross-references events from different sources (firewalls, endpoints, authentication logs) to detect coordinated attacks.

  - **Example**: A SIEM system detects multiple failed login attempts followed by a successful login from an unrecognized device, indicating a brute-force attack.

- Threat Intelligence Integration

  - SIEM enhances detection by integrating external threat intelligence feeds, identifying known

    - Malicious IP addresses and domains

    - Malware signatures and attack patterns

    - Indicators of Compromise (IoCs) from global threat reports

  - **Example**: If an internal system tries to communicate with a blacklisted IP, SIEM generates an alert.

- Machine Learning and AI for Advanced Threat Detection

  - SIEM systems use AI-driven analytics to recognize sophisticated attack patterns:

    - **Supervised Learning**: Uses labeled datasets to identify threats based on past attack trends

    - **Unsupervised Learning**: Detects unknown threats by identifying unusual behavior not previously seen

  - **Example**: AI-powered SIEM identifies an employee suddenly accessing multiple sensitive records at once—possibly signaling an insider threat.

Threat Response

Real-Time Alerting and Escalation: SIEM provides immediate alerts based on security incidents, categorized by severity and escalated through various communication channels (email, SMS, Slack, ticketing systems).

- **Prioritized Alerts**: Ensures security teams focus on the most critical threats first, reducing alert fatigue.
- **Example**: If a SIEM detects ransomware encrypting files, it immediately notifies the SOC team while triggering predefined response actions.

Incident Investigation and Analysis: SIEM provides a centralized platform for deep-dive forensic analysis and rapid investigation.

- Log Analysis
  - Examines the entire sequence of events that led to an attack.
  - Helps analysts track how attackers gained access and what actions they took.
  - **Example**: Security analysts investigate why a user account was suddenly granted elevated privileges before unauthorized database modifications.
- Data Visualization and Dashboards
  - Graphical representations of attack trends, security alerts, and system vulnerabilities.
  - **Example**: A financial institution uses SIEM dashboards to visualize unauthorized login attempts and credential stuffing attacks across multiple branches.
- Advanced Search and Filtering
  - Allows security teams to search specific logs or filter data based on key attributes (time, location, user, IP).
  - **Example**: Analysts quickly locate suspicious admin logins that originated from an unfamiliar IP in another country.

Automated Incident Response and Orchestration: Some SIEM platforms offer Security Orchestration, Automation, and Response (SOAR) capabilities to automate threat mitigation.

- Automated Actions
  - Quarantines infected systems.

- Blocks malicious IP addresses in firewall rules.
- Disables compromised user accounts.
- **Example:** SIEM detects a phishing email with a known malware payload and automatically isolates affected endpoints.

Forensics and Post-incident Investigation: SIEM stores security logs over extended periods for forensic analysis and compliance auditing.

- **Historic Data Review:** Helps reconstruct attack timelines, aiding in regulatory investigations.
- **Example:** After a data breach, SIEM logs reveal the exact entry point, allowing security teams to patch vulnerabilities.

Key Advantages of SIEM for Threat Detection and Response

- Proactive Threat Detection
  - Identifies cyber threats before they escalate into full-blown incidents.
  - **Example:** SIEM detects an employee sending large amounts of sensitive data to a personal email, preventing data leaks.
- Reduced Mean Time to Detect (MTTD) and Mean Time to Respond (MTTR)
  - Faster identification and containment of security threats.
  - **Example:** SIEM enables a global enterprise to detect an active malware infection and isolate affected machines in minutes instead of hours.
- Improved Security Posture
  - Continuously monitors security controls to prevent misconfigurations and compliance violations.

- **Example**: SIEM alerts when cloud storage permissions are misconfigured, preventing accidental data exposure.
- Enhanced Situational Awareness
  - Provides real-time visibility into security events across an organization's infrastructure.
  - **Example**: A retail company tracks login patterns and discovers that a compromised vendor account is being used for fraudulent transactions.

Conclusion

SIEM is essential for modern cybersecurity operations, providing real-time threat detection, automated incident response, and forensic investigation capabilities. By leveraging SIEM effectively, organizations can

- Proactively detect threats before they cause damage.
- Reduce incident response time through automation.
- Improve compliance with industry regulations.
- Enhance security visibility across their entire IT environment.

As cyber threats evolve, implementing a well-tuned SIEM is critical for maintaining a strong, resilient security framework.

Key Takeaways

SIEM is a cybersecurity solution that **collects, correlates, and analyzes log data** from various IT infrastructure sources (firewalls, servers, applications, etc.) to provide a centralized view of security events.

- **Core Functionality**
  - **Data Collection**: Gathers security logs and events from across the IT environment
  - **Event Correlation**: Analyzes collected data to find patterns and relationships between events, indicating suspicious activity

- **Threat Detection**: Uses analytics and machine learning to identify threats like malware, ransomware, and insider threats
- **Alert Generation**: Notifies security teams in real time about potential threats
- **Incident Response Facilitation**: Provides tools for investigating and responding to incidents
- **Compliance Reporting**: Assists with meeting regulatory compliance requirements

- **Key Benefits**
  - **Improved Threat Detection**: Proactively identifies and responds to security threats
  - **Reduced Security Risks**: Minimizes the impact of security breaches
  - **Enhanced Security Posture**: Boosts overall security and compliance
  - **Faster Incident Response**: Speeds up investigation and resolution times
  - **Cost Savings**: Reduces incident costs and improves operational efficiency

- **Threat Detection with SIEM**
  - **Anomaly Detection**: Identifies unusual behavior (user behavior analytics, network traffic analysis, log correlation)
  - **Threat Intelligence Integration**: Enhances detection by incorporating external threat feeds (e.g., malicious IPs, malware signatures)
  - **AI/ML**: Utilizes machine learning (supervised and unsupervised) to detect sophisticated and unknown attack patterns

- **Threat Response with SIEM**

  - **Real-Time Alerting:** Provides immediate, prioritized alerts based on incident severity.

  - **Incident Investigation:** Offers a centralized platform for deep-dive forensic analysis, log examination, data visualization, and advanced search.

  - **Automated Response (SOAR):** Some SIEMs offer capabilities to automate threat mitigation actions (e.g., quarantining systems, blocking IPs, disabling accounts).

  - **Forensics and Post-incident Investigation:** Stores logs for historic data review, aiding in reconstructing attack timelines.

- **Overall Impact:** SIEM is crucial for modern cybersecurity, providing **proactive threat detection, reduced mean time to detect (MTTD) and respond (MTTR), improved security posture, and enhanced situational awareness**, making it a critical component for a resilient security framework.

CHAPTER 15

Artificial Intelligence (AI) and Machine Learning (ML) in Cybersecurity

Artificial intelligence (AI) and machine learning (ML) have redefined cybersecurity by shifting from reactive defense to proactive threat mitigation. These technologies analyze vast datasets, identify patterns, and detect anomalies faster and more accurately than traditional security methods. By continuously learning from data, AI and ML can predict and prevent cyberattacks in real time, identifying suspicious behaviors before they escalate into breaches. This capability significantly enhances threat detection, response times, and overall security posture, making AI-driven cybersecurity an essential pillar of modern digital defense.

AI and ML are transforming the cybersecurity landscape by enabling faster, more accurate, and more proactive threat detection and response. As these technologies continue to evolve, they will play an increasingly critical role in helping organizations stay ahead of the ever-evolving threat landscape.

AI and ML are revolutionizing cybersecurity by enabling faster and more accurate threat detection and response. Here's a breakdown:

How AI and ML Are Used in Cybersecurity

1. Threat Detection

    AI and ML can analyze network traffic, user behavior, and system logs to identify unusual patterns that might indicate a potential cyberattack, even for previously unknown threats (zero-day exploits).

- **Anomaly Detection**
  - **User Behavior Analytics (UBA)**: Detecting abnormal user activity, like unusual login times or large file transfers
  - **Network Traffic Analysis**: Identifying suspicious network traffic patterns, such as port scans, DDoS attacks, and data exfiltration
  - **Log Analysis**: Correlating events from different sources to identify potential threats
- **Malware Detection**
  - **Identifying New and Evolving Malware**: Analyzing code and behavior to detect previously unknown malware variants
  - **Sandboxing**: Isolating and analyzing suspicious files in a safe environment to determine their behavior
- **Phishing Detection**
  - **Identifying and Blocking Phishing Emails and Websites**: Analyzing email content, sender addresses, and links to identify and block phishing attempts

2. Threat Response
   - **Incident Response Automation**: Automating tasks like quarantining infected systems, blocking malicious IP addresses, and initiating remediation actions
   - **Vulnerability Assessment**: Identifying and prioritizing vulnerabilities in systems and applications
   - **Security Orchestration and Automation (SOAR)**: Automating security workflows and streamlining incident response processes

3. Proactive Security
   - **Predictive Analytics**: Predicting future cyberattacks based on historical data and current trends
   - **Vulnerability Management**: Prioritizing vulnerabilities based on their potential impact and likelihood of exploitation

Benefits of AI and ML in Cybersecurity

- **Improved Threat Detection**: Faster and more accurate detection of threats, including advanced and evolving attacks.
- **Reduced Response Times**: Faster identification and response to security incidents.
- **Reduced Costs**: Automating tasks and improving efficiency can reduce the cost of cybersecurity operations.
- **Enhanced Security Posture**: Proactive identification and mitigation of threats can significantly improve an organization's overall security posture.

Challenges and Considerations

- **Data Quality and Bias**: The accuracy of AI and ML models depends heavily on the quality and diversity of the training data.
- **Explainability**: It can be difficult to understand how AI and ML models make decisions, which can make it challenging to explain and troubleshoot issues.
- **Adversarial Attacks**: Attackers can use AI to create sophisticated attacks that can evade detection by AI-powered defenses.

AI/ML Applications in Threat Detection and Response

AI and ML offer numerous benefits in threat detection and response:

1. Improved Threat Detection

    - **Faster and More Accurate Identification**: AI/ML algorithms can analyze vast amounts of data quickly, identifying subtle patterns and anomalies that might be missed by human analysts. This leads to faster detection of threats, including zero-day attacks and advanced persistent threats (APTs).

- **Detection of Novel Threats**: AI/ML models can learn and adapt to new and emerging threats, such as new malware variants and sophisticated phishing techniques.
- **Reduced False Positives**: By analyzing data more comprehensively, AI/ML can help reduce the number of false alarms, freeing up security teams to focus on real threats.

2. Enhanced Response

- **Automated Response**: AI/ML can automate routine security tasks, such as quarantining infected systems, blocking malicious IP addresses, and initiating remediation actions. This frees up security teams to focus on more strategic tasks.
- **Faster Incident Response**: By automating threat detection and response processes, AI/ML can significantly reduce the time it takes to contain and mitigate security incidents.
- **Improved Incident Investigation**: AI/ML can help security teams analyze and investigate security incidents more effectively by providing insights into the root cause of the attack and identifying the attacker's tactics, techniques, and procedures (TTPs).

3. Proactive Security

- **Predictive Analytics**: AI/ML can be used to predict future cyberattacks based on historical data and current trends. This allows organizations to proactively implement preventative measures and strengthen their defenses.
- **Vulnerability Assessment**: AI/ML can help identify and prioritize vulnerabilities in systems and applications, allowing organizations to focus their remediation efforts on the most critical issues.

4. Cost Savings

- **Reduced Operational Costs**: By automating routine tasks and improving efficiency, AI/ML can help reduce the cost of cybersecurity operations.

- **Reduced Impact of Security Incidents**: Faster detection and response can minimize the impact of security incidents, such as data breaches and system outages.

Ethical Considerations of AI/ML in Cybersecurity

While AI and ML in cybersecurity present exciting possibilities, these also raise significant ethical considerations which are as follows:

1. Bias and Discrimination

    - **Data Bias**: AI/ML models are trained on data. If this data reflects existing societal biases (e.g., racial, gender, socioeconomic), the models can perpetuate and even amplify those biases. This could lead to unfair or discriminatory outcomes, such as

        - **False Positives**: Targeting certain groups or individuals unfairly

        - **Denial of Service**: Blocking access to resources for specific groups

    - **Mitigation**

        - **Data Diversity**: Ensure training data is diverse and representative of the real world.

        - **Regular audits**: Regularly audit AI/ML models for bias and discrimination.

        - **Explainability:** Increase transparency and understanding of how AI/ML models make decisions.

2. Privacy Concerns

    - **Data Privacy**: AI/ML models often rely on large amounts of data, raising concerns about data privacy and potential misuse.

    - **Surveillance**: The use of AI/ML for surveillance purposes can raise concerns about privacy violations and mass surveillance.

- **Mitigation**

  - **Data Minimization**: Only collect and use the data necessary for the specific task.

  - **Data Anonymization and Pseudonymization**: Protect user privacy by anonymizing or pseudonymizing data.

  - **Transparency and Accountability**: Be transparent about data collection and use practices.

3. Job Displacement

   - **Automation**: AI/ML can automate many cybersecurity tasks, potentially leading to job displacement for some security professionals.

   - **Mitigation**

     - **Reskilling and upskilling**: Invest in training and education programs to help security professionals adapt to new roles and technologies.

     - **Focus on Human-AI Collaboration**: Leverage AI/ML to augment human capabilities rather than replace them.

4. Accountability and Trust

   - **Algorithmic Accountability**: Determining who is responsible for the actions and decisions of AI/ML systems can be challenging.

   - **Trust and Transparency**: Building and maintaining trust in AI/ML systems requires transparency and accountability.

   - **Mitigation**

     - Develop clear guidelines and ethical frameworks for the development and deployment of AI/ML in cybersecurity.

     - **Establish clear lines of responsibility for the actions of AI/ML systems.**

5. Security of AI/ML Systems

   - **Adversarial attacks**: Attackers can manipulate AI/ML systems by poisoning training data, exploiting vulnerabilities in the models themselves, or generating adversarial examples (inputs designed to fool the AI/ML system).

   - **Mitigation**
     - **Robust Model Development and Testing**: Develop and test AI/ML models to be resilient against adversarial attacks.
     - **Continuous Monitoring and Evaluation**: Continuously monitor and evaluate the performance of AI/ML systems to detect and mitigate threats.

It's important to note:

- These are just some of the ethical considerations of AI and ML in cybersecurity.
- There is no easy solution to these challenges.
- Ongoing dialogue and collaboration between researchers, developers, policymakers, and the public are crucial to addressing these issues and ensuring the ethical and responsible development and deployment of AI/ML in cybersecurity.

Key Takeaways

It is best described as a paradigm shift. AI and ML are fundamentally changing cybersecurity from a reactive approach to a **proactive one**, enabling real-time prediction and prevention of cyberattacks.

- **Enhanced Threat Detection**
  - **Anomaly Detection**: AI/ML identifies unusual patterns in user behavior, network traffic, and system logs (e.g., login times, large file transfers, port scans, DDoS attacks, data exfiltration).

- **Malware Detection**: It detects new and evolving malware by analyzing code and behavior, including using sandboxing for suspicious files.

- **Phishing Detection**: AI/ML identifies and blocks phishing attempts by analyzing email content, sender addresses, and links.

- **Streamlined Threat Response**

  - **Automation**: Automates tasks like quarantining systems, blocking malicious IPs, and initiating remediation

  - **Vulnerability Assessment**: Helps identify and prioritize system and application vulnerabilities

  - **SOAR**: Automates security workflows and streamlines incident response

- **Proactive Security**

  - **Predictive Analytics**: Forecasts future cyberattacks based on historical data and current trends

  - **Vulnerability Management**: Prioritizes vulnerabilities based on potential impact and likelihood of exploitation

- **Key Benefits**

  - **Improved Threat Detection**: Faster and more accurate identification of threats, including zero-day and advanced persistent threats (APTs).

  - **Reduced Response Times**: Quicker identification and containment of security incidents.

  - **Reduced Costs**: Automation and efficiency improvements lower operational expenses.

  - **Enhanced Security Posture**: Proactive mitigation significantly improves overall security.

- **Ethical Considerations**

  - **Bias and Discrimination**: AI/ML models can perpetuate societal biases if trained on unrepresentative data, potentially leading to unfair targeting or denial of service. Mitigation involves data diversity, regular audits, and explainability.

  - **Privacy Concerns**: Reliance on large datasets raises concerns about data privacy and surveillance. Mitigation includes data minimization, anonymization, and transparency.

  - **Job Displacement**: Automation of tasks may lead to job displacement. Mitigation focuses on reskilling, upskilling, and human–AI collaboration.

  - **Accountability and Trust**: Challenges exist in determining responsibility for AI/ML decisions and building trust. This requires clear ethical frameworks and accountability.

  - **Security of AI/ML Systems**: AI/ML systems are vulnerable to adversarial attacks (e.g., data poisoning, model exploitation). Mitigation requires robust model development, testing, and continuous monitoring.

CHAPTER 16

The Internet of Things (IoT) Security

The Internet of Things (IoT) refers to the interconnected network of physical objects that are embedded with sensors, software, and network connectivity, allowing them to collect and share data. These devices connect over the internet and can be used to transmit data, perform data analysis, and control one another remotely.

IoT is transforming the way we live, work, and interact with the world around us by connecting everyday objects and enabling them to work together seamlessly.

Here's a simple breakdown:

- **Think Beyond Computers**: IoT goes beyond traditional computers to include everyday objects like thermostats, light bulbs, cars, and even refrigerators.

- **Sensors Are Key**: These devices have sensors that gather information about their surroundings (temperature, humidity, location, etc.).

- **Connectivity Is Crucial**: They connect to the internet, allowing them to communicate with each other and with other systems.

- **Data Is the Lifeblood**: IoT devices generate massive amounts of data that can be analyzed to gain valuable insights and automate processes.

Key Characteristics of IoT

- **Interconnectivity**: Devices communicate and interact with each other.

- **Intelligence**: Embedded intelligence enables devices to make decisions and perform actions autonomously.

- **Scalability**: IoT networks can grow and adapt to accommodate a large number of devices.

Examples of IoT in Action

- **Smart Homes**: Controlling lights, thermostats, and appliances remotely
- **Wearable Technology**: Fitness trackers, smartwatches, and health monitoring devices
- **Connected Cars**: Self-driving cars, telematics, and in-car entertainment systems
- **Industrial IoT (IIoT)**: Smart factories, predictive maintenance, and supply chain optimization
- **Smart Cities**: Traffic management, waste management, and environmental monitoring

IoT Security Challenges and Vulnerabilities

IoT security is a critical aspect of cybersecurity in the modern world. As the number of connected devices continues to grow, it is essential to prioritize security measures to protect individuals, businesses, and critical infrastructure from cyber threats.

IoT security refers to the practices and technologies used to protect Internet of Things (IoT) devices and the networks they use.

Here's a breakdown:

- What it encompasses:
  - **Protecting Devices**: Securing the firmware, operating systems, and applications running on IoT devices
  - **Securing Data**: Protecting sensitive data transmitted by and stored on IoT devices
  - **Securing Networks**: Protecting the communication channels used by IoT devices
  - **Ensuring Privacy**: Protecting user privacy and data confidentiality

- Why it's crucial:

  - **Growing Attack Surface**: The increasing number of connected devices creates a larger attack surface for cybercriminals.

  - **Critical Infrastructure**: Many IoT devices are used in critical infrastructure (e.g., healthcare, transportation, energy), making security breaches potentially life-threatening.

  - **Data Breaches**: IoT devices can be a source of sensitive data, making them targets for data breaches.

- Key challenges:

  - **Limited Resources**: Many IoT devices have limited processing power and memory, making it difficult to implement robust security measures.

  - **Lack of Standardization**: There is no single standard for IoT security, making it difficult to ensure interoperability and security across different devices and platforms.

  - **"Internet of Skulls"**: Many IoT devices are designed with little or no security in mind, creating significant vulnerabilities.

Securing IoT Devices and Networks

The rapid proliferation of IoT devices has introduced significant security risks. Below is a breakdown of key vulnerabilities and measures to mitigate them.

1. Device-Level Vulnerabilities

   - **Weak or Default Passwords**: Many IoT devices are shipped with default credentials, making them easy targets for brute-force attacks.

   - **Insecure Software**: Devices often run outdated firmware or lack security updates, exposing them to exploits.

   - **Limited Processing Power and Memory**: Many IoT devices lack the computational resources to support robust security protocols like encryption and intrusion detection.

2. Network-Level Vulnerabilities

   - **Unencrypted Communication**: Many IoT devices transmit data in plaintext, making it susceptible to interception.
   - **Lack of Authentication and Authorization**: Weak access controls enable unauthorized actors to manipulate or access devices.
   - **Denial-of-Service (DoS) Attacks**: Attackers can flood IoT networks with traffic, causing devices to crash or malfunction.

3. Data Privacy and Security

   - **Data Breaches**: IoT devices collect vast amounts of personal and business data, making them attractive targets for cybercriminals.
   - **Lack of Data Encryption**: Data stored or transmitted without encryption can be intercepted and exploited.
   - **Privacy Concerns**: IoT devices often collect sensitive user data, raising concerns about unauthorized surveillance and data misuse.

4. Other Security Challenges

   - **Supply Chain Attacks**: Compromised components during manufacturing can introduce vulnerabilities before a device is even deployed.
   - **Physical Security Risks**: Many IoT devices operate in unsecured environments, leaving them vulnerable to tampering or theft.
   - **Lack of Standardization**: The absence of universal security frameworks makes it difficult to ensure consistent protection across devices and platforms.

Mitigating IoT Security Risks

- **Strong Passwords and Authentication**: Implement unique, complex passwords, and enable multifactor authentication (MFA).
- **Regular Software Updates**: Ensure all firmware and software are updated with the latest security patches.

- **Secure Network Connections**: Use encryption protocols like TLS/SSL to protect data in transit.

- **Data Privacy and Security**: Apply strong encryption methods for both stored and transmitted data.

- **Secure Device Development**: Build security into the device life cycle, including secure boot mechanisms and hardened operating systems.

- **Adoption of IoT Security Standards**: Follow industry best practices like NIST's IoT security framework or ISO/IEC 27030.

- **User Education**: Raise awareness about IoT security threats, and encourage users to adopt safe practices.

By addressing these vulnerabilities and implementing proactive security measures, organizations can significantly reduce IoT-related threats and enhance overall cybersecurity resilience.

Key Takeaways

The Internet of Things (IoT) involves **interconnected physical objects** (beyond computers) embedded with sensors and software, enabling them to **collect and share data** over the internet.

- **Key Characteristics of IoT**
  - **Interconnectivity**: Devices communicate and interact with each other.
  - **Intelligence**: Devices can make autonomous decisions and perform actions.
  - **Scalability**: IoT networks can easily expand to accommodate many devices.
- **IoT Security Challenges and Vulnerabilities**
  - **Growing Attack Surface**: The sheer number of connected devices significantly increases potential targets for cyberattacks.

- **Critical Infrastructure Risk**: Many IoT devices operate in critical sectors (e.g., healthcare, energy), making breaches potentially life-threatening.

- **Data Breaches**: IoT devices collect vast amounts of sensitive data, making them prime targets.

- **Limited Resources**: Many devices lack the processing power and memory for robust security measures.

- **Lack of Standardization**: No universal security standards exist, leading to inconsistent protection.

- **"Internet of Skulls"**: Many devices are designed with little or no security, creating inherent vulnerabilities.

• **Specific Vulnerabilities**

- **Device-Level**: Weak/default passwords, insecure/outdated software, limited processing power for security protocols

- **Network-Level**: Unencrypted communication, weak authentication/authorization, vulnerability to Denial-of-Service (DoS) attacks

- **Data Privacy**: Risk of data breaches due to lack of encryption and concerns over unauthorized surveillance

- **Other Challenges**: Supply chain attacks, physical security risks, and the overall lack of standardization

• **Mitigating IoT Security Risks**

- **Strong Authentication**: Implement unique, complex passwords and multifactor authentication (MFA).

- **Regular Updates**: Keep all firmware and software patched and up-to-date.

- **Secure Connections**: Use encryption protocols (e.g., TLS/SSL) for data in transit.

- **Data Encryption**: Encrypt both stored and transmitted data.

- **Secure Development**: Build security into the entire device life cycle, from design to deployment.

- **Adopt Standards**: Follow established IoT security frameworks (e.g., NIST, ISO/IEC 27030).

- **User Education**: Raise awareness about IoT threats and promote safe practices among users.

CHAPTER 17

Blockchain and Cryptocurrency Security

Blockchain security is a comprehensive risk management system for a blockchain network. It uses cybersecurity frameworks, assurance services, and best practices to reduce risks against attacks and fraud. Blockchain technology produces a structure of data with inherent security qualities. It's based on principles of cryptography, decentralization, and consensus, which ensure trust in transactions. In most blockchains or distributed ledger technologies (DLT), the data is structured into blocks, and each block contains a transaction or bundle of transactions.

CHAPTER 17 BLOCKCHAIN AND CRYPTOCURRENCY SECURITY

Each new block connects to all the blocks before it in a cryptographic chain in such a way that it's nearly impossible to tamper with. All transactions within the blocks are validated and agreed upon by a consensus mechanism, ensuring that each transaction is true and correct.

Blockchain technology enables decentralization through the participation of members across a distributed network. There is no single point of failure, and a single user cannot change the record of transactions. However, blockchain technologies differ in some critical security aspects.

Understanding Blockchain Technology

Blockchain technology provides a robust foundation for secure, transparent, and efficient digital transactions. While it continues to evolve, its transformative potential spans multiple industries.

Blockchain Explained

- **Distributed Ledger**: A digital ledger replicated across multiple computers, ensuring no central authority has control.
- **Decentralization**: Eliminates the need for intermediaries (e.g., banks), enhancing security and reducing manipulation risks.
- **Immutability**: Once recorded, data on the blockchain is nearly impossible to alter or erase, ensuring trustworthiness.
- **Transparency**: Depending on the blockchain type, transactions can be publicly verifiable, fostering accountability.

How It Works

- **Transactions**: A user initiates an action (e.g., cryptocurrency transfer, contract execution).
- **Block Creation**: The transaction is grouped into a "block" with others.
- **Verification**: A network of computers validates the block through consensus mechanisms (e.g., mining or staking).
- **Chain Formation**: Once verified, the block is added to the blockchain, creating a permanent, chronological record.

Key Features

- **Enhanced Security**: Decentralization and cryptographic protection make hacking extremely difficult.
- **Greater Transparency**: Public blockchains provide open access to transaction histories, increasing trust.

- **Cost Reduction**: Eliminates intermediaries, cutting down on processing fees and transaction costs.
- **Operational Efficiency**: Automation via smart contracts and real-time data updates optimizes processes.

Applications

- **Cryptocurrencies**: Bitcoin, Ethereum, and digital assets rely on blockchain for secure transactions.
- **Supply Chain Management**: Tracks goods, prevents fraud, and ensures authenticity.
- **Finance and Banking**: Enables decentralized finance (DeFi), cross-border payments, and smart contracts.
- **Healthcare**: Protects patient records and streamlines data sharing.
- **Voting Systems**: Secures election integrity with transparent, verifiable digital voting.
- **Real Estate**: Simplifies property transactions and guarantees ownership records.

Blockchain's ability to enhance security, efficiency, and trust makes it a game-changer in digital transformation across industries.

Security Challenges and Vulnerabilities in Blockchain

While blockchain technology offers significant advantages, it's crucial to be aware of the security challenges and vulnerabilities. Ongoing research and development are essential to ensure the continued security and robustness of blockchain systems.

1. 51% Attacks
    - **Concept**: An attacker gains control of more than 50% of the network's computing power (hash rate).

- **Impact**: Allows the attacker to

  - **Double-Spend**: Spend the same cryptocurrency multiple times.
  - **Reverse Transactions**: Revert legitimate transactions.
  - **Manipulate the Blockchain**: Control the order of transactions and block creation.

- **Mitigation**: Proof-of-Work (PoW) and Proof-of-Stake (PoS) consensus mechanisms aim to make 51% attacks prohibitively expensive or difficult.

2. Smart Contract Vulnerabilities

- **Bugs and Exploits**: Errors in the code of smart contracts can be exploited by attackers to

  - **Drain Funds**: Steal cryptocurrency from users.
  - **Manipulate Outcomes**: Alter the intended behavior of the contract.
  - **Cause Denial-of-Service**: Disrupt the functionality of the blockchain.

- **Mitigation**: Thorough code audits, rigorous testing, and formal verification techniques are crucial.

3. Phishing and Social Engineering

- **Targeting Users**: Attackers exploit human psychology to trick users into

  - **Revealing Private Keys**: Access to private keys grants full control over cryptocurrency holdings.
  - **Visiting Malicious Websites**: Phishing websites can steal credentials or install malware.

- **Mitigation**: Strong password practices, two-factor authentication, and user education are essential.

4. Data Privacy Concerns

    - **Public Ledgers**: Although pseudonymous, blockchain transactions can be analyzed to reveal patterns and potentially link them to real identities.

    - **Data Breaches**: If private keys or personal information are compromised, it can have serious consequences.

    - **Mitigation**: Privacy-enhancing technologies like zero-knowledge proofs and homomorphic encryption are being explored.

5. Scalability and Performance Issues

    - **Transaction Throughput**: Some blockchains struggle to handle a high volume of transactions, leading to slow confirmation times and increased fees.

    - **Scalability Solutions**: Layer-2 solutions, such as sidechains and state channels, are being developed to improve scalability.

6. Environmental Concerns

    - **Proof-of-Work (PoW)**: Some PoW-based blockchains consume significant amounts of energy, raising environmental concerns.

    - **Mitigation**: Proof-of-Stake (PoS) and other energy-efficient consensus mechanisms are gaining traction.

7. Regulatory Uncertainty

    - **Evolving Regulations**: The regulatory landscape for blockchain and cryptocurrency is constantly evolving, creating uncertainty for businesses and developers.

    - **Compliance Challenges**: Navigating complex and changing regulations can be challenging.

It's important to note that the blockchain community is actively working on addressing these challenges through ongoing research and development.

Securing Cryptocurrencies and Blockchain Applications

Securing cryptocurrencies and blockchain applications is paramount. Here's a breakdown of key strategies:

1. Strong Cryptography

   - **Public-Key Cryptography**: Underpins most blockchains. It uses a pair of keys:

     - **Public Key**: For receiving funds.

     - **Private Key**: For authorizing transactions.

     - **Importance**: Safeguarding private keys is crucial as they grant sole control over funds.

   - **Hashing Algorithms**: Securely generate unique digital fingerprints (hashes) for each block.

     - **Purpose**: Ensures data integrity and prevents tampering

2. Secure Key Management

   - **Hardware Wallets**: Store private keys offline on dedicated devices (like Ledger or Trezor).

     - **Benefits**: Highly secure, minimizes the risk of online attacks

   - **Software Wallets**: Store keys digitally on your computer or mobile device.

     - **Considerations**: More vulnerable to malware and online attacks

   - **Paper Wallets**: Store private keys offline on a piece of paper.

     - **Pros**: Simple and inexpensive

     - **Cons**: Risk of physical damage or loss

   - **Key Rotation**: Regularly changing private keys enhances security.

3. Consensus Mechanisms

    - **Proof-of-Work (PoW)**: Miners solve complex computational puzzles to validate transactions.
        - **Pros**: Highly secure, resistant to attacks
        - **Cons**: Energy-intensive
    - **Proof-of-Stake (PoS)**: Validators stake their cryptocurrency to validate transactions.
        - **Pros**: More energy-efficient than PoW
    - **Other Mechanisms**
        - **Delegated Proof-of-Stake (DPoS)**: Elects delegates to validate transactions
        - **Proof-of-Authority (PoA)**: Relies on a preselected set of validators

4. Smart Contract Security

    - **Thorough Audits**: Independent security experts review smart contract code for vulnerabilities.
    - **Formal Verification**: Mathematically prove the correctness of smart contract logic.
    - **Testing**: Rigorous testing in a controlled environment to identify and fix bugs.

5. User Education

    - **Phishing Awareness**: Educate users about phishing scams and social engineering attacks.
    - **Safe Key Handling Practices**: Emphasize the importance of secure key storage and management.
    - **Best Practices**: Promote best practices for interacting with blockchain applications.

6. Regulatory Compliance

    - **Know Your Customer (KYC) and Anti-Money Laundering (AML) Regulations**
        - **Purpose**: Prevent illicit activities like money laundering and terrorist financing.
        - **Implementation**: Implement robust KYC/AML procedures.

7. Continuous Monitoring and Improvement

    - **Regular Security Assessments**: Conduct ongoing security audits and penetration testing.
    - **Stay Updated**: Keep up-to-date with the latest security threats and best practices.

By implementing these security measures, individuals and organizations can significantly enhance the safety and security of their cryptocurrency holdings and blockchain applications.

Key Takeaways

- **Wallet Security Is Paramount**
    - **Hardware Wallets**: Most secure; private keys are offline.
    - **Software Wallets**: Convenient but more vulnerable to online attacks.
    - **Paper Wallets**: Simple offline storage, but prone to physical damage/loss.
    - **Key Rotation**: Regularly change private keys to enhance security.
- **Consensus Mechanisms Drive Security**
    - **Proof-of-Work (PoW)**: Very secure but energy-intensive.
    - **Proof-of-Stake (PoS)**: More energy-efficient.
    - **Other Mechanisms**: Delegated Proof-of-Stake (DPoS) and Proof-of-Authority (PoA) offer variations.

- **Smart Contract Security Is Critical**
    - **Audits**: Independent experts review code for vulnerabilities.
    - **Formal Verification**: Mathematically prove correctness.
    - **Testing**: Rigorous testing to find and fix bugs.
- **User Education Is Key**
    - Teach users about phishing and social engineering.
    - Emphasize safe key handling and storage.
    - Promote best practices for interacting with blockchain applications.
- **Regulatory Compliance Is Essential**
    - Implement Know Your Customer (KYC) and Anti-Money Laundering (AML) procedures to prevent illicit activities.
- **Continuous Vigilance**
    - Conduct regular security assessments and penetration testing.
    - Stay updated on the latest threats and best practices.

CHAPTER 18

Zero Trust Architecture

Zero Trust Architecture (ZTA) is a security framework (as shown below) that verifies every access request and prevents cyberattacks. It's designed to ensure that only authorized users and devices can access a network's resources.

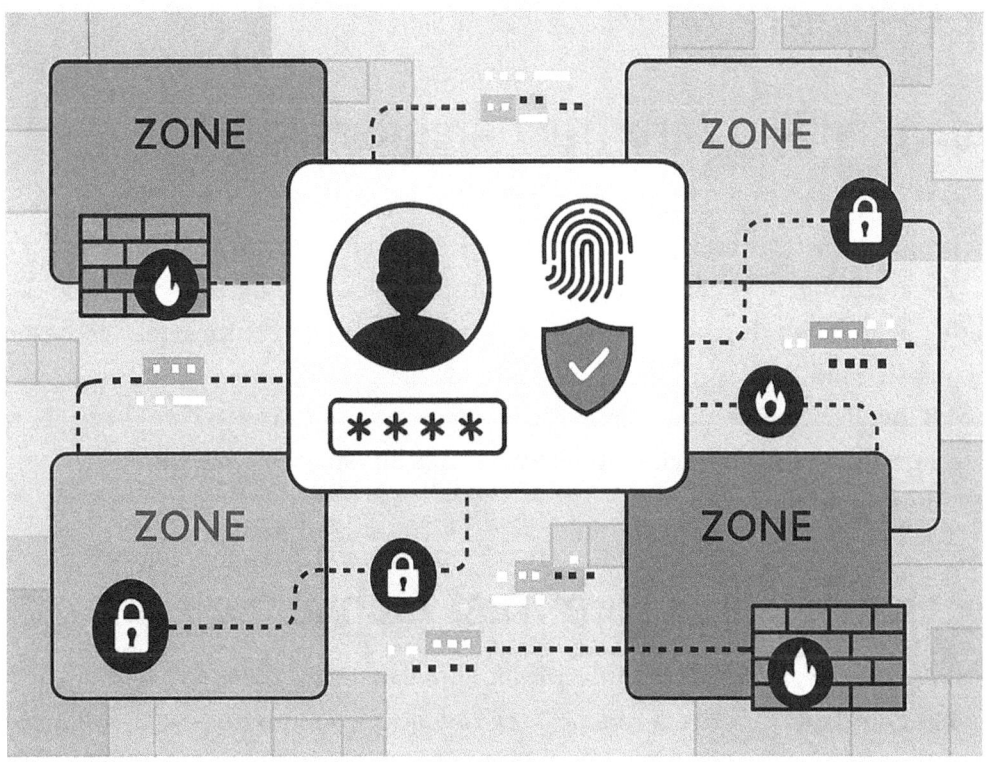

CHAPTER 18   ZERO TRUST ARCHITECTURE

Zero Trust Architecture is a strategy for designing and implementing IT systems that assumes no user or device is trustworthy by default. It's also known as perimeterless security.

ZTA refers to the implementation, practical application, and design that enforces Zero Trust principles in an organization's IT infrastructure. It provides the technical framework and structure that organizations use to enforce Zero Trust. ZTA includes various security technologies, such as

- Identity and access management (IAM)
- Multifactor authentication (MFA)
- Micro-segmentation
- Encryption
- Real-time monitoring

ZTA outlines how these principles are applied across an enterprise's systems, networks, and workflows to ensure that no entity (user, device, or application) gains access without thorough validation.

Understanding Zero Trust Architecture

Introduced in 2011 by John Kindervag, a former analyst at Forrester Research, Zero Trust Architecture has never been more critical. Digital transformation continues to accelerate, bringing us closer to the era of on-premises systems and software and ushering in multicloud environments, an exploding Internet of Things (IoT) ecosystem, and enhanced mobility.

Additionally, users demand direct access to resources from anywhere to collaborate and stay productive. Zero Trust Architecture makes this shift possible without compromising security.

Key Elements in a Zero Trust Architecture

The core principles of Zero Trust are typically associated with securing users or use cases like Zero Trust network access (ZTNA). However, a comprehensive Zero Trust Architecture encompasses users, applications, and infrastructure and materially enhances an organization's security posture.

- **Users**: Strong authentication of user identity, application of the principle of least privilege access, and verification of user device integrity are foundational parts of Zero Trust Architecture.

- **Applications**: A fundamental concept of Zero Trust Architecture is that applications cannot be trusted, and continuous monitoring at runtime is necessary to validate their behavior. Applying Zero Trust to applications removes implicit trust between various application components when they talk to each other.

- **Infrastructure**: Zero Trust Architecture addresses all security related to infrastructure (e.g., routers, switches, cloud, IoT, and supply chain).

Three Principles of Zero Trust?

The Zero Trust Architecture is based on three foundational principles: verification, least privilege access, and assumption of breach.

1. Continuously Monitor and Validate

   Resource usage should be continuously monitored to detect unusual behavior. Organizations should verify users' authenticity by authenticating and authorizing them based on all available data points, including location, user identity, service or workload, and data classification. Multifactor authentication, device health checks, and application whitelisting are recommended for verifying a user's identity, device posture, and application integrity.

2. Enforce Least Privileged Access

   The principle of least privilege restricts users' access rights to only the data, applications, and services they need to perform their authorized functions. This Zero Trust Architecture principle is enforced using granular access controls, just-in-time (JIT), and just-enough access (JEA).

Risk-based, adaptive access policies also help balance security and productivity. Following the principle of least privilege helps minimize potential exposure or damage from insider threats or compromised user accounts.

3. Assume Breach

   Zero Trust Architecture is based on the assumption that security breaches are inevitable and the threats that cause them can be inside and outside an organization's network perimeter. A key objective of Zero Trust Architecture is to minimize the blast radius of a breach when it occurs.

   This entails micro-segmenting sensitive resources, using end-to-end encryption, continuously monitoring user and device behavior for anomalies, and implementing robust incident response and recovery mechanisms.

The Five Pillars of Zero Trust

The US Cybersecurity and Infrastructure Security Agency (CISA) developed the five pillars of Zero Trust to guide organizations in implementing a robust Zero Trust Architecture (ZTA). These pillars address the growing threat landscape by ensuring that no user, device, network, application, or data is inherently trusted. Organizations must continuously verify, monitor, and enforce least privilege access controls across all digital environments.

Identity

Identity refers to the unique attributes that define both human and nonhuman users (e.g., employees, contractors, service accounts, and automated scripts).

Zero Trust Approach

- **Never Trust, Always Verify**: Every access request must be authenticated, authorized, and continuously monitored.

- **Granular Access Control**: Implement identity-based policies that grant access based on specific needs rather than blanket permissions.

Best Practices

- **Single Sign-On (SSO)**: Streamline authentication for users while improving security.

- **Multifactor Authentication (MFA)**: Require multiple verification methods before granting access.

- **Identity and Access Management (IAM)**: Centralize and enforce access controls across all environments.

- **Zero Standing Privileges (ZSP)**: Minimize long-term access to critical systems, and grant time-based permissions when needed.

Example:
An employee accessing cloud applications is prompted to verify their identity using MFA and device compliance checks before being granted access.

Devices

A device is any hardware that connects to an organization's network, including laptops, mobile devices, servers, IoT devices, and personal BYOD assets.

Zero Trust Approach

- **Continuous Monitoring**: Devices must be verified before and during each session.

- **Device Posture Assessment**: Ensure devices comply with security policies before granting access.

Best Practices

- **Device Inventory**: Maintain a real-time database of all registered devices and their security status.

- **Endpoint Detection and Response (EDR)**: Monitor for anomalies and block compromised devices.

- **Zero Trust Network Access (ZTNA)**: Restrict device access to only necessary resources.

- **Automated Patching**: Keep device firmware and security configurations updated.

CHAPTER 18 ZERO TRUST ARCHITECTURE

Example:

A remote employee using a personal laptop must pass a device security check (e.g., updated OS, encrypted storage) before accessing the corporate VPN.

Networks

A network refers to all communication channels, including internal networks, remote connections, wireless networks, and cloud-based infrastructures.

Zero Trust Approach

- **Assume the Network Is Compromised**: Limit exposure by segmenting and encrypting traffic.
- **Verify Before Connecting**: Enforce strict authentication for all network communications.

Best Practices

- **Micro-segmentation**: Divide networks into isolated zones to limit unauthorized lateral movement.
- **End-to-End Encryption**: Encrypt all data traffic to prevent interception (TLS/SSL, IPSec).
- **Network Access Control (NAC)**: Validate all devices before granting network access.
- **Behavioral Analytics**: Continuously monitor network traffic for anomalies.

Example:

A finance department user is restricted to accessing financial databases only and is denied access to engineering systems, even within the same organization.

Applications and Workloads

Applications and workloads include all software, cloud services, and computing processes that run on an organization's infrastructure.

Zero Trust Approach

- **Eliminate Implicit Trust**: Applications must undergo continuous monitoring for suspicious behavior.
- **Secure Software Supply Chain**: Verify the integrity of applications before deployment.

Best Practices

- **Runtime Application Self-Protection (RASP)**: Automatically detects and prevents real-time application threats.

- **Zero Trust Application Access**: Grant temporary access per request rather than persistent access.

- **Container Security**: Protect cloud workloads and microservices from unauthorized access.

- **DevSecOps Integration**: Embed security into the entire software development life cycle (SDLC).

Example:
A user launching a virtual machine in AWS must pass an identity verification step, role-based access control (RBAC), and multilayer encryption before deployment.

Data

Data includes structured and unstructured information stored across devices, applications, databases, networks, and cloud environments.

Zero Trust Approach

- **Data Is the Ultimate Target**: Protect it at rest, in transit, and in use.

- **Apply Least Privilege Access**: Users can only access data required for their specific tasks.

Best Practices

- **Data Loss Prevention (DLP)**: Prevent sensitive data leaks by enforcing usage policies.

- **File and Database Encryption**: Ensure that stored data is protected against unauthorized access.

- **Access Logging and Monitoring**: Track all interactions with sensitive data for audit and compliance.

- **Data Masking and Tokenization**: Anonymize critical data to prevent exposure in unauthorized environments.

Example:
A marketing team member is denied access to customer financial data but is granted access to customer demographics and campaign results.

CHAPTER 18   ZERO TRUST ARCHITECTURE

Why the Five Pillars of Zero Trust Matter

1. **Reduces Attack Surface**: Prevents attackers from moving laterally across networks

2. **Prevents Insider Threats**: Ensures employees only access what they need

3. **Secures Remote Work and Cloud Services**: Extends security beyond traditional perimeters

4. **Enhances Compliance and Governance**: Meets regulatory requirements like GDPR, HIPAA, and NIST

5. **Improves Incident Response**: Provides real-time threat detection and automated remediation

Final Thoughts

The five pillars of Zero Trust provide a structured approach for securing identities, devices, networks, applications, and data. By removing implicit trust and enforcing continuous authentication and authorization, organizations can effectively reduce cyber risks and enhance security resilience.

Zero Trust is not a single technology, it is a mindset. Organizations that embrace continuous verification will be best positioned to defend against evolving cyber threats.

Seven Core Pillars of Zero Trust Architecture

The seven core pillars of Zero Trust Architecture are derived from more detailed frameworks like the Department of Defense (DoD) Zero Trust Reference Architecture, adding two additional focus areas. These seven pillars include the five above and emphasize two critical elements: automation and security operations.

1. **Threats Visibility and Analytics**

   A comprehensive monitoring system actively tracks all user activities, device interactions, network traffic, and other relevant data to identify any anomalies and suspicious behaviors. This data is continuously analyzed to swiftly detect and respond to any potential threats, ensuring the safety and security of our system.

2. **Automation and Orchestration**

    ZTA leverages automated systems to implement and uphold security protocols, as well as to promptly address potential security risks in real time. This approach enhances the efficiency and precision of the response to potential security incidents.

Steps to Implementing Zero Trust Architecture

Implementing Zero Trust Architecture (ZTA) requires a structured approach that redefines how security is enforced across the organization. It involves adopting new technologies, processes, and mindsets to ensure that no user, device, or system is trusted by default. The following diagram and sections show a step-by-step guide to implementing Zero Trust Architecture:

Steps to Zero Trust Architecture Implementation

CHAPTER 18 ZERO TRUST ARCHITECTURE

1. Define the Attack Surface

   Defining your attack surface should be the first item on your Zero Trust checklist. To do this, you want to home in on the areas you need to protect. This way, you will be able to implement policies and deploy tools across your entire network. Focus on your most valuable digital assets.

- **Sensitive Data**: The sensitive data that an organization collects and stores, such as its customers' and employees' personal information, can be easily stolen by thieves.

- **Critical Applications**: These are the applications and data that are vital to your business operations.

- **Physical Assets**: Physical assets such as POS terminals, IoT devices, and medical equipment can also be stolen by thieves.

- **Corporate services**: These include the various components of an organization's infrastructure that support the day-to-day operations of its employees and executives.

2. Implement Controls Around Network Traffic

   The way traffic flows across your network will depend on the various dependencies that each system has. For instance, if an organization has a database that holds information about its customers, then many systems would need to access this data.

   The way requests are routed through a database is very important to ensure that they are protected from unauthorized access. This is because the information in the database is delicate and sensitive. Understanding the details of the network architecture will help you determine which network controls should be implemented and where to place them.

3. Create a Zero Trust Policy

   After you have architected the network, you will want to design your Zero Trust policies. This is most effectively done using what is known as the Kipling method: who, what, when, where, why, and how for every user, device, and network that wants to gain access.

4. Architect a Zero Trust network

   A Zero Trust network is designed to protect specific areas of the network. In most cases, a next-generation firewall will be used as a tool to segment the network.

CHAPTER 18   ZERO TRUST ARCHITECTURE

Although Zero Trust is often associated with securing only users, a comprehensive approach is also needed to protect the various components of an organization's infrastructure.

1. Before you start implementing a Zero Trust strategy, it's important that the users are secure. This includes implementing a variety of security measures such as multifactor authentication and the use of low-access policies.

2. Zero Trust in applications is a concept that eliminates the implicit trust that various components of them have when interacting with one another. It requires continuous monitoring to ensure that the applications are following proper behavior.

3. The various components of an organization's infrastructure, such as switches, routers, IoT, supply chain, and the cloud, should also be protected from unauthorized access using an enterprise-wide Zero Trust strategy.

5. Monitor Your Network

   One of the most critical steps that you can take to ensure that your network is secure is to monitor its activity. It can help you identify potential issues and provide valuable insight into the performance of your network. Pay attention to the following:

   - **Reports**: Reports can be used to flag anomalous behavior. You can then analyze the data to learn how your system or employee is affected by your Zero Trust system.

   - **Analytics**: The data collected by your system can be used to provide insight into how well it functions. This is useful when you need to monitor the behavior of your users and the performance of certain components of the network.

   - **Logs**: The logs produced by your system can provide you with a permanent record of activity. They can be analyzed manually or with the help of analytical tools, which can identify patterns and anomalies.

How to Implement Zero Trust Architecture

Zero Trust Architecture (ZTA) is a security model that assumes no user, device, or system should be trusted by default. Implementing ZTA requires a structured approach, combining technology, policy, and continuous monitoring.

Step-by-Step Guide to Implementing ZTA

- Identify Assets
  - Create an inventory of all on-premises, cloud, and remote assets.
  - Classify assets based on sensitivity and vulnerability.
- Verify Devices and Users
  - Implement multifactor authentication (MFA) for user verification.
  - Use device posture assessments (e.g., embedded chips, behavioral analytics) to confirm legitimacy.
- Map Workflows
  - Define who, when, and why access is granted to assets.
  - Establish granular access policies based on roles and responsibilities.
- Define and Automate Policies
  - Enforce context-aware access controls (e.g., device type, location, user role).
  - Automate access approvals and denials using firewalls, IAM, and SIEM tools.

  Test, Monitor, and Maintain
  - Conduct penetration testing to validate ZTA effectiveness.
  - Continuously monitor user behavior and adjust policies to mitigate threats.
  - Implement regular software updates to optimize security and performance.

Examples of Zero Trust Architecture in Action

Organizations across industries adopt ZTA to secure their operations:

- Financial Sector
  - Banking networks use ZTA to restrict unauthorized access and detect insider threats.
  - Stock exchanges apply Zero Trust to prevent fraud and monitor high-risk transactions.
- Healthcare
  - Hospitals secure patient records with ZTA, ensuring only authorized personnel access sensitive data.
  - Pharmaceutical companies implement Zero Trust to protect clinical trial research from cyber espionage.
- Remote Workforce Security
  - Companies replace traditional VPNs with ZTA, ensuring employees access only necessary resources.
  - ZTA prevents shadow IT by blocking unauthorized applications.
- Cloud and IoT Security
  - Ecommerce platforms use ZTA to prevent data exfiltration by restricting access to customer records.
  - IoT manufacturers apply Zero Trust to isolate compromised devices and prevent botnet attacks.

Key Benefits of Zero Trust Architecture

- Enhanced Security
  - Least privilege access ensures users and devices only access necessary data.
  - Reduces insider threats by continuously verifying trust.

- Protection Against Data Breaches

  - Requires authentication for every request, minimizing lateral movement

  - Assumes "breach mentality," ensuring no implicit trust exists

- Improved Visibility and Monitoring

  - Real-time logging detects suspicious activity early.

  - Audit trails help meet compliance standards.

- Reduced Risk of Advanced Persistent Threats (APTs)

  - Micro-segmentation isolates network segments, limiting attacker movement.

  - Strong identity validation minimizes exposure to nation-state attacks.

- Scalability

  - Accommodates growing cloud-based applications and remote workforces

  - Supports multicloud environments securely

- Improved Incident Response

  - Security teams isolate and contain compromised resources quickly.

  - Automated response mechanisms enhance remediation efforts.

- Regulatory Compliance

  - Aligns with GDPR, HIPAA, and PCI-DSS, reducing compliance risks

  - Enforces strict access control, MFA, and continuous monitoring

- Securing Remote Work and Cloud Applications

  - Ensures employees and partners securely access cloud-based applications

  - Replaces traditional VPNs, preventing unauthorized access

- Extends Security Beyond the Network Perimeter
  - Software-defined perimeters secure access across multiple locations.
  - Users' permissions follow them, preventing credential abuse.

Conclusion

Zero Trust Architecture is a necessity of modern security. By verifying every user, device, and request, ZTA ensures organizations remain resilient against cyber threats. Organizations that adopt and continuously refine ZTA are better positioned to prevent breaches, meet compliance requirements, and support an increasingly remote and cloud-based workforce.

Key Takeaways

ZTA is a security framework that assumes no user, device, or application can be trusted by default, regardless of its location (inside or outside the network). It's also known as "perimeterless security."

- **How It Works**: ZTA verifies every access request, continuously monitors resource usage, and enforces the **principle of least privilege**.
- **Key Technologies**: ZTA relies on identity and access management (IAM), multifactor authentication (MFA), micro-segmentation, encryption, and real-time monitoring.
- **Driving Factors**: ZTA is crucial in modern environments with multicloud setups, IoT proliferation, and remote work, enabling secure access from anywhere.
- **Three Foundational Principles**
  1. **Continuously Monitor and Validate**: Every access request is authenticated and authorized based on all available data (user, location, device health, etc.).

2. **Enforce Least Privileged Access**: Users only get access to the data, applications, and services strictly necessary for their authorized functions. This minimizes potential damage from breaches.

3. **Assume Breach**: ZTA operates on the premise that breaches are inevitable. Its goal is to minimize the "blast radius" of a breach through micro-segmentation, encryption, and continuous monitoring.

Zero Trust is not a single technology; it's a **mindset of continuous verification** that is essential for defending against evolving cyber threats.

CHAPTER 19

Cybersecurity by Design

In an era marked by relentless cyberattacks, rising software supply chain risks, and increasingly complex digital infrastructures, security can no longer be an afterthought. The traditional approach of retrofitting cybersecurity measures late in the product life cycle—often after deployment or public exploitation—has repeatedly proven ineffective. The consequences of this reactive mindset are not merely technical; they are strategic, financial, reputational, and regulatory.

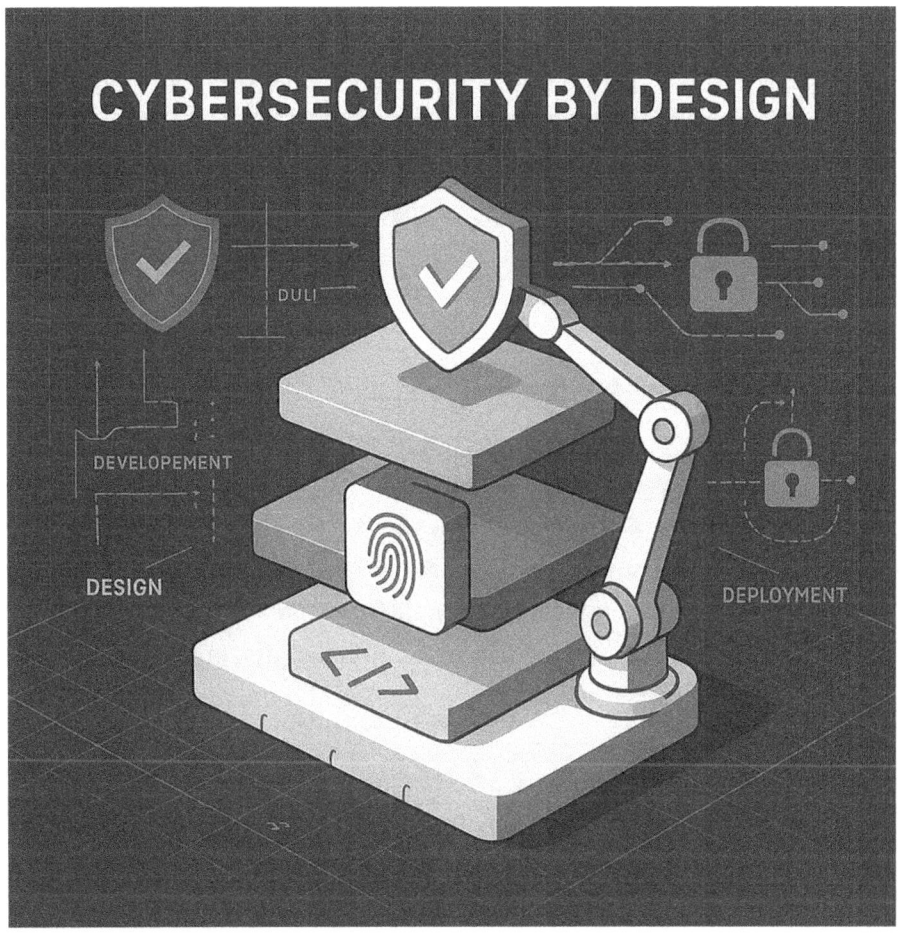

Secure by Design offers a fundamentally different mindset—one that embeds security into the DNA of a product or system from day one. It elevates cybersecurity from a technical bolt-on to a core business requirement, equal in importance to performance, scalability, usability, and cost.

Prioritizing Security from Inception

The most critical aspect of Secure by Design lies in its emphasis on the design phase of a product's development life cycle. This is the stage where fundamental architectural decisions are made, where potential risks can be identified and mitigated most effectively, and where the cost of remediation is significantly lower. By embedding security considerations into the initial blueprints, companies can drastically decrease the number of exploitable flaws that might otherwise slip through the cracks and reach the market for widespread use or consumption.

Imagine building a house: it's far more efficient and robust to design a strong foundation, secure locks, and fire safety systems into the original architectural plans, rather than trying to retrofit them after the house is built and occupied. Similarly, in software and hardware development, attempting to bolt on security features late in the game often results in weaker defenses, higher costs, and a greater risk of overlooking critical vulnerabilities. Secure by Design advocates for this "build it in, don't bolt it on" mentality.

Redefining Security As a Core Business Requirement

Products built with Secure by Design principles start from the premise that customers' security is not optional. It is not a premium feature. It is not conditional on additional fees or configurations. Instead, it is foundational. This represents a significant philosophical shift: rather than designing for functionality first and layering on security later, Secure by Design means the product *cannot function without security* being inherently integrated.

Organizations that take this approach build trust and resilience simultaneously. Secure by Design is not just about writing more secure code—it is about making security a first-class citizen in every decision, from architectural choices to third-party dependencies to how defaults are configured.

The Design Phase Is the Critical Juncture

The design phase of a product's life cycle is where the greatest leverage exists for security impact. Decisions made here—such as software architecture, identity models, encryption schemes, API structures, and third-party integrations—have long-lasting implications for the product's risk posture. Flaws introduced during design are often the most difficult and expensive to fix later in the development life cycle.

By incorporating Secure by Design principles early, teams can

- **Minimize exploitable flaws** before they ever reach production.

- **Reduce the attack surface** by making intentional choices around data exposure and control paths.

- **Integrate controls** that enable future monitoring, forensics, and incident response.

- **Align with regulatory expectations** (e.g., NIST, CISA, ISO/IEC 27001) before compliance becomes a crisis.

Threat modeling, secure architecture reviews, and risk-informed decision-making should be standard elements of the design process. Security should not be invited to the table—it should already have a seat there.

Security Should Work Out of the Box

Secure by Design products are *secure by default*. This means that even if users never touch the configuration settings, the product should still protect their data, ensure system integrity, and defend against common threat vectors.

Key characteristics of Secure by Design products include

- **Secure Defaults**

  Out-of-the-box configurations should favor security. Open ports, weak encryption, anonymous access, and verbose error messages should be disabled unless explicitly enabled with full awareness of the implications.

- **No Paywall for Protection**

  Security-critical features such as multifactor authentication (MFA), single sign-on (SSO), audit logging, and secure update mechanisms should be available to all customers at no extra cost. Organizations should not be forced to choose between security and budget.

- **Built-in Observability**

  Logging, monitoring, and alerting capabilities should be built-in and easy to integrate with existing security operations. Without visibility, defenders are blind.

- **Continuous Hardening**

  Systems should be designed to support future patching, configuration lockdowns, and defense-in-depth enhancements without major refactoring.

Secure by Design in Practice

Being Secure by Design isn't about checking boxes—it's about cultural transformation. Here's how leading organizations put it into practice:

- **Cross-functional Collaboration**: Security architects, product managers, UX designers, and software engineers work together to embed security into feature design and user journeys.

- **Developer Empowerment**: Development teams are equipped with secure coding tools, automated testing frameworks, and access to internal security champions.

- **Zero Trust Foundations**: Systems are architected to assume breach and enforce least privilege, strong identity verification, and continuous access evaluation.

- **Supply Chain Scrutiny**: Dependencies, libraries, and third-party services are vetted and monitored continuously for risk exposure.

- **Customer-Centric Transparency**: Security commitments are communicated openly to customers, with documentation that explains protections, expected behavior, and incident response channels.

Regulatory and Industry Support for Secure by Design

The Secure by Design approach is not just a best practice—it is increasingly a regulatory expectation. Agencies such as the **Cybersecurity and Infrastructure Security Agency (CISA)** and international coalitions have released Secure by Design guidelines encouraging (and in some sectors, mandating) security to be considered at the earliest stages of product development.

Moreover, large enterprises are beginning to demand Secure by Design commitments from their vendors, tying procurement decisions to a supplier's ability to demonstrate embedded security practices.

Moving from Aspiration to Action

Embracing Secure by Design requires leadership commitment, cultural change, and structural support. To move from aspiration to reality, organizations should

- Adopt **security as a strategic objective**, not just a technical function.

- Incorporate **Secure Software Development Life Cycle (SSDLC)** practices into product and engineering workflows.

- Develop **security champions programs** to scale expertise across teams.

- Measure and track **design-time security decisions**, not just incident response metrics.

- Treat **security failures** as opportunities for improvement, not just blame.

By adopting Secure by Design, companies demonstrate a commitment to their customers' safety and privacy, building trust and fostering long-term relationships. It transforms security from a cost center into a competitive advantage, establishing a reputation for reliability and responsibility in the marketplace.

Key Takeaways

Secure by Design is not a buzzword—it is an ethical, economic, and operational imperative. In a digital ecosystem where customers increasingly expect security to be seamless and guaranteed, building secure products from the start is not just smart engineering—it's smart business.

By adopting Secure by Design principles, organizations don't just reduce their own risk. They raise the standard for the entire ecosystem, helping to create a more trustworthy, resilient digital future.

CHAPTER 20

Data Privacy

In today's hyper-connected digital ecosystem, data has become the lifeblood of modern enterprises. Every digital interaction—whether on social media, ecommerce platforms, or search engines—leaves behind a trail of information that can be collected, analyzed, and monetized. This reality forces us to confront critical questions: What is data privacy? Why does it matter? And how do we protect it? The answers determine not just individual security but the trust and integrity of the digital ecosystem itself.

CHAPTER 20 DATA PRIVACY

With the increasing reliance on data for personalization, analytics, automation, and decision-making, organizations also inherit a profound responsibility: **protecting the privacy of individuals**. While cybersecurity focuses on securing systems, networks, and applications from unauthorized access, **data privacy** ensures that personal and sensitive data is collected, processed, stored, and shared in a lawful, transparent, and ethical manner.

This chapter explores the foundational principles of data privacy, regulatory obligations, practical implementation strategies, and the critical role it plays in enterprise trust and risk management.

Understanding Data Privacy vs. Data Security

Although often used interchangeably, **data privacy** and **data security** are distinct but interrelated disciplines:

Aspect	Data Privacy	Data Security
Focus	Rights of individuals over their personal data	Protection of data from unauthorized access or breaches
Objective	Ensure data is collected and used lawfully and transparently	Safeguard data from loss, theft, corruption, or misuse
Driven by	Ethics, compliance, user trust	Threat landscape, technical controls, resilience
Examples	GDPR compliance, consent management, data minimization	Encryption, firewalls, access control, intrusion detection

In essence, data privacy governs **why** and **how** data is used, while data security governs **how well** it is protected.

In today's hyper-connected world, personal data is currency.

Data privacy refers to an individual's right to control how their personal information is collected, used, and shared. It encompasses a range of concerns, including

- **Who Has Access to Your Data**: This includes not only companies and organizations but also potential hackers and identity thieves.

- **What Type of Data Is Being Collected**: Information collected can range from basic contact details to highly sensitive data such as medical records and financial information.

- **How Your Data Is Being Used**: Are companies using your data to personalize ads, track your online behavior, or make decisions that affect your life?

- **Whether You Have Control Over Your Data**: Can you access, correct, or delete your data? Can you choose whether or not your data is collected in the first place?

Data privacy is not just a matter of personal preference; it is a fundamental right that protects us from a variety of harms. Without data privacy, we risk

- **Identity Theft**: Criminals can use stolen personal information to open fraudulent accounts, make unauthorized purchases, and even commit crimes in your name.

- **Financial Loss**: Data breaches can expose your bank account numbers, credit card details, and other financial information, leading to theft and fraud.

- **Discrimination**: Companies may use your data to make unfair or biased decisions about you, such as denying you a loan or job opportunity.

- **Loss of Control**: When your data is collected and used without your knowledge or consent, you lose control over your own life and choices.

While data privacy challenges are significant, there are steps one can take to protect oneself:

- **Be Mindful of What You Share Online**: Think carefully before posting personal information on social media or other websites.

- **Use Strong Passwords and Enable Two-Factor Authentication**: This makes it harder for hackers to access your accounts.

- **Read Privacy Policies Carefully**: Understand how companies collect, use, and share your data before agreeing to their terms.

- **Use Privacy-Enhancing Tools**: Consider using a VPN, ad blocker, or privacy-focused browser to limit tracking and protect your online activity.

- **Stay Informed**: Keep up-to-date on data privacy news and best practices.

Global Regulatory Landscape and the Role of Laws and Regulations

Privacy regulations have proliferated globally in response to public demand for greater control over personal information. In addition to individual actions, laws and regulations play a crucial role in protecting data privacy. Some of the most influential laws include

- **General Data Protection Regulation (GDPR)**: EU regulation that defines strict rules for processing personal data, including consent, breach notification, data subject rights, and data transfers

- **California Consumer Privacy Act (CCPA)/CPRA**: US law providing California residents with rights to know, access, delete, and opt out of the sale of their personal data

- **Health Insurance Portability and Accountability Act (HIPAA)**: US law protecting medical information

- **Personal Data Protection Law (PDPL)**: Enacted in multiple countries (e.g., Saudi Arabia, UAE, India) to align with international privacy standards

- **China's Personal Information Protection Law (PIPL)**: Highly prescriptive data privacy law with strict data localization and cross-border data sharing rules

Core Principles of Data Privacy

Whether guided by regulation or best practices, data privacy programs should be anchored in several core principles:

1. **Lawfulness, Fairness, and Transparency**: Data must be processed lawfully and openly communicated to users.

2. **Purpose Limitation**: Data should only be used for the stated, specific purpose for which it was collected.

3. **Data Minimization**: Collect only the data necessary to achieve the stated objective.

4. **Accuracy**: Ensure data is kept accurate and up-to-date.

5. **Storage Limitation**: Retain data only as long as needed; enforce retention policies.

6. **Integrity and Confidentiality**: Protect data using appropriate security measures.

7. **Accountability**: Be able to demonstrate compliance with privacy obligations.

Implementing a Data Privacy Program

Building a robust data privacy program requires alignment across people, processes, and technology. Key components include

A. **Data Discovery and Classification**

- Identify what personal or sensitive data exists.
- Map data flows to understand how data moves across systems and jurisdictions.
- Classify data by sensitivity and regulatory impact.

B. **Privacy Governance**

- Appoint a **Data Privacy Officer (DPO)** or assign responsibilities to legal, compliance, or security leaders.
- Establish a cross-functional **privacy governance committee**.
- Define policies on consent, usage, retention, and third-party data sharing.

C. **Privacy Impact Assessments (PIA)**

- Conduct PIAs for new systems, projects, or vendors that handle personal data.
- Identify and mitigate privacy risks before implementation.

D. **Consent and Preference Management**

- Implement mechanisms for users to give, revoke, or modify consent.
- Provide clear privacy notices and choice options.

E. **Vendor and Third-Party Risk Management**

- Evaluate third-party data processors for compliance with privacy obligations.
- Include data protection clauses in contracts and conduct audits.

F. **Data Subject Rights Management**

- Enable users to exercise their rights to access, correct, delete, or port their data.
- Ensure responses to requests meet regulatory deadlines.

G. **Privacy by Design and Default**

- Embed privacy considerations into system design and development life cycles.
- Default to the most privacy-protective settings unless the user chooses otherwise.

Privacy-Enhancing Technologies (PETs)

Technology can be both the problem and the solution. PETs help protect data while preserving its utility:

- **Encryption (at Rest and in Transit)**: Protects data from unauthorized access

- **Data Masking and Tokenization**: Obfuscates sensitive fields for safe use in non-production environments

- **Differential Privacy**: Adds statistical noise to datasets to prevent reidentification

- **Federated Learning**: Allows AI model training without centralizing personal data

- **Homomorphic Encryption**: Enables computation on encrypted data without decrypting it

Building a Culture of Privacy

No technology or process can succeed without **a privacy-aware culture**. CISOs and CXOs must

- Promote **employee training** on data handling, phishing, insider risk, and regulatory requirements.

- Integrate privacy considerations into **product development, marketing, HR, and analytics**.

- Foster **transparency and trust** by publishing clear privacy policies and responding openly to incidents.

- Conduct **tabletop exercises** simulating privacy breaches and regulator inquiries.

Leadership Insight: Data privacy is not just a compliance issue; it's a **brand differentiator**. Enterprises that respect user privacy earn long-term trust and loyalty.

Responding to Privacy Incidents

Data breaches involving personal data trigger not only security responses but also privacy obligations:

- **Breach Notification**: Notify regulators and data subjects within stipulated timelines (e.g., 72 hours under GDPR).

- **Forensic Analysis**: Understand what data was accessed, how, and by whom.
- **Regulatory Engagement**: Cooperate with data protection authorities.
- **Remediation and Lessons Learned**: Close gaps and update privacy controls.

8. The Future of Data Privacy

As technology evolves—AI, IoT, biometrics, quantum computing—so too will privacy challenges:

- **AI and Automated Decision-Making**: Ensuring transparency and fairness in how personal data is used by algorithms
- **Cross-Border Data Transfers**: Managing compliance with emerging data localization requirements
- **Synthetic and Derived Data**: Regulating use of generated data that still reflects individual behaviors
- **Personal Ownership Models**: Emergence of self-sovereign identity (SSI) and data trusts

Key Takeaways

Data privacy is not a check-the-box exercise—it's a strategic imperative that intersects with legal risk, customer trust, brand reputation, and business continuity. For CISOs and CXOs, investing in a proactive privacy program is not only a regulatory necessity but a competitive advantage.

As the digital enterprise expands its data footprint, protecting individuals' privacy will define not just your security posture but your values.

Data privacy is an **individual's right to control** how their personal information is **collected, used, and shared**. This includes knowing who has access, what data is collected, how it's used, and having control over it.

1. **Why It Matters (Risks Without It)**

   - **Identity Theft**: Criminals can use stolen data for fraudulent activities.

   - **Financial Loss**: Breaches can expose financial details, leading to fraud.

   - **Discrimination**: Companies might use data to make unfair or biased decisions.

   - **Loss of Control**: Personal data used without consent diminishes individual autonomy.

2. **Protecting Your Data**

   - **Be Mindful Online**: Think before sharing personal information on social media.

   - **Strong Security**: Use **strong passwords** and **two-factor authentication (2FA)**.

   - **Read Privacy Policies**: Understand how companies handle your data.

   - **Use Privacy Tools**: Consider VPNs, ad blockers, and privacy-focused browsers.

   - **Stay Informed**: Keep up with data privacy news and best practices.

3. **Role of Laws and Regulations**

   - **GDPR (EU)**: Sets high standards for data protection and individual control.

   - **CCPA (California)**: Grants consumers rights regarding collected data and opting out of data sales.

   - These laws are crucial but require ongoing effort from everyone to be fully effective.

PART V

Cybersecurity Tabletop Exercises (TTXs)

This section provides a practical approach to cyber readiness and resilience. A cybersecurity tabletop exercise (TTX) is a simulated, discussion-based activity designed to test an organization's incident response capabilities in a low-risk, no-fault environment. Unlike a full-scale drill, a TTX does not involve actual systems but rather a facilitated conversation among key stakeholders about how they would respond to a hypothetical cyber-attack scenario.

CHAPTER 21

Tabletop Exercise: A Critical Tool for Incident Preparedness

A **cybersecurity tabletop exercise (TTX)** is a structured, discussion-based simulation where key personnel gather to assess and refine their responses to a hypothetical cyberattack or disruptive security event. These exercises provide organizations with a **low-risk environment** to evaluate their incident response capabilities, enhance team coordination, and identify potential weaknesses before a real crisis occurs.

CHAPTER 21   TABLETOP EXERCISE: A CRITICAL TOOL FOR INCIDENT PREPAREDNESS

Why Conduct a Cybersecurity TTX?

Tabletop exercises serve as an invaluable tool for organizations to

- **Test and Improve Incident Response Plans**: By walking through various scenarios, teams can uncover gaps, weaknesses, and areas for improvement in their response strategy.

- **Clarify Roles and Responsibilities**: Participants gain a clearer understanding of their individual roles and how they must coordinate with others during an actual incident.

- **Enhance Communication and Collaboration**: TTXs foster interdepartmental coordination, ensuring that technical teams, leadership, and legal/compliance teams are aligned.

- **Increase Cybersecurity Awareness**: Employees become more familiar with cyber threats, response procedures, and the importance of proactive security measures.

- **Improve Decision-Making Under Pressure**: Simulated incidents help leadership and response teams practice critical decision-making in a controlled setting.

How a Typical TTX Works

A well-executed TTX follows a structured approach to maximize learning and preparedness:

1. **Planning Phase**
   - The planning team develops a **realistic** and **relevant** scenario tailored to the organization's industry and risk profile.
   - Objectives and success criteria are established.
   - Key participants, including IT, security, legal, HR, communications, and executive leadership, are identified.

2. **Execution Phase**
   - Facilitators present the incident scenario in stages, gradually escalating the situation.
   - Participants discuss their immediate and long-term responses, considering technical, operational, legal, and reputational aspects.
   - Injects (additional unexpected developments) may be introduced to simulate real-world complexity.

3. **Debriefing and Lessons Learned**

    - After the exercise, facilitators lead a structured debrief to review key takeaways.
    - Teams identify what worked well, what needs improvement, and actionable steps to enhance preparedness.
    - Findings are documented, and updates to the incident response plan are implemented.

Common Cybersecurity TTX Scenarios

Organizations can tailor their TTXs to address specific threats, such as

- **Ransomware Attack**: A scenario where critical data is encrypted and held hostage, requiring teams to evaluate recovery, legal, and negotiation strategies
- **Data Breach**: An incident involving unauthorized access to sensitive customer or company data, triggering incident response, disclosure requirements, and reputational management
- **Denial-of-Service (DoS/DDoS) Attack**: A simulated attack that disrupts online services, requiring IT teams to assess mitigation and business continuity strategies
- **Insider Threat**: A situation where a rogue employee or contractor compromises security, necessitating forensic investigation, HR involvement, and legal considerations
- **Supply Chain Compromise**: A third-party vendor breach that impacts organizational security, highlighting the need for vendor risk management

Key Benefits of Conducting Regular TTXs

By integrating TTXs into their cybersecurity strategy, organizations can

1. **Enhance Incident Response Readiness**: Ensure teams are well prepared to respond quickly and effectively.

2. **Strengthen Communication and Coordination**: Improve collaboration between technical teams, leadership, and external stakeholders.

3. **Increase Awareness and Threat Intelligence**: Equip employees with knowledge of evolving cyber risks.

4. **Reduce the Impact of a Real Cyberattack**: Minimize operational, financial, and reputational damage.

5. **Ensure Regulatory and Compliance Preparedness**: Meet legal obligations and industry standards (e.g., GDPR, NIST, ISO 27001, CISA guidelines).

Key Takeaways

Cybersecurity threats continue to evolve, making proactive preparedness essential. Regularly conducting cybersecurity tabletop exercises helps organizations build resilience, reduce vulnerabilities, and respond effectively when a real attack occurs. Investing in simulated crisis training today can prevent costly breaches and disruptions in the future.

A cybersecurity tabletop exercise (TTX) is a discussion-based simulation where key personnel assess and refine their responses to a hypothetical cyberattack. It provides a low-risk environment to evaluate incident response capabilities and identify weaknesses.

CHAPTER 22

David vs. Goliath: Cybersecurity's Constant Struggle

The biblical tale of David and Goliath, a story of an underdog's triumph against overwhelming odds, resonates powerfully in the realm of cybersecurity. While the battlefield has shifted from a valley to the digital landscape, the core narrative of smaller, seemingly outmatched entities facing colossal adversaries remains strikingly relevant. In cybersecurity, "David" represents small- to medium-sized businesses (SMBs) and even individual users, while "Goliath" embodies sophisticated cybercriminals, nation-state actors, and well-organized hacking groups.

The disparity in resources is stark. Goliath commands vast armies of skilled hackers, cutting-edge tools, and seemingly limitless funding. They can launch complex, multipronged attacks, leveraging zero-day exploits and advanced persistent threats (APTs) to penetrate even the most fortified defenses. David, on the other hand, often struggles with limited budgets, a shortage of dedicated security personnel, and a reliance on outdated systems. They might be seen as easy targets, a stepping-stone to a larger prize, or simply collateral damage in a large-scale attack. Yet, the cybersecurity landscape isn't a simple story of inevitable Goliath victories. David has weapons in their arsenal, too. Just as David used his slingshot to fell the giant, smaller organizations can leverage strategic thinking, agility, and a focus on the fundamentals to punch above their weight.

David's Strategic Advantages

- **Agility and Adaptability**: Unlike large, bureaucratic organizations, SMBs can often react more quickly to emerging threats. They can implement new security measures and adapt their strategies with greater speed and flexibility.

- **Focus on Fundamentals**: A strong foundation in cybersecurity basics can be surprisingly effective. This includes regular patching, strong password policies, employee training on phishing awareness, and robust backup and recovery procedures. Sometimes, the simplest defenses are the most effective.

- **Leveraging Managed Security Services**: Outsourcing cybersecurity to specialized providers can give SMBs access to expertise and tools they might not otherwise be able to afford. Managed Security Service Providers (MSSPs) can provide 24/7 monitoring, threat intelligence, and incident response capabilities.

- **Embracing Cloud Security**: Cloud-based security solutions can be more cost-effective and scalable than on-premise infrastructure, allowing smaller organizations to access enterprise-grade security tools without breaking the bank.

- **Community and Collaboration**: Sharing threat intelligence and collaborating with other organizations can help SMBs stay ahead of the curve. Industry groups and online forums can provide valuable insights and best practices.

Goliath's Vulnerabilities

While Goliath possesses significant advantages, they are not invincible. Their size and complexity can sometimes be a weakness. Large organizations can be slow to adapt, and their sprawling networks can present a larger attack surface. Furthermore, Goliaths often focus on high-profile targets, sometimes overlooking smaller, less defended organizations that can serve as a backdoor.

Leveling the Playing Field

The cybersecurity industry is constantly evolving, with new tools and technologies emerging to help David fight back. Artificial intelligence, machine learning, and automation are making it easier for smaller organizations to detect and respond to threats. Threat intelligence platforms provide valuable insights into emerging attacks, allowing organizations to proactively defend themselves.

The Ongoing Battle

The David and Goliath story in cybersecurity is not a one-time event; it's an ongoing struggle. As Goliath develops new and more sophisticated attack methods, David must adapt and innovate to stay ahead. The key takeaway is that size and resources are not the only determinants of success. Strategic thinking, agility, a focus on fundamentals, and a willingness to embrace new technologies can empower even the smallest organization to defend against the most formidable cyber threats. The battle is constant, but David can, and often does, win.

Key Takeaways

- **The Core Analogy**: In cybersecurity, "David" represents **small- to medium-sized businesses (SMBs) and individual users**, while "Goliath" embodies **sophisticated cybercriminals, nation-state actors, and organized hacking groups** with vast resources.

- **Resource Disparity**: Goliaths have immense funding, advanced tools, and skilled personnel, enabling complex attacks (e.g., zero-day exploits, APTs). Davids often face **limited budgets, staff shortages, and outdated systems**, making them seem like easy targets.

- **David's Strategic Advantages**: Despite resource limitations, SMBs can leverage
    - **Agility**: Faster adaptation to new threats and implementation of security measures.

- **Focus on Fundamentals**: Strong basic cybersecurity practices like regular patching, strong passwords, employee phishing training, and robust backups are highly effective.

- **Managed Security Services (MSSPs)**: Outsourcing provides access to expert 24/7 monitoring, threat intelligence, and incident response at a more affordable cost.

- **Cloud Security**: Cost-effective and scalable access to enterprise-grade security tools without significant on-premise infrastructure investment.

- **Community and Collaboration**: Sharing threat intelligence and best practices with industry peers.

Goliath's Vulnerabilities: Their large size and complexity can lead to slow adaptation, a larger attack surface, and a tendency to overlook smaller organizations that can serve as backdoors.

Glossary of Cybersecurity Terms

Abbreviation	Description	Analogy
MFA	Multifactor Authentication: Adds extra layers of security when logging in	Like using both a key and a fingerprint to unlock your house
SOC	Security Operations Center: A team that monitors and responds to security incidents	Like a neighborhood watch team keeping an eye on suspicious activity
EDR	Endpoint Detection and Response: Detects threats on devices like laptops and phones	Like a home alarm system that detects break-ins and alerts you
DLP	Data Loss Prevention: Ensures sensitive information isn't leaked or stolen	Like labeling and locking up sensitive documents in a secure cabinet
NIST	National Institute of Standards and Technology: Provides cybersecurity guidelines	Like a recipe book for baking a perfectly secure cake
SOC 2	Service Organization Control 2: Evaluates data security in cloud services	Like a health inspection report ensuring the restaurant (cloud service) is clean and safe
IAM	Identity and Access Management: Manages who can access what in the system	Like a bouncer checking IDs at a club, letting only authorized people in
VPN	Virtual Private Network: Encrypts internet traffic for secure communication	Like a secure tunnel that hides what you're sending and receiving online
SIEM	Security Information and Event Management: Collects and analyzes security data	Like a control room displaying and analyzing multiple security camera feeds at once

(*continued*)

GLOSSARY OF CYBERSECURITY TERMS

Abbreviation	Description	Analogy
PAM	Privileged Access Management: Protects accounts with special system privileges	Like giving the master key only to trusted employees in a hotel
CISO	Chief Information Security Officer: Leads the organization's cybersecurity efforts	Like a general overseeing the army to defend a castle
SSL/TLS	Secure Sockets Layer/Transport Layer Security: Encrypts data between a user and a server	Like sealing a letter in an envelope before mailing it
DNS	Domain Name System: Translates domain names (e.g., google.com) into IP addresses	Like a phonebook that connects a person's name to their phone number
IoT	Internet of Things: Devices connected to the internet (e.g., smart bulbs)	Like having all your household appliances talking to each other over Wi-Fi
WAF	Web Application Firewall: Protects web applications from attacks	Like a security guard stopping troublemakers at the gate of an amusement park
RDP	Remote Desktop Protocol: Allows remote access to a computer	Like having a remote control to operate a computer from far away
XSS	Cross-Site Scripting: A type of attack that injects malicious code into websites	Like graffiti artists sneaking in and spray-painting on a billboard
SQLi	SQL Injection: A database attack where hackers insert malicious queries	Like someone sneaking a poison note into a chef's recipe book
DoS/DDoS	Denial of Service/Distributed Denial of Service: Attacks that overwhelm systems to make them unavailable	Like a mob of prank callers jamming a customer service hotline
APT	Advanced Persistent Threat: A prolonged, targeted cyberattack	Like a professional burglar staking out and breaking into a high-security mansion

(*continued*)

GLOSSARY OF CYBERSECURITY TERMS

Abbreviation	Description	Analogy
PII	Personally Identifiable Information: Sensitive data that can identify a person (e.g., SSN)	Like your personal diary that contains all your secrets
HIPAA	Health Insurance Portability and Accountability Act: Protects patient healthcare data.	Like a rulebook ensuring doctors don't share your medical information without permission
GDPR	General Data Protection Regulation: Protects data privacy in the EU	Like a strict librarian ensuring no one takes your private book without asking
SOC 1	Service Organization Control 1: Focuses on financial reporting and IT controls	Like an accountant ensuring your bank is handling your money correctly
PKI	Public Key Infrastructure: Uses keys and certificates to secure communication	Like giving someone a padlock (public key) and keeping the key (private key) yourself
MITM	Man-In-The-Middle: An attack where someone secretly intercepts communications	Like someone eavesdropping on your phone call and pretending to be one of the callers
CSRF	Cross-Site Request Forgery: Tricks a user into performing actions without their consent	Like someone forging your signature to transfer money
Firewall	A security system that monitors and controls incoming/outgoing traffic	A security guard at a gated community checking visitors
Phishing	A cyberattack that tricks people into revealing sensitive info	A scam call pretending to be your bank to get your PIN
Malware	Malicious software designed to harm or exploit a device or network	A virus that spreads through a school, making students sick
Encryption	Converting data into a secure format to prevent unauthorized access	Locking a diary with a special code only the owner can read

(continued)

GLOSSARY OF CYBERSECURITY TERMS

Abbreviation	Description	Analogy
Zero Trust	A model that assumes no entity inside/outside a network is trusted	A bouncer checking IDs at a club, even for regulars
Multi-Factor Authentication	A security method requiring multiple verification steps	A bank requiring both a card and a fingerprint to withdraw
Denial-of-Service Attack	An attack that overwhelms a system, making it unavailable	Traffic congestion so bad that no one can drive
Ransomware	Malicious software that encrypts files and demands ransom	A kidnapper locking someone in a room and demanding payment
Patch	A software update fixing security vulnerabilities or bugs	A repairman fixing a broken lock to prevent break-ins
Social Engineering	Manipulating people to divulge confidential information	A con artist tricking someone into giving up house keys
Intrusion Detection System	A system that detects and alerts on suspicious activity	A home security alarm notifying of an attempted break-in
Privilege Escalation	Gaining unauthorized higher-level access to a system	A student sneaking into the teacher's lounge to access files
Virtual Private Network (VPN)	A secure tunnel that encrypts data for safe communication	A private tunnel letting you safely talk across a busy highway
Data Breach	An incident where confidential data is accessed/stolen	A thief stealing personal records from a doctor's office
Man-in-the-Middle Attack	An attack where a hacker intercepts and alters communication	A mailman secretly opening and rewriting your letters

Resources and References

1. National Institute of Standards and Technology: https://www.nist.gov/cyberframework
2. International Organization for Standardization: https://www.iso.org/standard/27001
3. MITRE Corporation: https://www.mitre.org/
4. Control Objectives for Information Technologies (COBIT): https://www.isaca.org/resources/cobit#1
5. The Open Worldwide Application Security Project: https://owasp.org/
6. The CIS Controls: A Framework for Effective Cybersecurity by SANS Institute

Index

A

ABAC, *see* Attribute-Based Access Control (ABAC)
Accellion, 16
Access control, 36, 50, 54, 57, 58
Advanced Persistent Threats (APTs), 11, 24, 67, 130, 271
AI, *see* Artificial intelligence (AI)
Amazon Web Services (AWS), 5
Anti-Malware software, 31
Antivirus, 31
Apache Log4J, 17
Application Security, 211, 213
APTs, *see* Advanced Persistent Threats (APTs)
Artificial intelligence (AI), 9, 11, 12, 130, 137, 229
    accountability and trust, 234
    benefits, 231
    bias and discrimination, 233
    challenges and considerations, 231
    cost saving, 232
    cybersecurity landscape, 229
    dialogue and collaboration, 235
    job displacement, 234
    malware, 230
    mitigation, 233, 234
    phishing, 230
    predictive Analytics, 232
    privacy concerns, 233
    proactive security, 230, 232
    security teams, 232
    threat detection, 229
    threat response, 230
    uses, 229
    vulnerabilities, 230, 232
Attribute-Based Access Control (ABAC), 57
Authentication, 36, 56–58, 63
Authorization, 36, 57, 59
AWS, *see* Amazon Web Services (AWS)

B

Blockchain security, 247
    challenges and vulnerabilities
        data privacy concerns, 252
        51% attacks, 250, 251
        phishing and social engineering, 251
        smart contract vulnerabilities, 251
    regulatory uncertainty, 252
    scalability and performance issues, 252
Blockchain technology, 248, 249
    applications
        cryptocurrencies, 250
        finance and banking, 250
        healthcare, 250
        real estate, 250
        supply chain management, 250
        voting systems, 250
    block creation, 249
    chain formation, 249

Blockchain technology (*cont.*)
   cost reduction, 250
   decentralization, 249
   distributed ledger, 249
   enhanced security, 249
   immutability, 249
   operational efficiency, 250
   transparency, 249
   verification, 249
Board of directors, 81
Board of members, cyber risk, 81
Business Acumen, 120

C

California Consumer Privacy Act (CCPA), 185
   vs. GDPR, 187
   obligations, 186
   provisions, 186
   relationship, 187
Capital One, 16
CCPA, *see* California Consumer Privacy Act (CCPA)
Center for Internet Security (CIS) controls, 148–150, 177
Chief Information Officer (CIO), 101
Chief Information Security Officer (CISO), 85, 127
   AI/ML algorithms, 130
   business leader, 85, 88, 89
   challenges, 129
   and CIO, 102–104, 106
   cloud security, 130, 131
   compliance advocate, 137
   C-suite, 104
   culture champion, 137
   and CXOs, 101, 104
   cybersecurity efforts, 105
   cybersecurity mesh, 131
   definition, 85
   DevSecOps, 131
   emerging technologies, 137
   executive alignment, 106
   functions, 127–129
   IoT, 131
   key metrics, 138
   KPIs, 138
   leadership qualities, 138
   navigating evolving threats, 137
   quantum computing, 131, 138
   requirements, 119
   responsibilities, 86, 87, 105, 122
   risk management, 137
   security pillars, 105, 106
   skills and competencies
      Business Acumen, 120
      communication and interpersonal skills, 120, 121
      considerations, 121
      decision-making, 121
      leadership and management skills, 121
      negotiation and influencing skills, 121
      technical expertise, 119
   strategic business partner, 137
   strategic initiatives, 88
   strategic priorities, 105
   technology infrastructure and innovation, 101
   typical day, 87
   vulnerabilities, 85
   zero trust security, 130

INDEX

Chief Information Security Officers (CISOs), 5
China's Personal Information Protection Law (PIPL), 284
CIA, *see* Confidentiality, integrity, and availability (CIA)
CIO, *see* Chief Information Officer (CIO)
Ciphertext, 61
CIS controls, *see* Center for Internet Security (CIS) controls
CISO, *see* Chief Information Security Officer (CISO)
CKC, *see* Cyber Kill Chain (CKC)
CLI, *see* Command Line Interface (CLI)
Cloud-based environments, 83
Cloud-based security, 300
Cloud computing, 5, 206, 214
Cloud computing models, 208
Cloud environments, 137
Cloud security, 94, 119, 130, 131, 205–207, 212, 214–216
   cloud computing, 205
   compliance and governance, 211
   concepts, 205
   controls and practices, 212
   data, 210
   key Aspects, 206
   matters, 211
   measurement, 207
   remote servers, 205
   services, 206
   traditional computing, 205
Cloud Security Posture Management (CSPM), 131
Cloud services and platforms, 5
COBIT, *see* Control Objectives for Information and Related Technologies (COBIT)
Colonial Pipeline, 17
Command Line Interface (CLI), 173
Compliance, 91–93
Confidentiality, integrity, and availability (CIA), 8, 28, 54
Content security policy (CSP), 168, 169
Control Objectives for Information and Related Technologies (COBIT), 147, 148, 177
Crisis communication, 114
   cybersecurity, 116
   key aspects, 115
Cross-site scripting (XSS), 167
Cryptocrime, 16
Cryptocurrencies
   consensus mechanisms, 254
   continuous monitoring and improvement, 255
   hashing algorithms, 253
   public-key cryptography, 253
   regulatory compliance, 255
   secure key management, 253
   smart contract security, 254
   user education, 254
Cryptography, 60
   applications, 63
   concept, 62
   digital lives, 61
   encryption, 61–63
   security objectives, 61
   symmetric-key algorithms, 60
CSP, *see* Content security policy (CSP)
CSPM, *see* Cloud Security Posture Management (CSPM)
CXO-level executives, 82
Cyberattacks
   business, 25
   consequences, 25

INDEX

Cyberattacks (*cont.*)
   critical infrastructure, 26
   individuals, 25
Cyber breaches, 6, 16
Cybercrime, 14, 15
Cybercriminals, 9, 12, 24, 25, 70, 81, 82
Cyber Espionage, 11
Cyber insurance, 16
Cyber Kill Chain (CKC), 154, 177
   countermeasures, 154
   detection, 155
   vs. MITRE ATT&CK, 155, 163
   perimeter/malware, 154
   prevention, 155
   Red Team threat emulations, 155
   response, 155
   security posture, 154
   stages, 156
      command and control (C2), 161
      communication channels, 161
      delivery, 158, 159
      evasion techniques, 161
      exploitation, 159
      impact, 163
      installation, 160
      objectives, 162
      post-exploitation tools, 162
      reconnaissance, 156, 157
      remote manipulation, 161
      weaponization, 158
   structured approach, 163
Cyber risk, 82
Cybersecurity, 1, 3, 275
   advocacy, 99, 100
   AI, 11
   AI-powered attacks, 12
   APTs, 11
   architecture, 4, 95

   awareness, 9, 37, 97
   board meetings, 6
   CIA, 8
   collaboration, 112
      importance, 114
      key aspects, 113
   communication, 99, 100, 109
      board level, 110
      effective communication, 112
      key metrics/reporting, 110, 111
      relationships, 111
      risk assessments/prioritization, 111
      security awareness, 111
      tailoring the message, 110
      technical teams and leadership, 110
   concepts, 64
   constant struggle, David *vs.*
      Goliath, 299–301
   cost efficiency, 5
   crisis communication, 116
   cyberattacks, 25, 26
   cybercriminals, 12
   data centers, 3
   data privacy, 282
   definition, 8
   distributed data, 5
   global cost, 21, 22
   holistic approach, 64
   human factor, 9
   importance, 6, 9
   incident response, 99
   incident response communication, 116
   IOT, 11
   and IT, 102
   key metrics, 133, 134
   KPIs, 133, 135, 136
   landscape, 9, 33
   legacy approach, 3

malware, 10
measures, 10
multilayered approach, 5
organized crime, 10
policies, 96
posture, 23
proactive measures, 27
professionals, 6, 97
real-world consequences, 26
reporting, 133, 136
risks, 6
roles, 96
Secure by Design, 276
    built-in observability, 278
    continuous hardening, 278
    design phase, 277
    design-time security decisions, 279
    incorporate SSDLC, 279
    no paywall for protection, 278
    in practice, 278
    principles, 277
    regulatory and industry
      support, 279
    secure defaults, 277
    security champions programs, 279
    treat security failures, 279
security operations, 99
spending, 15
strategies, 33
statistics, 15, 16
teams, 97, 98
technologies, 94
threat landscape, 24
threats, 10
training, 37
types of data compromised, 23
ubiquity of technology, 24
workforce, 15

yourself and your business,
    protection, 26
Cybersecurity and Infrastructure Security
    Agency (CISA), 279
Cybersecurity concepts
    access control, 36
    data security, 36
    incident response, 37
    network security, 36
    risk assessment and
      management, 35, 64
Cybersecurity culture, 95, 96
    executive level, 96
    landscape, 95
    PCs, 95
    practices, 97
Cybersecurity frameworks (CSF), 27, 139,
    140, 176
Cybersecurity key metrics, 200
Cybersecurity landscape, 20
Cybersecurity leaders
    business acumen, 132
    emerging technologies, 132
    ethical considerations, 133
    leadership and communication, 132, 133
    proactive and predictive security, 133
Cybersecurity market, 16
Cybersecurity mesh, 131
Cybersecurity operations, 226
Cybersecurity principles
    accountability, 30
    availability, 28–30
    confidentiality, 28, 29
    defense in depth, 31
    integrity, 28, 29
    least privilege, 30, 31
    proactive risk management, 32
    transparent communication, 32

INDEX

Cybersecurity program
    assessment and planning, 198
    considerations, 200
    implementation, 199
    monitoring and maintenance, 199
Cybersecurity regulatory compliance, 179
    auditing systems, 181
    audits and investigations, 181
    benefits, 181
    considerations, 181
    controls and measures, 179
    documentation, 181
    and governance, 179, 182
    integrity, 180
    policies and procedures, 180
    resource allocation, 180
    risk management framework, 180
    risks, 179
    roles and responsibilities, 180
Cybersecurity threats
    AI/ML, 12
    cybercrime, 15
    data breaches, 15
    evolution, 13
    geopolitical tensions, 12
    human factor, 13
    impacts, 14
    quantum computing, 12
    resilience, 13
Cybersecurity TTX, 293
    clarify roles and responsibilities, 295
    data breach, 296
    decision-making under pressure, 295
    DoS/DDoS attack, 296
    enhance communication and collaboration, 295
    increase cybersecurity awareness, 295
    insider threat, 296
    key benefits, 297
    low-risk environment, 293
    Ransomware attack, 296
    supply chain compromise, 296
    test and improve incident response plans, 294
Cyber threats, 67
    categories, 75
    consequences, 73, 74
    DDoS attacks, 72
    DoS attacks, 71
    malicious actors, 68
    Malware, 68
    phishing attacks, 69
    social engineering, 70
    sophistication, 9
    vigilance, 75
    zero-day exploit, 72, 73
Cyber warfare, 11, 12

D

Data backup and recovery, 36
Data breaches, 6, 10, 15, 18–20, 24, 26
Data centers, 3, 83
Data encryption, 36, 54
Data Flow Diagram (DFD), 44
Data loss prevention (DLP), 5, 29, 36, 54, 120, 134
Data privacy, 55, 281–283
    AI and automated decision-making, 288
    challenges, 283
    concepts, 55
    considerations, 56
    core principles, 284, 285
    cross-border data transfers, 288
    vs. data security, 282

implementation, data privacy program
    consent and preference
        management, 286
    data discovery and
        classification, 285
    data subject rights
        management, 286
    PIAs, 286
    privacy by design and default, 286
    privacy governance, 285
    vendor and third-party risk
        management, 286
laws and regulations, 55, 284
    CCPA/CPRA, 284
    GDPR, 284
    HIPAA, 284
    PDPL, 284
    PIPL, 284
PETs, 286, 287
principles, 55
privacy-aware culture, 287
privacy obligations, 287
privacy regulations, 284
synthetic and derived data, 288
Data processing, 55
Data protection, 58
Data Protection Officers (DPOs), 56
Data security, 36, 54, 94, 120, 212, 282
    importance, 54
    key aspects, 54
    measures, 54
DC Health Link, 17
DDoS, *see* Distributed denial-of-service (DDoS)
Deep-dive forensic analysis, 224
Deepfakes, 12, 198
Dell, 19
Denial-of-Service (DoS) attacks, 67, 71, 242

DevSecOps, 131, 137
DFD, *see* Data Flow Diagram (DFD)
Digital landscape, 80
Digital transformation, 3
    COVID-19 pandemic, 7
    definition, 6
    impact, 33
    into secure digital transformation, 7, 8
Digital world, 67
Distributed denial-of-service
    (DDoS), 67, 72
Distributed ledger technologies
    (DLT), 247
DLP, *see* Data loss prevention (DLP)
DLT, *see* Distributed ledger
    technologies (DLT)
DoS attacks, *see* Denial-of-Service
    (DoS) attacks
DPOs, *see* Data Protection Officers (DPOs)
DREAD framework, 42

E

Electronic Arts, 17
Encryption, 59, 61–64
Endpoint Security, 94
Enterprise risk management (ERM), 144
Equifax, 16
ERM, *see* Enterprise risk
    management (ERM)
Executive leaders, 79
Executive leadership, 80, 82

F

Facebook, 16, 17
False Positive Rate (FPR), 134
Fidelity Investments, 17

INDEX

Firewalls, 31, 36, 59
FPR, *see* False Positive Rate (FPR)

G

GCP, *see* Google Cloud Platform (GCP)
GDPR, *see* General Data Protection Regulation (GDPR)
General Data Protection Regulation (GDPR), 182, 284
    compliance, 185
    European Union (EU), 182
    impact, 184
    principles, 183
    rights of Individuals, 184
Google Cloud Platform (GCP), 5

H

Hashing, 29, 63
Health Insurance Portability and Accountability Act of 1996 (HIPAA), 188, 284
    impact, 190
    key aspects, 189
    provisions, 190
HIPAA, *see* Health Insurance Portability and Accountability Act of 1996 (HIPAA)

I, J

IaaS, *see* Infrastructure-as-a-service (IaaS)
IAM, *see* Identity and access management (IAM)
ICMR, *see* Indian Council of Medical Research (ICMR)

Identity and access management (IAM), 94, 172, 173, 212
Identity theft, 25
IDPS, *see* Intrusion Detection and Prevention Systems (IDPS)
IDS, *see* Intrusion Detection Systems (IDS)
IDT, *see* Incident detection time (IDT)
IIoT, *see* Industrial IoT (IIoT)
Incident detection time (IDT), 134, 138
Incident response, 37, 50, 86, 93, 94, 99
Incident response communication, 114
    cybersecurity, 116
    key aspects, 115, 116
Incident response plan, 30
Incident Response Planning and Handling (IRPH), 51, 52
    benefits, 53
    considerations, 53
    stages, 52, 53
Incident response time (IRT), 134, 138
Indian Council of Medical Research (ICMR), 18
Industrial IoT (IIoT), 240
Industry analysts, 21
Information Security Management System (ISMS), 146, 177
Information technology (IT), 3
Infrastructure-as-a-service (IaaS), 5, 208
Infrastructure Security, 210, 213
Integris Health, 17
Internet Control Message Protocol (ICMP), 71
Internet of Things (IoT), 9, 11, 24, 72, 131, 137
    connected cars, 240
    connectivity, 239
    intelligence, 239
    interconnectivity, 239

key characteristics, 243
scalability, 240
security (*see* IoT security)
sensors, 239
in smart cities, 240
in smart homes, 240
wearable technology, 240
Internet Protocol (IP), 71
Intrusion Detection and Prevention Systems (IDPS), 36, 50, 59
Intrusion Detection Systems (IDS), 31
IoT security, 240
    challenges, 241, 242
    critical infrastructure, 241
    data breaches, 241
    ensure privacy, 240
    growing attack surface, 241
    mitigate IoT security risks, 242–244
    protect devices, 240
    secure IoT devices and networks
        data privacy and security, 242
        device-level vulnerabilities, 241
        network-level vulnerabilities, 242
    securing data, 240
    securing networks, 240
IP, *see* Internet Protocol (IP)
IRPH, *see* Incident Response Planning and Handling (IRPH)
IRT, *see* Incident response time (IRT)
ISMS, *see* Information Security Management System (ISMS)
ISO 27001, 146, 147, 177
IT, *see* Information technology (IT)

K

Kaseya, 17
Key indicators, 177

Key performance indicators (KPIs), 133, 135, 136, 138, 200
KPIs, *see* Key performance indicators (KPIs)

L

Least Privilege, 36, 57, 59
LINDDUN framework, 43–45

M

Machine learning (ML), 12, 130, 137, 223, 229
    See also Artificial intelligence (AI)
Malware, 15, 68, 75
Managed Security Service Providers (MSSPs), 300
Marriott International, 16
Mean time to detect (MTTD), 134, 138, 225
Mean time to resolve (MTTR), 134, 138
MFA, *see* Multifactor authentication (MFA)
MGM Resorts ransomware attack, 82
Microsoft, 17
Microsoft Azure, 5
Microsoft Exchange Server, 16
MITRE ATT&CK framework, 150, 177
    cyber adversaries, 150
    navigator, 153, 154
    phases
        collection, 153
        command and control (C2), 153
        credential access, 152
        defense evasion, 152
        discovery, 152
        execution, 151

INDEX

MITRE ATT&CK framework (*cont.*)
    exfiltration, 153
    impact, 153
    initial access, 151
    lateral movement, 152
    persistence, 151
    privilege escalation, 152
    reconnaissance, 151
    resource development, 151
  tactics, 153
  techniques, 153
MSSPs, *see* Managed Security Service Providers (MSSPs)
MTTD, *see* Mean time to detect (MTTD)
MTTR, *see* Mean time to resolve (MTTR)
Multifactor authentication (MFA), 36, 172

N

National Institute of Standards and Technology (NIST), 140
National security threats, 26
Network Monitoring Metrics, 201
Network security, 36, 58, 94, 119
  access and authentication, 58, 59
  awareness, 60
  data encryption, 59
  importance, 60
  perimeter security, 59
  principles, 58
  security monitoring, 60
  traffic protection, 59
  vulnerability management, 59
Network traffic analysis, 222
NIST, *see* National Institute of Standards and Technology (NIST)
NIST CSF, 141, 176

components
  core, 141–143
  profiles, 143
  tiers, 143
functions, 143
  detect (DE), 145
  govern (GV), 144
  identify (ID), 145
  protect (PR), 145
  recover (RC), 146
  respond (RS), 146
purpose, 146

O

Open Worldwide Application Security Project (OWASP), 163
OWASP, *see* Open Worldwide Application Security Project (OWASP)
OWASP Top 10, 164, 177
  broken access control, 165
  cryptographic failures, 166
  data integrity failure, 173, 174
  identification and authentication failures, 171–173
  injections, 166
    angular, 168
    attackers, 166
    forms, 167
    react, 167
    vue, 168
    XSS, 167
  insecure design, 168, 169
  monitoring failures, 174, 175
  security logging, 174, 175
  security misconfiguration, 169, 170
  software failure, 173, 174
  SSRF, 175, 176

tools, 176
vulnerabilities, 164, 165
vulnerable and outdated components, 171

P

PaaS, *see* Platform as a Service (PaaS)
PASTA framework, *see* Process for attack simulation and threat analysis (PASTA) framework
Patching, 50
Patch management, 59
Payment Card Industry Data Security Standard (PCI DSS), 192
    aspects, 192
PCI DSS, *see* Payment Card Industry Data Security Standard (PCI DSS)
PCs, *see* Personal computers (PCs)
PDPL, *see* Personal Data Protection Law (PDPL)
Personal computers (PCs), 95
Personal Data Protection Law (PDPL), 284
PETs, *see* Privacy-enhancing technologies (PETs)
Phishing, 10, 69, 70
PIA, *see* Privacy Impact Assessments (PIA)
Pillars, Zero Trust
    applications and workloads, 262, 263
    data, 263
    device, 261, 262
    identity, 260, 261
    network, 262
Platform as a Service (PaaS), 209
PoLP, *see* Principle of Least Privilege (PoLP)

PoW-based blockchains, 252
Principle of Least Privilege (PoLP), 30, 31
Privacy-aware culture, 287
Privacy-enhancing technologies (PETs), 286, 287
Privacy Impact Assessments (PIA), 286
Process for attack simulation and threat analysis (PASTA) framework, 45, 46
Public cloud platforms, 83

Q

Quantum computing, 12, 131, 138

R

Ransomware, 10
Ransomware attacks, 24, 26
RAT, *see* Remote access Trojan (RAT)
RBAC, *see* Role-based access control (RBAC)
Remote access Trojan (RAT), 151
Response metrics, 201
Return on investment (ROI), 97, 136
Risk assessment, 35, 64
Risk management, 35, 37, 48, 64, 91, 92
Risk mitigation, 35
Robust cybersecurity program, 200
ROI, *see* Return on investment (ROI)
Role-based access control (RBAC), 31, 54, 57

S

SaaS, *see* Software as a Service (SaaS)
Sarbanes-Oxley Act of 2002 (SOX), 191
    compliance, 192
    impact, 192
    provisions, 192

INDEX

SDLC, *see* Software development life cycle (SDLC)
SEC, *see* Securities and Exchange Commission (SEC)
Secure digital transformation, 83
Secure Software Development Life Cycle (SSDLC), 279
Securities and Exchange Commission (SEC), 6
Security controls, 214
Security Information and Event Management (SIEM), 32, 50, 60, 94, 217
    advantages, 225
    benefits, 219
    configuration and tuning, 221
    considerations, 221
    critical insights, 218
    implementing and managing, 220
    management and maintenance, 221
    planning and assessment, 220
    security threats, 218, 222
    selection and deployment, 220
Security leaders, 117
Security measures, 3
Security operations, 93, 94
Security Orchestration, Automation, and Response (SOAR), 224
Security Posture, 225
Security team, 107
    communication and collaboration, 108
    considerations, success, 109
    leadership and mentorship, 108
    motivation and recognition, 108
    performance management, 109
    recruitment and hiring, 107, 108
    team composition, 108
Sensors, 239
Server-side request forgery (SSRF), 175, 176
Shared Responsibility Model, 211
SIEM, *see* Security Information and Event Management (SIEM)
Situational awareness, 226
SOAR, *see* Security Orchestration, Automation, and Response (SOAR)
Social engineering, 67, 70, 75
Software as a Service (SaaS), 5, 83, 209
Software development life cycle (SDLC), 48
SolarWinds, 16
SOX, *see* Sarbanes-Oxley Act of 2002 (SOX)
SSDLC, *see* Secure Software Development Life Cycle (SSDLC)
SSRF, *see* Server-side request forgery (SSRF)
Stakeholder management, 112
    importance, 114
    key aspects, 112
Strategic planning, 87
    Amazon, 90
    definition, 89
    elements, 89, 90
    governance, 90, 91
    organizations, 90
STRIDE framework, 39–41
Strong security program, 195
    assessment features, 197
    audits and assessments, 197
    cyber threats and protect, 197
    GDPR and CCPA, 198
    implementing and maintaining, 196
    improvement and adoption, 198
    organizations, 197

risk assessments, 195
Supply chain attacks, 24

T

Tabletop exercise (TTX), 293, 295–297
    execution phase, 295
    planning phase, 295
    structured debrief, 296
    See also Cybersecurity TTX
Tactics, techniques, and procedures (TTPs), 150, 177
Technical expertise, 120
Technologies, 120
Third-party systems, 4
Threat actors, 82
Threat detection
    intelligence integration, 223
    log correlation and analysis, 223
    MI and AI, 223
    and response, 213
    UBA, 222
Threat intelligence, 120
Threat landscape, 65–67, 74, 75
Threat modeling, 32, 35, 37
    architecture overview, 38
    assets, 38
    countermeasure, 46
    decompose application and identify threats, 39
    DREAD framework, 42
    LINDDUN framework, 43–45
    monitoring, 48
    objectives and scope, 38
    PASTA framework, 45, 46
    results/awareness, 47
    risk and impact, 46
    STRIDE framework, 39–41
    threat actors, 39
    threats and vulnerabilities, 42
    validate/review/iterate, 47
Threat response
    graphical representations, 224
    ransomware, 224
    search and filtering, 224
T-Mobile, 17, 19
Traditional network models, 83
TTPs, *see* Tactics, techniques, and procedures (TTPs)
TTX, *see* Tabletop exercise (TTX)
Twitter (X), 17, 18
2FA, *see* Two-factor authentication (2FA)
Two-factor authentication (2FA), 172, 283

U

UBA, *see* User Behavior Analytics (UBA)
UnitedHealth Group's ChangeHealth, 17
User Awareness Metrics, 201
User Behavior Analytics (UBA), 222

V

Virtual private networks (VPNs), 4, 36, 59
VPNs, *see* Virtual private networks (VPNs)
Vulnerabilities, 73
Vulnerability management
    benefits, 51
    considerations, 51
    definition, 49
    stages, 50, 51
Vulnerability Management Metrics, 201

W

World Economic Forum, 14

INDEX

X
XSS, *see* Cross-site scripting (XSS)

Y
Yahoo, 16

Z
Zero Trust Architecture (ZTA), 7, 257
    applications, 259
    benefits
        enhanced security, 270
        improved visibility and monitoring, 271
        incident response, 271
        protection against data breaches, 271
        reduced risk, APTs, 271
        regulatory compliance, 271
        scalability, 271
        secure remote work and cloud-based applications, 271
    in cloud and IoT security, 270
    digital transformation, 258
    direct access, 258
    in financial sector, 270
    in healthcare, 270
    implementation, 265, 269
        architect Zero Trust network, 267, 268
        control around network traffic, 267
        create Zero Trust Policy, 267
        define attack surface, 266, 267
        monitor network, 268
        step-by-step guide, 265, 269
    infrastructure, 259
    perimeterless security, 258
    pillars of Zero Trust (*see* Pillars, Zero Trust)
    principles
        adaptive access policies, 260
        assumption, security breaches, 260
        continuous monitor and validate, 259
        enforce least privileged access, 259
    in remote workforce security, 270
    security technologies, 258
    threats visibility and analytics, 264, 265
    users, 259
Zero Trust Model, 95
Zero Trust network access (ZTNA), 258, 261
Zero Trust policies, 267
Zero trust security, 130, 137
ZTA, *see* Zero Trust Architecture (ZTA)
ZTNA, *see* Zero Trust network access (ZTNA)

GPSR Compliance

The European Union's (EU) General Product Safety Regulation (GPSR) is a set of rules that requires consumer products to be safe and our obligations to ensure this.

If you have any concerns about our products, you can contact us on

ProductSafety@springernature.com

In case Publisher is established outside the EU, the EU authorized representative is:

Springer Nature Customer Service Center GmbH
Europaplatz 3
69115 Heidelberg, Germany